THE
COMPLETE BLUE
MAX

THE COMPLETE BLUE MAX

A Chronological Record of the Holders of the Pour le Mérite, *Prussia's Highest Military Order, from* 1740 to 1918

Kevin Brazier

Pen & Sword
MILITARY

First published in Great Britain in 2013 by
Pen & Sword Military
an imprint of
Pen & Sword Books Ltd
47 Church Street
Barnsley
South Yorkshire
S70 2AS

ISBN 978 1 84884 86 0

Typeset in Centaur by
Phoenix Typesetting, Auldgirth, Dumfriesshire, DG2 0XE

Printed and bound in England by
MPG Printgroup

Pen & Sword Books Ltd incorporates the Imprints of Pen & Sword Aviation, Pen &
Sword Family History, Pen & Sword Maritime, Pen & Sword Military, Pen & Sword
Discovery, Wharncliffe Local History, Wharncliffe True Crime, Wharncliffe
Transport, Pen & Sword Select, Pen & Sword Military Classics, Leo Cooper, The
Praetorian Press, Remember When, Seaforth Publishing and Frontline Publishing

For a complete list of Pen & Sword titles please contact
PEN & SWORD BOOKS LIMITED
47 Church Street, Barnsley, South Yorkshire, S70 2AS, England
E-mail: enquiries@pen-and-sword.co.uk
Website: www.pen-and-sword.co.uk

CONTENTS

For my brother David,
much missed.

ACKNOWLEDGEMENTS

My initial thanks must go to Rupert Harding for his continuing confidence in commissioning me to write another book on medals. I must thank Lance Renetzke for his knowledge of German Army ranks and Jill Sugden for her many hours of research. My special thanks go to Joe Dever for taking the photographs of my *Pour le Mérite*.

I must thank Terry Hissey for his help and for proof-reading the finished work. I am most grateful also to the Photographic Department of the Imperial War Museum. I must thank the staff at many of the museums I have been in contact with.

I must thank my editor, Sarah Cook, for her many hours of hard work, and for putting up with my endless last-minute changes. Last, but by no means least, Teresa, my long-suffering wife.

If anyone has any further information on the *Pour le Mérite*, please contact the author at kib1856@yahoo.com

PREFACE

This book, my third, principally tells the stories of the eighty-one airmen who were awarded the *Pour le Mérite*, better known as the Blue Max, and said to have been so called as the blue of the medal matched the blue eyes of Max Immelmann, one of its first recipients.

The first thing you may notice about this book is that it is not in exactly the same format as the previous two in the series, which is due in part to the fact that the *Pour le Mérite* was not usually awarded for a single action but rather for reaching a level of achievement. Also many holders have no known graves and the unknown whereabouts of their medals makes doing such a list pointless.

Some men were awarded it for as few as seven victories, while others were awarded it despite not having shot down a single aircraft; these were usually awarded by the Kaiser personally for some great act of bravery or significant achievement. Some of these men were not even fighter pilots but observers or airship commanders, and two were generals. The usual number of victories required was initially eight, but that figure was raised to sixteen by January 1917, and eventually to twenty later in that year, as more and more men were awarded the medal and it was felt it was becoming too widespread. I have also included the twenty-six men who shot down the required number of enemy aircraft but did not receive the medal. The rolls of honour list recipients of the award as far back as 1740 but only the First World War airmen's stories are told.

After the *Pour le Mérite* the next award would be the Oak Leaves to the *Pour le Mérite*, which were for extraordinary achievements, but not a single airman was ever to receive them; von Ludendorff wanted them awarded to Manfred von Richthofen, but this never happened. It would seem this award was only for high-ranking officers.

The Germans fought a very defensive air war, initially because, having developed a machine-gun that could fire through the propeller, they were not allowed to fly over enemy lines for fear of it falling into Allied hands. Then, as the war went on, they realised that they were able to recover most of their downed pilots. This also helped with the confirmation of victories, as in the German Army Air Service only confirmed claims could be credited. German pilots could not share a victory and disputes over claims were not uncommon; these were usually resolved by the senior pilot being awarded the 'kill'. However, some pilots were happy to allow a novice to take the credit to help them get started. The Germans, French and Americans did not count 'out of control' victories (where a pilot dived away to escape from the enemy) but the British did; the British also counted 'probable kills'. Also, it must be noted that the British command did not like the idea of its pilots keeping a tally and many final scores were only worked out long after the end of the war.

German *Jastas* were known as 'circuses' because they used tents and would pack up to move along the front line from time to time. The fact that German fighters were flamboyantly painted has led to some totally erroneous suppositions as to why this was done. The main reason was to overcome problems with air-to-air communication and identification. Each *Jasta* had a basic theme so they could be distinguished from one another, and individual pilots would then add their own personal markings, letters or initials (either their own or those of their girlfriends); pilots who had served in the army often used numbers from their old regiments. All of this helped with confirmation of victories, and added to the 'circus' theme in the eyes of the Allies, although painting aircraft different colours was frowned upon by the High Command initially.

German fighter units were not like their Allied counterparts. For one thing they were smaller in size, rarely having more than ten or twelve pilots on strength, as opposed to eighteen or more in a British squadron. Whereas the British unit was based on three flights, plus a squadron commander, each *Jasta* just had its leader, although that depended on whether he was a flying leader or someone who had achieved the position through rank. The rank system was paramount in the German military and even some highly successful fighter pilots continued to be NCOs, sometimes never being commissioned. There was also a vast difference between regular and reserve commissions (for the duration of the war). While reserve officers could command units, more often the preference was for officers with permanent ranks, whether they were successful pilots or not. Some *Jastas* had leaders who had shot down just one or two, while commanding pilots with much greater scores.

Rank was not automatic in the Germany military either. Pilots were either NCOs or Leutnants. A few would make it to Oberleutnant, but not many. Command of a unit did not entail an automatic promotion. In the RFC/RAF a flight commander was always a captain, while a commanding officer was always a major. In comparison, few *Jasta* commanders reached the rank of Hauptmann and most would see out the war as mere Leutnants, despite long periods in command.

CHAPTER 1

A Short History of the Medal

On 8 May 1667 in the Germanic principality of Brandenburg Prince Friedrich Wilhelm founded the Order of Generosité (aka the 'Gracecross'), a military and civil order that was created for rewarding loyal subjects for outstanding service. Initially it was a simple gold cross with a precious stone in the middle, but in 1685 the medal took on a new look that was very like the Order of St John. The basic design is that of an eight-pointed Maltese Cross, enamelled in sky blue, with an eagle with upswept wings between each arm. The upper arm bears a hand-painted letter 'F' (for Friedrich) surmounted by the electoral crown. The other three arms have the words 'Gene', 'Rosi' and 'Te' on them. The reverse was plain blue enamel. It was worn around the neck from a long black ribbon 1½ inches (38mm) wide.

On 9 January 1740 the award was renamed and established as the *Orden Pour le Mérite* by Friedrich II (the Great). The most obvious change was the wording: the 'F' and the crown were retained on the upper arm, but now it became 'Pour' on the left arm, 'leMe' on the right arm and 'rite' on the lower arm, originally in italics but changed in 1832 to the Roman style; the whole medal is 52mm wide. Silver stripes were also added to the black ribbon. The wording is in French because it was the favoured court language at the time. Holders of the Order of Generosité were allowed to continue wearing it, but if they were awarded the *Pour le Mérite* they were required to return it. The medal saw many inconsistencies in appearance and construction between 1740 and the 1800s. The *Pour le Mérite* with 'Brilliants' was a special award that was encrusted with diamond-like gems.

On 18 January 1810 the *Pour le Mérite* was reserved as a military order. It could be (and was) awarded more than once to the same person, and in fact was awarded three times to one person. On 10 March 1813 the Oak Leaves were established by Wilhelm III in memory of his wife Queen Louise, and would be awarded for extraordinary achievements; these were gold, but later were made from silver and measured 17mm by 20mm. From 17 December 1817 the Oak Leaves ribbon would have another silver stripe, down the centre. The 'Peace Class' of the *Pour le Mérite* was created in 1842 for Art and Science, and women were eligible for this award. Between 1842 and 1913 no fewer than 324 awards were made, including three to the military. The 'Crown' attachment came next, established by Wilhelm

IV in 1844. This was for those who had held the *Pour le Mérite* for fifty years and was first awarded to Generalmajor du Pac de Badens et Sombrelle of France. The Crown was gold and measured 17mm by 14mm. On 18 September 1866 the Grand Cross and Star were established by Wilhelm I; only ever awarded five times, it was never awarded again after his death. The Grand Cross was twice the size of the *Pour le Mérite* and a companion Star was worn on the breast. On 27 January 1903 the Kaiser bestowed the *Pour le Mérite* on the gunboat SMS *Iltis* in recognition of the bravery of her entire crew during the Boxer uprising; this is the only time that the award has been given in this way. In its 173 years up to the First World War the *Pour le Mérite* had been awarded 4,743 times.

There was no set criteria for the award of the medal. The Army General Headquarters staff provided recommendations to the Kaiser's military cabinet and the awards were determined by the Adjutant General's department. However, the Kaiser could (and did) award it directly in reward for glorious or decisive victories, and often for a single act. During the war a total of 687 awards were made.

On 9 November 1918 all imperial orders were abolished with the Kaiser's abdication. The Peace Class was reinstituted on 31 May 1952 and survives to this day.

CHAPTER 2

Roll of Honour: a chronological list of *Pour le Mérite* holders, 1740–1812

D etails for this period are difficult to find and only a few names appear here before 1792, but for each year the number of awards made will be given and known holders listed. Ranks for this period are not easy to find, and thus only a few entries will start with them. Most entries start with the name; where first names are also unknown, these entries only have the surname. Surnames are in CAPITALS. This is followed by the date of the award if known. Any further awards are noted in brackets with the date, with the Oak Leaves indicated as (OL), Brilliants as (B), and the Crown as (C). If the award of the Oak Leaves or the Crown was made at the same time as the *Pour le Mérite*, it is shown as (with OL), or (with Crown).

The award could be (and was) awarded to the same person more than once, although it is possible that some of the 'second awards' could be the Oak Leaves. If two or more awards have been made on the same date, then they are listed in alphabetical order.

1740

19 awards, including:

Oberst Hans von HACKE 9–I–1740 (one of the first three ever awarded)

State Minister Samual von MARSCHALL 9–I–1740 (one of the first three ever awarded)

Oberstleutnant Friedrich Wilhelm Marquis de VARENNE 9–I–1740 (one of the first three ever awarded)

Hauptmann Franz Egmond de CHASÔT (with B) 1740 (exact date unknown)

1741

19 awards

1742

132 awards

1743

4 awards

1744

3 awards

1745

67 awards

1746

4 awards

1747

53 awards, including:

Count Francesco ALGAROTTI 1747

Pierre Louis Moreau de MAUPERTIUS 1747

1748

5 awards

1749

1 award

1750

3 awards, including:

Francois Marie Arouet de VOLTAIRE 25–9–1750

(withdrawn on 16–3–1753)

1751

6 awards

1752

6 awards

1753

5 awards

1754

4 awards

1755

1 award

1756

52 awards

1757

87 awards, including:

von BÜLOW 5–11–1757

von der GOLTZ 5–11–1758

Johann Jakob von WUNSCH 1757 (exact date unknown)

1758

24 awards

1759

21 awards

1760

54 awards, including:

Ernst Ludwig von PFUEL 1760

1761

20 awards

1762

67 awards, including:

Czar PETER III 4–1762 (first award to a Russian)

1767

1 award

1768

7 awards

1771

1 award

1772

1 award

1773

2 awards

1774

37 awards

1775

15 awards

1776

7 awards

1777

1 award

1778

64 awards

1779

15 awards

1780

4 awards

1781

1 award

1783

6 awards

1784

1 award

1785

1 award

1786

18 awards

1787

42 awards

1788

9 awards

1789

62 awards, including:

Gebhard Lieberecht von BLUCHER 1789

Julius August Reinhold von GRAWERT 1789

Johann Ernst Graf von KUNHEIM 1789

1790

4 awards, including:

Colonel Charles GORDON 3–6–1790 (first award to a Briton)

1791

16 awards

1792

99 awards including:

Hieronymus BRUCKNER 1792

Karl Wilhelm von BYERN 1792

Georg Ludwig Friedrich Freiherr von DALWIG 1792

Friedrich Wilhelm Heinrich DECKER 1792

August Friedrich von DROSSEL 1792

Friedrich Albrecht Gotthilf Freiherr von ENDE 1792

Karl Gustav von ERICHSEN 1792

Otto Leopold Ehrenreich von GLODEN 1792

Karl Ferdinand von GORTZ 1792

Ludwig August Emil Franz von GUIONNEAU 1792

Gottfried Ludwig Mathias von HARTMANN 1792

Ludwig Ferdinand Friedrich von HEISING 1792

Levin Karl von HEISTER 1792

Friedrich Jakob von HOLTZENDORFF 1792

Johann Christian von HUNDT 1792

Karl Friedrich Siegmund von KAMEKE 1792

Hans Maximilian von KOPPERN 1792

Friedrich Gottlieb von LAURENS 1792

Mathias Julius von LAURENS 1792

Karl Heinrich August Graf von LINDENAU 1792

Peter Ewald von MALSCHITZKI 1792

Friedrich Wilhelm Heinrich von PELET 1792

Franz Otto von PIRCH 1792

Heinrich Ernst Edler von der PLANITZ 1792

August Wilhelm von PLETZ 1792

Siegmund Moritz von PRITTWITZ und GAFFRON 1792

Johann Otto Heinrich von SCHMIDT 1792 (OL 31–5–1814)

Hans Karl Ludolf von STRANTZ 1792

Friedrich Bogislav Graf TAUENTZIEN von WITTENBERG 1792

Karl Philipp von UNRUH 1792

Karl Friedrich von VOSS 1792

Leutnant Karl Wieprecht Hans Friedrich Graf von ZEITEN 5–12–1792
   (C18–7–1844)

1793

358 awards, including:

Ludolph August Friedrich von ALVENSLEBEN 1793

Ferdinand Friedrich Duke of ANHALT-KOTHEN-PLESS 1793

Karl Anton Andreas von BOGUSLAWSKI 1793

Ernst Friedrich Otto von BONIN 1793

Karl Leopold Heinrich Ludwig von BORSTELL 1793

Karl Friedrich Peter von BROCKHAUSEN (sometimes misspelt
    BROCKHHAUSEN) 1793

Karl Wilhelm von BUNTING 1793

Arvid Conrad von CARNALL 1793

Christian Wilhelm von CHLEBOWSKY 1793

Daniel Noah Ludwig von CROUSAZ 1793

Philipp Georg von DIETHERDT 1793

Karl Ludwig Jakob EDLER von LECOQ 1793

Karl Christian von ELSNER 1793

Karl Christian Burghard von ESEBECK 1793

Friedrich Wilhelm Leopold Freiherr von GAUDI 1793

Christian Alexander Freiherr von HAGKEN 1793

Albrecht Georg Ernst Karl von HAKE 1793

Johann August von HARROY de TECHREAUX 1793

Johann Kaspar von der HEYDEN 1793

Prince Georg Friedrich Heinrich HOHENLOHE-INGELFINGEN 1793

Hans Christoph Ernst von KALCKREUTH 1793

Georg Christian Friedrich von KAMEKE 1793

Andreas Georg Friedrich von KATZLER 1793

Franz Friedrich Karl Ernst von KLUX 1793

Johann Christoph von KNOBELSDORFF 1793

Karl Leopold von KOCKRITZ 1793

Karl Friedrich KOHN von JASKI 1793

Friedrich Wilhelm Ludwig von KRUSEMARCK 1793

Heinrich von der LAHR 1793

August Christoph Heinrich von LEGAT 1793

Gottlieb Peter LEHMANN 1793

Johann Christian Wilhelm von LENTKEN 1793

Karl Christian Reinhold von LINDENER 1793

Karl Friedrich Ludwig von LOBENTHAL 1793

Wilhelm Peter Franz Graf von LOUCEY 1793

Johann Leopold von LUCK und SALISCH 1793

Karl Friedrich von MASSOW 1793

Johann Adorf Prince of NASSAU-USINGEN 1793

David von NEUMANN 1793

Christian Friedrich von der OSTEN 1793

Otto Albrecht Philip Ludwig von der OSTEN 1793 (OL 2–10–1815)

Karl Ludwig von PFUEL 1793

Wilhelm Ludwig von PUTTKAMER 1793

Eugen von RAUMER 1793

Karl Wilhelm von SANITZ 1793

Karl August von SCHAFFER 1793

Dietrich Lebrecht von SCHIMONSKI 1793

Moritz Ludwig Wilhelm von SCHOELER 1793

Ernst Christian Friedrich von SCHRAMM 1793

Johann Friedrich Gustav von STOCKHAUSEN 1793

Christian Georg Ludwig von STRACHWITZ 1793

Friedrich Wilhelm Alexander von TSCHAMMER und OSTEN 1793

Konrad Heindrich von WEDEL 1793

Hans Ernst Christoph von WERDER 1793

Karl Ludwig von WUTHENAU 1793

Christian Gottlieb Georg von ZSCHOCK 1793

Johann Christian von ZWEIFFEL 1793

1794

355 awards, including:

Karl Friedrich Heinrich Graf von der GOLTZ 19–1–1794 (first award),
    (13–4–1814, unclear if this award was the OL or a second award with
    OL)

Philipp Friedrich Ferdinand von ARNIM 1794

Ernst Friedrich Wilhelm von BANDEMER 1794

Josef Albrecht von BIEBERSTEIN-PILCHOWSKI 1794

Karl Anton Ernst von BILA 1794

Wilhelm Johann Freiherr von BLUMENSTEIN 1794

Philipp Julius Freiherr von BOINEBURG zu LENGSFELD 1794

Bogislav Ernst von BONIN 1794

Karl Philipp Traugott von BRIESEN 1794

Karl Friedrich von BRUSEWITZ 1794

Heinrich Friedrich Ernst von CORVIN-WIERSBITZKI 1794

Christoph Friedrich Otto von DIERICKE 1794

Rudolf Gottlieb Freiherr von DYHERRN 1794

Johann Friedrich Wilhelm von FIEBIG 1794

Ulrich Karl von FROREICH 1794

Wilhelm Leopold von FROREICH 1794

Friedrich Daniel von GLASER 1794

Johann Freiherr von HINRICHS 1794

Karl Friedrich von HOLTZENDORFF 1794 (OL 2–10–1815)

Heinrich Wilhelm von HORN 1794

Gebhard Friedrich Gottlob von INGERSLEBEN 1794

Friedrich Daniel Wilhelm von IRWING 1794

Philipp von IVERNOIS 1794

Wilhelm Gottfried von JOCHENS 1794

Friedrich Georg von KALL 1794

Gotthilf Benjamin KEIBEL 1794

Karl Ludwig Ferdinand von KLUCHTZNER 1794

Christian Friedrich von KNEBEL 1794

Leopold Ernst Gustav von KOSCHEMBAHR 1794

Ernst Christian Wilhelm Ludwig von KUROWSKY 1794

Balthasar Wilhelm Christoph von LARISCH 1794

Claude Francois Joseph LE BAUL de NANS et LAGNY 1794

Alexander Friedrich Albrecht Freiherr von LEDEBUR 1794

Ernst Julius von MAGUSCH 1794

Helmuth Dietrich Freiherr von MALTZAHN 1794

Johann Ludwig MARKOFF 1794

Hans Christoph von NATZMER 1794

Moritz August von OBERNITZ 1794

Bernhard Vollrad Dietrich von OLDENBURG 1794

Friedrich Gottlieb von OSWALD 1794

Johann Christian von PONTANUS 1794

Heinrich Konstantin Anton von POYDA 1794

Heinrich August Freiherr von REITZENSTEIN 1794

Kaspar Friedrich von RENTZEL 1794

Ernst Andreas von ROEHL 1794

Johann Gabriel von ROSENSCHANZ 1794

Johann Friedrich Freiherr von SCHENCK zu SCHWEINSBERG 1794

Christian Ludwig SCHIMMELPFENNIG von der OYE 1794

Johann Christian Ludwig von SCHMIDT 1794

Ernst Emanuel Siegmund von SCHONING 1794

Dietrich Wilhelm von SCHULZ 1794

Ferdinand Ludwig von SJOHOLM 1794

Georg Dietrich von SOBBE 1794

Johann Karl August Freiherr von STREIT 1794

Karl Friedrich Ernst Graf TRUCHSESS zu WALDBURG 1794

Ernst Vollrad von VIEREGG 1794

Ludwig Ernst von VOSS 1794

Ernst Friedrich Christoph Wilhelm von WARBURG 1794

Erhard Gustav Graf von WEDEL 1794

Friedrich Wilhelm von WERDER 1794

Otto Ludwig von WOBESER 1794

Karl Heinz von ZIELINSKI 1794

Christoph Johann Friedrich Otto von ZIETEN 1794

1795
40 awards, including:

Ernst Philipp von GETTKANDT 1795

Christoph Friedrich von MOSCH 1795

Johann Fabian Wilhelm von SCHATZEL 1795

Johann Friedrich Wilhelm von SCHOELER 1795

Friedrich Georg Ludwig von SOHR 1795

1796

2 awards

1797

2 awards, including:

Generalmajor Fedor Petrovich DENISSOW VIII 16–I–1797

1798

3 awards, including:

Karl Heinrich von PACZENSKY und TENCZIN (sometimes misspelt
    PACZINSKY) 1798

Franz Friedrich von PUTTKAMER 1798

1799

5 awards, including:

Friedrich von LINGELSHEIM 1799

Johann Adam Siegmund von UTTENHOVEN (sometimes misspelt
    UTTENHOFEN) 1799

1800

2 awards

1801

55 awards, including:

Johann Adolf von LÜTZOW 1801

Christian Friedrich Wilhelm von PLOETZ 1801

Karl Friedrich Hermann von SPIRIT (aka von BERRIES) 1801

1802

20 awards, including:

Johann Casimir von AUER 1802

Ludwig Wilhelm August von EBRA 1802

Karl Friedrich Wilhelm von HAMBERGER 1802

Eberhard Friedrich Freiherr von MASS BACH 1802

Franz Heinrich Christian von PLOTZ 1802

Alexander Heinrich Christian von THILE 1802

Karl Gottlieb von TSCHEPE 1802

Ernst Philipp von WAGENFELD 1802

Johann Philipp Benjamin von WEGER 1802

Wilhelm Ernst August Freiherr von WINTZINGERODE 1802

1803

2 awards

1804

14 awards, including:

Abraham Franz von BAILLIODZ 1804

Ehrenreich Wilhelm Gottlieb von BETTER 1804

Wilhelm Ferdinand BOLTZIG 1804

Friedrich Wilhelm Graf von HERTZBERG 1804

Ulrich Leberecht von HEYKING 1804

Friedrich August von KAUFFBERG 1804

Friedrich August Erdmann KRAFFT 1804

Karl Ernst Ludwig von LETTOW 1804

Johann Bernhard von MANSTEIN 1804

Karl Peter von TRESKOW 1804

1805

7 awards, including:

Elias Maximilian Graf HENCKEL von DONNERSMARCK 1805

Karl Georg Friedrich von WOBESER 1805

1806

3 awards:

Alexei KULESCH 1806

Ferdinand Baptista von SCHILL 1806

August Friedrich Ludwig Freiherr von WRANGEL 1806

1807

453 awards, including:

Joseph Theodor Sigismund BACZKO 1807

Gustav Friedrich Wilhelm Freiherr von BARNEKOW 1807

Karl Wilhelm Reinhold von BECKEDORFF (sometimes misspelt
  BECKENDORFF) 1807

Johann Peter Paul BEIER 1807 (OL 2–10–1815)

Hans Karl Friedrich Franz von BELOV 1807

Theodor Werner Christian von BELOW 1807

Friedrich Ludwig von Dionys BLANCKENBURG 1807

Ernst Gottlieb Kurt von BORCKE 1807

Julius Gustav Friedrich von BOTH 1807

Friedrich August Karl von BRANDENSTEIN 1807 (OL 2–10–1815)

Louis Mathias von Gottlieb Nathanael BRAUCHITSCH 1807

Karl Wilhelm Ernst Freiherr von CANITZ und DALLWITZ 1807
  (OL 11–10–1831)

Vollmar Friedrich Karl Heinrich von CLAUSEWITZ 1807
  (OL 31–5–1814)

Karl Wilhelm Gustav von COSEL 1807

Friedrich Karl Emil Graf DOHNANYI-SCHLOBITTEN 1807

Friedrich von EISENHARDT 1807

Wilhelm Alexander Freiherr von der GOLTZ 1807

Friedrich Wilhelm Graf von GOTZEN 1807

Johann Leberecht Christoph von GRAVENITZ 1807

Karl Wilhelm Georg von GROLMAN 1807

Tido August von HAGEN 1807

Ernst Wilhelm von HAMILTON 1807

August Wilhelm von HERTIG 1807

Herman Frederick Prince of HOHENZOLLERN-HECHINGEN 1807

Hans Jakob Furchtegott von Casimir HULSEN 1807

Ernst August von KAMPTZ 1807

Johann Karl Jakob von KEMPHEN 1807 (OL 2–10–1815)

Friedrich Karl von der KNESEBECK 1807

Karl Leberecht Friedrich Freiherr von KRAFFT 1807

Johann Wilhelm KRAUSENEK 1807 (OL 2–10–1815)

Geoffrey Ludwig Heinrich von L'ESTOCQ 1807

Johann Leopold von Constantinople LARISCH 1807

Johann Philipp August Freiherr von LEDEBUR 1807

Friedrich Ernst von LOEBELL 1807 (first award), 1812 (second award),
    (OL 31–5–1814)

Ludwig Adolf Wilhelm von LÜTZOW 1807 (OL 2–10–1815)

Hans Christoph Ludwig von der MULBEN 1807

Johann Karl Jakob von MUTIUS 1807

Wilhelm Dubislav von NATZMER 1807

Wilhelm August Graf NEIDHARDT von GNEISENAU 1807

Friedrich Christoph Ludwig von Viktor OERTZEN 1807

Adolf Friedrich von OPPEN 1807

Friedrich Christian Angel von PETER-DORFF 1807

Karl Heinrich Christian Ludwig von PIPE 1807

Wilhelm Gottlieb Christian von PLATEN 1807

Joseph von Nicodemus PODBIELSKI 1807

Karl Ludwig Heinrich Freiherr von PREUSSER (sometimes misspelt
    PRUSSIA) 1807

Johann Gustav Georg von RAUCH 1807 (OL 3–6–1814)

Leopold August Eduard von RECKOW 1807

Karl Wilhelm von Sigismund ROTTENBURG 1807

Gerhard Johann David von SCHARNHORST 1807

Karl Dietrich Ludwig von SCHMALENSEE 1807

Georg Friedrich Wilhelm von SCHOENERMARCK 1807

Ernst Julius Freiherr SCHULER von SENDEN 1807

Engelhardt Louis STACH-GOLTZ-HOME 1807

Karl Friedrich of St Francis STEINMETZ 1807

Wilhelm Ludwig of Bogislav STONE-WEIR 1807

Friedrich von SZERDAHELY 1807

Ernst Ludwig von TIPPELSKIRCH 1807 (OL 2–10–1815)

Friedrich Wilhelm von Christoph UNRUH 1807

Karl Friedrich Heinrich von WEDEL 1807

Friedrich Heinrich Graf von WRANGEL 1807 (OL 13–9–1848)

Johann David Ludwig Graf YORCK von WARTENBERG 1807

Karl Ludwig von ZASTROW 1807

Konstantin Gottlieb Leberecht ZEPELIN 1807 (OL 14–1–1816)

Ernst Ludwig Otto von ZIETEN 1807

1808
53 awards

1809
68 awards, including:

Colonel GOERGOLIJ 9–2–1809 (with B)

1810
7 awards, including:

Michael Heindrich von LOSTHIN 12–6–1810 (OL 2–10–1915)

1811
4 awards

1812
78 awards, including:

Ludwig Casimir AUER 1812

Gustav Friedrich Eugen BELOV 1812

Karl August Ferdinand BORCKE 1812

Karl Friedrich Wichmann von BOSE 1812

Wilhelm Friedrich Graf von BRANDENBURG 1812

Karl Heinrich von BROESIGKE 1812

17

Wilhelm Benedict von CLAUSEWITZ 1812 (OL 18–6–1816)

Christian Ernst Theodor von EICKE 1812

Friedrich Wilhelm von FUNCK 1812 (OL 3–11–1815)

Ludwig Freiherr von HUCHTENBRUCK und QUADT 1812

Alexander Ludwig Georg Moritz von JURGASS-ELECTIONS 1812

Karl August Wilhelm Graf von KANITZ 1812

Karl Friedrich Erdmann von KRACHT 1812

Ernst Ludwig Christian von KYCKPUSCH 1812

August Christian Friedrich von LEGAT 1812

Friedrich Wilhelm Graf von LEPEL 1812

Georg Wilhelm von LETTOW 1812

Karl Friedrich Gustav von LILLJESTROM 1812

Johann Friedrich Konstantin von LOSSAU 1812

Ernst Heindrich Wilhelm von PERBANDT 1812

Erhard Friedrich Leopold von RODER 1812

Ferdinand Wilhelm Karl von SCHACK 1812

Hans Wilhelm von SCHACK 1812

Anton Friedrich Florian von SEYDLITZ-SHORTLY-BACH 1812

Johann Georg Emil von SHOWER 1812

Karl Friedrich Christian Freiherr von STEINACKER 1812

Rudolph Wenzislaus von Anton STENGEL 1812

Friedrich Ludwig Emil Karl Freiherr von STIERN 1812

Karl Alexander von TRESCKOW 1812

Philip Friedrich Wilhelm von UTTENHOVEN (sometimes misspelt
    UTTENHOFEN) 1812

Ferdinand Friedrich Wilhelm von WINNING 1812

Karl Wilhelm von WNUCK 1812

The total number of awards up to 1812 is 2,654. (Included in this total are
ninety-seven awards made between 1740 and 1786 where the exact year of issue
is unknown.)

CHAPTER 3

Roll of Honour: a complete chronological list of all *Pour le Mérite* holders, 1813–1913

Ranks for this period are not easy to find, and thus only a few entries will start with them. Most entries start with the name; where first names are also unknown, these entries only have the surname. Surnames are in CAPITALS. This is followed by the date of the award. Any further awards are noted in brackets with the date, with the Oak Leaves indicated as (OL), Brilliants as (B), the Crown as (C), and the Peace Class as (P). If the award of the Oak Leaves or the Crown was made at the same time as the *Pour le Mérite* it will be shown as (with OL), or (with Crown). The Grand Cross and Star is shown as (GCS). Where the date of the *Pour le Mérite* is unknown but the date of the Oak Leaves is known, I have put the award in on the Oak Leaves date; these entries will be in *italics*.

The award could be (and was) awarded to the same person more than once, although it is possible that some of the 'second awards' could be the Oak Leaves. If two or more awards have been made on the same date, then they are listed in alphabetical order.

1813

Johann Ernst Ferdinand von EISENHART 18–2–1813

Karl Siegismund Erhard von KNOBLOCH 18–2–1813

Karl Heinrich RERDANZ 18–2–1813

Magnus Friedrich von SCHACK 18–2–1813

Karl Adolf Ferdinand von STANTZ 18–2–1813

Friedrich Heinrich August von WITZLEBEN 18–2–1813

Kurt Friedrich Heinrich von BORCKE 20–2–1813

Karl August Alexander von CRAYEN 20–2–1813

Johann GIESE 20–2–1813

August Karl Julius von MANTEUFFEL 20–2–1813

Wilhelm Heinrich von RUDORFF 20–2–1813

Karl Adolf Eduard von SZERDAHELI 20–2–1813

Heinrich Ernst Adolf WESTPHAL 20–2–1813

Wilhelm Kaspar Ferdinand Freiherr von DOERNBERG 10–4–1813

Andrei Ivanovich GORLENKOV 18–4–1813

Pavel Ivanovich BROSIN 13–5–1813

Alexei Igorovich DEDENIEV 13–5–1813

Semen Ivanovich DOBROVOLSKI 13–5–1813

Renatus Rodion Fedorovich GERNGROSS 13–5–1813

Prince Peter Dmitriovich GORTSHAKOV 13–5–1813

Ivan HIRSCH 13–5–1813

HOECK 13–5–1813

Maxim Konstantinovich KRISHANOVICH 13–5–1813

Alexander Ivanovich MARKOV III 13–5–1813

Peter Ivanovich MEDVIEDEV 13–5–1813

Igor Fedorovich NOLDKEN 13–5–1813

Vladimir Afanasseovich OBRUTSHEV 13–5–1813 (first award),
    13/18–10–1814 (second award)

Dmitri Tichonovich Michailovich PARENSSOV 13–5–1813

Nikolai Jevgienovich POSTELNIKOV 13–5–1813

Siegfried Georg Gebhard von QUITZOW 13–5–1813

Robert Igorovich RENNI 13–5–1813

Nikolai Vassilieovich SASONOV 13–5–1813

Nikolai Ivanovich SELIAVIN 13–5–1813

Gustaf Gustafovich STADEN 13–5–1813

Alexander Andreieovich STSHERBININ 13–5–1813

Igor Michailovich TRUBTSHENINOV 13–5–1813

VRANIZKI 13–5–1813

von ADERKAS 17–5–1813

Vassili BEHRENDS 17–5–1813

Prince DRULSKI-SAKOLINSKI 17–5–1813

Anton Jevstafieovich ENGELHART 17–5–1813

Karl Petrovich GUTJAHR 17–5–1813

Alexander Iljit ILJINSKI 17–5–1813

Franz Danilovich OLSHEVSKI 17–5–1813

Ivan OSERSKI 17–5–1813

Siegismund Ferdinandovich POSTELS 17–5–1813

Ivan Ivanovich SCHLETER 17–5–1813

Lev Astafieovich ASTAIEV 18–5–1813

Bogdan Jamelianovich von BRIESKORN 18–5–1813

Georg Wilhelm von HOFMANN 18–5–1813

Stepan Jemelianovich IVANOV 18–5–1813 (first award),
    11–4–1814 (second award), 12–12–1814 (third award)

Fedor Fedorovich von KURSSEL 18–5–1813

Peter Johann Freiherr von LEDINGHAUSEN 18–5–1813

Andrei Ivanovich LIEBSTEIN 18–5–1813

Leopold von MACH II 18–5–1813 (first award), 11–7–1813 (second award)

Alexander Wilhelm von NEIDHARDT 18–5–1813

Karle Ivanovich RABEN 18–5–1813

Afanassi Jefimovich STSHELKAN 18–5–1813

Hans Otto WACHTEN 18–5–1813

Karl Friedrich Franz DALLMER 27–5–1813

Heinrich Gottlieb Konrad HEUDUCK 27–5–1813

August Johann von HOBE 27–5–1813

Christof Josef Friedrich von MICHAELIS 27–5–1813

Karl Friedrich von TIELE 27–5–1813

Johann David Ludwig von YORCK 27–5–1813 (OL, 10–6–1813)

Baron Lev Karlovich von BODE 11–6–1813

Heinrich Friedrich von DIEST 11–6–1813

GLASKO 11–6–1813

Nikolai Dmitrieovich GURIEV 11–6–1813

Martin Nikoliovich HARTING 11–6–1813

Michail Ivanovich KACHOVSKI 11–6–1813

Theodor Ludwig Graf von KELLER 11–6–1813

Arkadi Vassilieovich KOTSHUBEI 11–6–1813

Ivan Grigorieovich MASSALOV 11–6–1813

Vassili Wilhelm von zur MEHLEN 11–6–1813

Ivan Petrovich NOVOSSILZOV 11–6–1813

Ivan Ivanovich PACHERT 11–6–1813

Jakob Vassilieovich PETRULIN 11–6–1813 (first award),
    13/18–10–1814 (second award)

Baron Gustaf von RENNE 11–6–1813

Alexander Petrovich RESLEV 11–6–1813

Baron Andrei Fedorovich von ROSEN 11–6–1813

Ivan Petrovich SHABELSKI 11–6–1813

Peter Nikolaiovich TSHAGIN 11–6–1813

Dmitri Lvovich YGNAATIEV 11–6–1813

Vinzentius Ferrerius Kajetanus von LUPINSKI 14–6–1813

Moritz Ivanovich von BOETTICHER 17–6–1813

Ivan Fedorovich PETERSON 6–7–1813

BULLACH 11–7–1813

Apollon Vassilieovich GOLOFEIEV 11–7–1813

Alexei Alexieiovich MILOCHOV 11–7–1813

Adolf Erikus FEKGEBTREU 2–8–1813

POPOV 2–8–1813

Friedrich Wilhelm Heinrich von PROBST 2–8–1813

Stephen Danilovich PROTOPOPOV 2–8–1813

Ernst Friedrich von SAUCKEN 2–8–1813

Wilhelm Friedrich Karl Dresler von SCHARFFENSTEIN 2–8–1813

Karl Johann Ferdinand JULIUS 4–8–1813

Jevstafi Vladimirovich KAVER 4–8–1813

Fedor Stephanovich KOILENSKI 4–8–1813

Leonti Leotieovich REITZ 4–8–1813

Friedrich Wilhelm von DUNKER 8–8–1813

Georg Karl Leonhard Ludwig von STÜLPNAGEL 8–8–1813

Grigori Vassilieovich BESTUSHEV 11–8–1813

Michail GLUTSHKOVIUS 11–8–1813

Andrei Jefremovich LITOV 11–8–1813

MENIKOV 11–8–1813

Prince Nikolai Serieieovich MENSHIKOV 11–8–1813

Ludwig Franovich MICHAUD 11–8–1813

Count Ivan Alexieieovich MUSSIN-PUSHKIN 11–8–1813

PROSVIRKIN 11–8–1813

Alexander Ivanovich RACHMANOV 11–8–1813

Andrei Fedorovich RÜHL 11–8–1813

Friedrich August von RUMMEL 11–8–1813

Danilo Dmitrieovich SASSAJÄDKO 11–8–1813

Baron Igor Vassilieovich von SCHULZ 11–8–1813

Igor Vassilieovich SONTAG 11–8–1813

Nikolai Stephanovich VELIAMINOV 11–8–1813

Semen Igorovich ROGATSHEV 4–9–1813

SAMARIN 4–9–1813

Count Alexis NOAILLES 5–9–1813

Wieprecht Hans Karl Friedrich von ZIETEN 5–9–1813

Michail Fedorovich ACHLESTISHEV 6–9–1813

Igor Andreieovich AGTE (also spelt ACHTE) 6–9–1813

Fedor Petrovich BECKMANN 6–9–1813

Ivan Ivanovich BIAKOV 6–9–1813

Ilia Gavrilovich BIBIKOV 6–9–1813

August Friedrich Ludwig von BOETTICHER 6–9–1813

Ivan Fedorovich BOGDANOVICH 6–9–1813

Christofor Sergieieovich BORISSOV 6–9–1813

von BREMEN 6–9–1813

Baron Karl Vassilieovich von der BRINCKEN 6–9–1813

Karl Vassilieovich BRUCKENDAHL 6–9–1813

Friedrich Wilhelm von BÜLOW 6–9–1813

Igor Vassilieovich CHOLODOVISKI 6–9–1813

Nikolai Kyrillovich DOLOMANOV 6–9–1813

DREVICH 6–9–1813

Karl Karlovich von ESSEN 6–9–1813

Nikolai Fedorovich FILIPOV 6–9–1813

Friedrich Kaspar von GEISMAR 6–9–1813

GLIEBOV 6–9–1813

Fedor Nikolaieovich GLINKA 6–9–1813

Peter Vasilieovich GRIGORIEV 6–9–1813

Alexander Karlovich GÜNZEL II 6–9–1813

JEREOVSKI 6–9–1813

Karl Filippovich JUNCKER 6–9–1813

Ivan Michailovich KARPOV 6–9–1813

Pavel Dmitriovich KISSELEV 6–9–1813

Vassili Vassilieovich KOTSHUBEI 6–9–1813

KOVERNIEV 6–9–1813

Lev Fedorovich KRAMER 6–9–1813

Ivan Nikolaieovich KRASNOKUTSKI 6–9–1813

Igor Konstabtinovich KRISTOFOVICH 6–9–1813

KRIVONOSSOV 6–9–1813

Alexander Alexandrovich KRUS 6–9–1813

Vladimir Vassilieovich LEVSHIN 6–9–1813

LIUBUSHIN 6–9–1813

Woldemar Heinrich von LOEWNSTERN 6–9–1813

Vassili Ivanovich LOSSENKOV 6–9–1813

Ivan MAKALINSKI 6–9–1813

MATOV 6–9–1813

Vassili Alexandrovich von MENDEM 6–9–1813

Count Ossip Stephanovich de MENDOZA-BUTELLO 6–9–1813

Baron Igor Kasimirovich von MEYERDORFF 6–9–1813

MIAGKOV 6–9–1813

Alexei Grigorieovich MILORADOVICH 6–9–1813

Ivan Petrovich MIRKOVICH 6–9–1813

Alexander Leontieovich MOISSEIEV 6–9–1813

Ivan Semenovich MOROSOV 6–9–1813

Prince Alexander Vassilieovich MUSTAFIN 6–9–1813

NAGIN 6–9–1813

Yeugeni Petrovich NASIMOV 6–9–1813

Bogdan Bogdanovich NILUS 6–9–1813

Peter Ivanovich NOVAK 6–9–1813

Count Ossip Franzovich d'OLONNE 6–9–1813

Anton Danilovich OLSHEVSKI 6–9–1813

Adolf Friedrich von OPPEN 6–9–1813

Alexei Fedorovich ORLOV 6–9–1813

Baron Dmitri Jevgrafieovich von der OSTEN-SACKEN 6–9–1813

Matvei Ivanovich OSTRAGRADSKI 6–9–1813

Anton Fedorovich von PAIKUL (also spelt PAYKULL) 6–9–1813

Andrei Ivanovich PASHKOV 6–9–1813

Ossip Fedorovich PASKEVIVH 6–9–1813

PAVLOV 6–9–1813

Ferdinand Adamovich PAVLOVSKI II 6–9–1813

Ivan Alexieieovich PETROV 6–9–1813

Ivan Matvieieiovich PETROV 6–9–1813

POTVIG 6–9–1813

Alexander Nikolaieovich RAIEVSKI 6–9–1813

RAISKI 6–9–1813

Count Louis de ROCHECHOUART 6–9–1813

Ivan Petrovich SABA 6–9–1813

Michail Jakoleovich SABLIN 6–9–1813

Dmitri Andreieovich SCHEPING 6–9–1813

Fedor Nikita SCHULGAN 6–9–1813

Fedor Jefimovich SCHWARZ 6–9–1813

Andrei Andreieovich SELIVANOV II 6–9–1813 (first award)
    13/18–10–1814 (second award)

SELSAVIN III 6–9–1813

Timofei Andreieovich SHATALOV 6–9–1813

Ivan SHIROV 6–9–1813

Nikolai Martemianovich SIPIAGIN 6–9–1813

Peter Jakovieovich SOROKIN 6–9–1813

SVIERIEV 6–9–1813

TEPLOV 6–9–1813

Gotthard von TIESENHAUSEN 6–9–1813

TRAUTMANN 6–9–1813

Nikolai Jakimovich TREULEBEN 6–9–1813

Vassili Ivanovich TRIAPIZIN 6–9–1813

Prince Alexander Petrovich TRUBEZKOI II 6–9–1813

Andrei Petrovich TURSHANINOV 6–9–1813

Vassili Michailovich VNUKV 6–9–1813

Prince Sergei Grigorieovich VOLKONSKI 6–9–1813

Heinrich August Truchsess Graf zu WALDBURG-CAPUSTIGALL
    6–9–1813

Andrei WIRJUBOV 6–9–1813

BOGDANOV 7–9–1813

Nikolai Alexandrovich OKUNIEV 8–9–1813

Albert Le BLANC 10–9–1813

Jakob SÜCK 10–9–1813

Gustaf Ivanovich von BOETTICHER 13–9–1813

BRÜMMER 13–9–1813

Christian Ivanovich DIETERICHS III 13–9–1813

Faddei Antipovich DROSDOVSKI 13–9–1813

Alexei Fedorovich EMME 13–9–1813

Vassili Andreieiovich FANSHAVE 13–9–1813

Gustaf Vassilieovich GERBEL II 13–9–1813

David KANDIBA II 13–9–1813

Alexander Ivanovich KUSMIN 13–9–1813

Michail Vassilieovich SAVIESKIN 13–9–1813

Fedor Maximovich SCHULMANN 13–9–1813

Fedor Nikita SESLAVIN 13–9–1813

SOSNIN 13–9–1813

Michail Alexieieovich TEPLOV 13–9–1813

Frol Ossipovich DOLIVA-DOBROVOLSKI 15–9–1813

Prince Valerian Grigorieovich MADATOV 15–9–1813

Friedrich Thomas Freiherr ADLERCREUTZ 16–9–1813

Elias ARFVEDSON 16–9–1813

Magnus Friedrich Ferdinand von BJÖRNSTJERNA 16–9–1813

Karl Gustaf FORSELL 16–9–1813

Gustaf Abraham PEYRON 16–9–1813

Leonhard Axel REUTERSKJÖLD 16–9–1813

Karl Johann af WIRSÉN 16–9–1813

VOINOV 21–9–1813

Prince Kai Bei BOLATUK 24–9–1813

SOSNIN 24–9–1813

Michail TRESKIN 24–9–1813

Andrei Petrovich TURTSHANINOV 24–9–1813

Timofei Igorovich von BOCK 25–9–1813

Prince Friedrich Franz Anton von HOHENZOLLERN-HECHINGEN
    25–9–1813

Alexei Fedorovich ORLOV 25–9–1813

James N. CHARLES 28–9–1813

Henry Fredric COOKE 28–9–1813

George Lionel DAWSON 28–9–1813

Ernst Johann Christian von DÜRING 28–9–1813

George JAMES 28–9–1813

Peter Timofieovich SEKRETOV 1–10–1813

KUTEINIKOV VI 4–10–1813

Christof George Heinrich Franz von SOMMITZ 6–10–1813

Prince Karl Friedrich August von MECKLENBURG-STRELITZ
    9–10–1813

Emanuel Graf von MENSDORFF 9–10–1813

Karl Friedrich von dem KNESEBECK 19–10–1813

Karl Leopold Ludwig von BORSTELL 21–10–1813

POPOV 21–10–1813

Heinrich Ludwig August von THÜMEN 21–10–1813

Baron Gustaf Romamovich von UNGERN-STERNBERG 21–10–1813

Alexander Heinrich Gotthard von ZASTROW 21–10–1813

Karl CALL 25–10–1813

Adam Retsey de RETSE 25–10–1813

Alexander Petrovich BERGMANN 15–11–1813

Konstantin Stephanovich ANDREIEIVSKI 18–11–1813

Stanislav Stanislavieovich BRANICKE 18–11–1813

Nikolai Dmitrieovich DURNOVO 18–11–1813

Maxim Maximovich von GROTENHELM 18–11–1813

Konstantin Zarevich von IMERETIEN 18–11–1813

Jakob Matvieieovich von LAMSDORF 18–11–1813

Alexander Ivanovich MICHAILOSKI-DANILEVSKI 18–11–1813

Lev Alexieieovich PEROVSKI 18–11–1813

von RAMBURG 18–11–1813

Count Ludwig Viktor Leo de ROCHECHOUART 18–11–1813

Alexander Vassilieovich von STERHELM 18–11–1813

Baron Justus Philipp von WOLZOGEN 18–11–1813

Maximilian von BÖHM 28–11–1813

August Eberhard von GEORGII 28–11–1813

Prince Wenzel LIECHTENSTEIN 28–11–1813

Johann Baptist Graf PAAR 28–11–1813

Felix Graf WOYNA 28–11–1813

Baron Roman von AEXKULL-GYLLENBANDT 8–12–1813

AKSAKOV 8–12–1813

Alexander Ivanovich ALBRECHT 8–12–1813

Ivan Karlovich ARNOLDI 8–12–1813

ARTEMIEV 8–12–1813

Jefim Troimovich ARTIUCHOV 8–12–1813

Michail Nikolaieovich ASTACHOV 8–12–1813

Ernst Ludwig ASTER 8–12–1813

Lev Ivanovich ATRESHKOV 8–12–1813

Flagon Mironovich BASHMAKOV (also spelt BACHMAKOV)
    8–12–1813 (first award), 13/18–10–1814 (second award)

Alexei Alexanderovich BATASHEV 8–12–1813

Johann Jevstafieovich BAUMGARTEN 8–12–1813

Ivan Ivanovich BECK 8–12–1813

Fedor Ivanovich BELLINGHAUSEN 8–12–1813

Konstantin Alexandrovich BENDERSKI 8–12–1813

Michail Dmitrieovich BESTUSHEV-RIUMIN 8–12–1813

Ivan BICHALOV 8–12–1813

Konon Vassilieovich BICHALOV 8–12–1813

David Grigorieovich BIEGODOV 8–12–1813 (first award),
    16–12–1813 (second award)

BIELAIEVSKI 8–12–1813

Anton Antonovich BISTROM 8–12–1813

Gavrilo Vassilieovich BLANOV 8–12–1813

Alexander Nikolaieovich BOGDANOV 8–12–1813

Karl August Ferdinand von BORCKE 8–12–1813

Nikolai Ivanovich BORISSOV 8–12–1813

Alexander Ivanovich BRAMS 8–12–1813

Semen Petrovich BRESHINSKI 8–12–1813 (first award),
    13/18–10–1814 (second award)

BRÜCKENTAL 8–12–1813

Peter Dmitrieovich BULGARIN 8–12–1813

Count Viktor Ivanovich de CHAMBORANT 8–12–1813

Alexei Afanassieovich CHOMIAKOV 8–12–1813

Grigori Semenovich CHRAPOVIZSKI 8–12–1813

Pavel Vassiliovich DANILOV 8–12–1813

DAVIDOV I 8–12–1813

Jevdokim Vassiliovich DAVIDOV II 8–12–1813

Semen Semenovich DEMTSHENKOV 8–12–1813

Andrei Ivanovich DIETERICHS 8–12–1813 (with OL)

Andrei Ivanovich DIETRICHS 8–12–1813

Lavrenti Leontieovich DOBROVOLSKI 8–12–1813

Ivan DSEVONSKI 8–12–1813

DSHESHELINSKI 8–12–1813

Fedor Fedorovich DUROV 8–12–1813

Ivan Nikolaieovich DUROV 8–12–1813

Alexei Matvieieovich EISMONT 8–12–1813

FOMIN 8–12–1813

Peter Ivanovich FREIGANG 8–12–1813 (first award),
    12–12–1814 (second award)

Ivan Petrovich FRIEDBERG 8–12–1813

Peter Nikolaieovich FROLOV 8–12–1813

Afanassi Jakovleovich GALIONKA 8–12–1813

Jakob Fedorovich GANSKAU 8–12–1813

Semen Ossipovich GATOVSKI 8–12–1813

Yeugeni Alexandrovich GOLOVIN 8–12–1813

Prince Michail Dmitrieovich GORTSHAKOV 8–12–1813

Karl Wilhelm Georg von GROLMAN 8–12–1813

Dmitri Ulnovich von GROTHUSS 8–12–1813

GUBIN 8–12–1813

Alexander Klavdieieovich GUÉROIS 8–12–1813

Anton Antonovich HELMERSEN 8–12–1813

Heinrich Wilhelm von HORN 8–12–1813

Nikolai Nikolaieovich ITSHKOV 8–12–1813

Alexander Ivanovich JAKOVLEV 8–12–1813

Stepan Makarovich JAKOVLEV 8–12–1813 (with OL)

Vassili Vassiliovich JESCHIN 8–12–1813 (second award),
(date of first award unclear)

JESSAULOV 8–12–1813

JURGENEV 8–12–1813

Alexander Ivanovich KALININ 8–12–1813

Fedor Grigorieovich KALM 8–12–1813

KANATTSHIKOV 8–12–1813

Alexander Nikolaieovich KANTSHIALOV 8–12–1813

Ivan Fedorovich KAPUSTIN 8–12–1813

Nikanor Fedorovich KASHIRINOV 8–12–1813

Ivan Petrovich KASIN II 8–12–1813

Prince Grigori Vassilieovich KASTROIT-DREKALOVICH-
SKANDERBEK 8–12–1813

Konstantin Fomitch KELDERMANN 8–12–1813

Michail Gerassimovich KELDIJAREV 8–12–1813

Jermolai Fedorovich KERN 8–12–1813

Dmitri Andreovich KISSLOVSKI 8–12–1813

Ewald Johann von KLEIST 8–12–1813

Jevstafi Christoforovich KLINGENBERG 8–12–1813

Friedrich Karl Leopold von KLÜX 8–12–1813

Boris Jakovleovich KNIASHNIN 8–12–1813

Vassili Ivanovich KORSHAVIN 8–12–1813

Fedor Nikititsh KOTSHETOV 8–12–1813

KOVALEVSKI 8–12–1813

Michail Michailovich KOVANKOV 8–12–1813

Jakob Petrovich KRASSOVSKI 8–12–1813

Andrei Ivanovich KRISHANOVSKI 8–12–1813

Gustav Vassilieovich KROHNSTEIN 8–12–1813

Nikolai Andreieovich KURNOSSOV 8–12–1813

Stepan Ivanovich KUSMIN 8–12–1813

KUTSHEROV 8–12–1813

Stepan Ivanovich LESSOVSKI 8–12–1813

Dmitri Andreieovich LEVIN 8–12–1813

LISTOVSKI 8–12–1813

Alexander Petrovich LOPUCHIN 8–12–1813

Timofei Antonovich LÖWENHOF 8–12–1813 (first award),
    13/18–10–1814 (second award)

Dmitri Nikolaiovich LUKOMSKI 8–12–1813

Wichard Friedrich von LÜTZOW 8–12–1813

Michail Semenovich MAGDENKO II 8–12–1813

Ivan Vassilieovich MAKAZAROV 8–12–1813

Alexander Semenovich MALEIEV 8–12–1813

MALEVANOV 8–12–1813

Semen Semenovich MASARAKI 8–12–1813

MASSLOV 8–12–1813

Jakob Afanassieovich MEDINZOV 8–12–1813

Alexander Ivanovich MESSING 8–12–1813

Vassili Nikolaieovich MIAGKOV 8–12–1813

Sergei Ivanovich MIKULIN 8–12–1813

Andrei Nikolaieovich MILORADOVICH 8–12–1813

Porfiri Christoforovich MOLOSTVOV 8–12–1813

MOLTSHANOV 8–12–1813

Denis Denissovich MOSHENSKI 8–12–1813

Petrovich MURAVSKI 8–12–1813 (first award),
    12–12–1814 (second award)

Andrei Grigorieovich NAPENIN 8–12–1813

Sergei Vassilieovich NAPIEIZAN 8–12–1813

Heinrich Karlovich NARBUT 8–12–1813

Avim Vassilieovich NESTEROVSKI 8–12–1813

Karl NOLDE 8–12–1813

NOVIKOV 8–12–1813

Alexander Petrovich OBOLENSKI 8–12–1813

Prince Nikolai Petrovich OBOLENSKI 8–12–1813

Prince Vassili Petrovich OBOLENSKI 8–12–1813 (second award),
    (date of first award unclear)

Peter Semenovich OBUCHOVSKI 8–12–1813

Matvei Antonovich OLSHEVSKI 8–12–1813

Nikolai Jeremieieovich OSSIPOV 8–12–1813

PEREPIETSHIN 8–12–1813

Matvei Ivanovich PICHATSHEV 8–12–1813

PISHNIZKI 8–12–1813

Alexander Alexandrovich PISSAREV 8–12–1813

Ivan Ivanovich POCHVISNIEV 8–12–1813

Ivan Lawrenteovich POHL 8–12–1813

Danilo Petrovich POLOSSOV 8–12–1813

Vassili Jakovleovich PONEROVSKI 8–12–1813

Peter Igorovich POTAPOV 8–12–1813

Stanislaus Stanislavovich POTOCKI 8–12–1813

Pavel Onufrieovich PRIGARA 8–12–1813

Grigori Grigorieovich PROTASSOV 8–12–1813

Peter Sergieieovich PROTOPOPOV 8–12–1813

Alexei Alexanderovich PSHENITSHNOI 8–12–1813

Prince Yuri Petrovich RATEIEV 8–12–1813

Karl Pavlovich von REIBNITZ 8–12–1813

Karl Pavlovich von RENNENKAMPFF 8–12–1813 (first award),
13/18–10–1814 (second award)

Christofor Romanovich von REUTERN 8–12–1813

Ivan Bogdanovich RÖHREN 8–12–1813 (with OL)

Vladimir Ivanovich ROSEN 8–12–1813

Count Louis Franzovich de SAINT PRIEST 8–12–1813

Ivan Vassilieovich SAMOILOVICH 8–12–1813

Michail Vassilieovich SAVIESKIN 8–12–1813

SAVINITSH 8–12–1813

Fedor Fedorovich SCHUBERT 8–12–1813

Alexei Andreieovich SELIVANOV III 8–12–1813

Stepan SEMENSTSHENKOV 8–12–1813

Grigori Alexieieovich SERGIEIEV 8–12–1813

SHAMSHEV 8–12–1813

Jakob Sergieieovich SHELVINSKI 8–12–1813

Vassili Nikanrovich SHENSHIN 8–12–1813 (with OL)

Peter Alexandrovich SHOCHOV 8–12–1813

Nikolai Petrovich SHUBINSKI 8–12–1813

Ivan Fedorovich SHUMKOV 8–12–1813

Alexander Akimovich SHURAVLOV 8–12–1813

Sacher Sergieieovich SHUSHERIN 8–12–1813 (with OL), (first award),
13/18–10–1814 (second award), (unclear if a third award was made or
whether it was the OL)

von SIEGROTH 8–12–1813

Peter Gavrilovich SMOLKOV 8–12–1813

Martemian Andreieovich SOLOVOV 8–12–1813

Ivan Matvieieovich SPIRIDOV 8–12–1813

Michail Michailovich STANKOVICH 8–12–1813

Sachar Christoforovich STAVRAKOV 8–12–1813

Anton Ossipovich STEGMANN 8–12–1813

Peter Karlovich STRAHLMANN 8–12–1813

Prince Nikolai Grigorieovich STSHERBATOV 8–12–1813

Peter Onufrieovich SUCHOSANET II 8–12–1813

Sergei Charitonovich SUIEV 8–12–1813

Nikolai Ivanovich SUTHOF I 8–12–1813

Peter SUVOROV II 8–12–1813 (with OL)

Peter Ivanovich TARNOVSKI 8–12–1813

Afanassi Petrovich TARSHEVSKI 8–12–1813

Karl Karlovich TAUBE 8–12–1813

Peter Fedorovich TAZIN IV 8–12–1813 (first award),
    16–12–1813 (second award)

Igor Ivanovich TELIEGIN 8–12–1813

Pavel Lvovich TEMIROV 8–12–1813

Fedor Fedorovich TERNE 8–12–1813 (first award),
    12–12–1814 (second award)

Fedor Karlovich TIMRODT 8–12–1813

Vassili Grigorieovich TISHIN 8–12–1813

Pavel Semenovich TIUNIN 8–12–1813

Jevdokim Petrovich TOLMATSHOV 8–12–1813

Ignati Petrovich TOTSHINSKI 8–12–1813 (first award),
    17–2–1832 (second award)

Pavel Andreieovich TRAVIN 8–12–1813

Count Joseph Venanzone TRINCHIERI 8–12–1813

Michail Ivanovich TSHEODAIEV 8–12–1813

Grigori Ilit TSHERNOSUBOV 8–12–1813

Ivan Igorovich TSHURILOV 8–12–1813

Baron Peter Longinovich von UEXKULL-GYLLENBANDT 8–12–1813

Peter Alexandrovich UGRIUMOV 8–12–1813

Peter Sergieieovich USHAKOV 8–12–1813 (first award),
    13/18–10–1814 (second award)

Dmitri Nikolaieovich VALCHOVSKI 8–12–1813

Georg Wilhelm von VALENTINI 8–12–1813

Stepan Semenovich VASSELOVSKI 8–12–1813

Peter Ivanovich VERCHOVSKI 8–12–1813

Peter Prokofieovich VICHODSEVSKI 8–12–1813

Count Matvei Jureovich VIELHORSKI 8–12–1813

von VIETINGHOFF 8–12–1813 (first award), 11–4–1814 (second award)

Vladimir Michailovich VIKTOROV 8–12–1813

Adam Antonovich VINIARSKI 8–12–1813

Jakob Ivanovich VOLEVATSH 8–12–1813 (first award),
    13/18–10–1814 (second award)

Peter Lvovich VOLSHENSKI 8–12–1813

Vassili Michailovich VUNKOV 8–12–1813

Alexander Georg Ludwig Moritz Maximillian von WAHLEN-JÜRGASS
    8–12–1813

Michail Alexandrovich von WISIN 8–12–1813

Prince Alexander Konstabtinovich YPSILANTI 8–12–1813

Vassili BICHALOV 10–12–1813

Johann Heinrich KREUGER 10–12–1813

Karl August L'COQ 10–12–1813

SHIMANOV 10–12–1813

RASLOV 11–12–1813

On 11–12–1813 the award was also made to an unknown Russian adjutant
    with the rank of lieutenant

Magnus Graf BRAHE 12–12–1813

Karl Friedrich von CARDELL 12–12–1813

Gustaf Stanisaus von ENGESTRÖM 12–12–1813

Charles Jean de SURMAIN 12–12–1813

Anton Kasimirovich ARZISHEVSKI 16–12–1813

Fedor Sergieieovich ASANTSHEVSKI 16–12–1813

Jakob Ivanovich BAROZZIE 16–12–1813

Dmitri Ivanovich BIBIKOV 16–12–1813

Grigori Grigorieovich BIELOGRADSKI 16–12–1813

Karl Freidrich Salesius Freiherr von dem BUSSCHE-IPPENBURG
    16–12–1813

Dmitri Petrovich BUTURLIN 16–12–1813

Nikolai Petrovich CHANIKOV 16–12–1813

Grigori Sergieieovich CHOMUTOV 16–12–1813

Jason Semenovich CHRAPOVIZKI 16–12–1813

Pavel Stepanovich CHRIESTSHATIZKI 16–12–1813

Andrei Vassilovich DASHKOV 16–12–1813

Wilhelm Ludwig Viktor Henckel Graf von DONNERSMARCK
16–12–1813

Ossip Petrovich DU BOY (also spelt DEBOAR) 16–12–1813

Andrei Vassilieovich ENGELHART 16–12–1813

Rudolf (or Roman) Antonovich FREYMANN 16–12–1813

Alexander Michailovich GEDEONOV 16–12–1813

Prince Sergei Dmitrieovich GORTSHAKOV 16–12–1813

Alexei Jevdokimovich GREKOV XVII 16–12–1813

GRINKEVICH 16–12–1813

Michail Andreieovich HABBE 16–12–1813

Igor Ivanovich HELFREICH 16–12–1813

Ossip Alexandrovich HURKO (also spelt GURKO) 16–12–1813

Ivan Jakovieovich IKONNIKOV 16–12–1813

Ustin Timofieieovich IVASKEVICH 16–12–1813

JULIUS 16–12–1813

KAMENSKI 16–12–1813

Christofor Pavlovich KARSHIN 16–12–1813

Vladimir Karlovich von KNORRING 16–12–1813

August Fedorovich KOMSTADIUS 16–12–1813

Baron Ossip Ivanovich von KORFF I 16–12–1813

Semen Nikolaieovich KORSSAKOV 16–12–1813

Nikolai Fedorovich KOSLOV 16–12–1813

Grigori Andreieovich KOSTIN IV 16–12–1813

Alexander Grigorieovich KRASNOKTSKI 16–12–1813

Fedor Ivanovich KRATZ 16–12–1813

Nikolai KREKSHIN 16–12–1813

Michail Michailovich KUSNEZOV 16–12–1813

Ossip Ivanovich MANFREDI 16–12–1813

MUCHANOV 16–12–1813

Nikolai Fedorovich NAKOVALNIN 16–12–1813

Ivan Yurieovich NIKOLAIEV 16–12–1813

Kirill Nikititsh NIKONOV 16–12–1813

Ivan Fedorovich OLDENBORGEN 16–12–1813

Peter Petrovich PAISSEL 16–12–1813

Alexander Alexieieovich PANTSHULIDSEV 16–12–1813

Sergei Nikolaieovich PLOCHOVO 16–12–1813

Paul Karlovich von PRITTWITZ 16–12–1813

Andrei Fedorovich PROZIKOV 16–12–1813

Ivan Stanislavovich RAISKI 16–12–1813

Vassili Dmitrieovich RIKOV 16–12–1813

Nikolai Matvieieovich ROKOTOV 16–12–1813

Peter Vassilieovich SABANIEIEV 16–12–1813

Nikolai Antonovich Freiherr von SCHLIPPENBACH 16–12–1813

Jakob Fedorovich SCHLODHAUER 16–12–1813

Karl Grigorieovich SCHRÖDER 16–12–1813

Prince Nikolai Michailovich SHACHOVSKOI 16–12–1813

Yuri Ivanovich SHAMSHEV IV 16–12–1813

Maxim SHIMANOVSKI 16–12–1813

Alexander Fedorovich SHUBIN 16–12–1813

Karl Ivanovich von SIEVERS 16–12–1813

Ossip Ivanovich SMOLIAK 16–12–1813

Afanassi Ivanovich SOLOTAREV 16–12–1813

Jakob Michailovich STARKOV 16–12–1813

Michail Sergieieovich STCHULEPNIKOV 16–12–1813

Vladimir Karlovich STRAHLBORN 16–12–1813

Ivan Onufrieovich SUCHOSANET I 16–12–1813

Peter Ivanovich TARASSOV 16–12–1813

Nikolai Jakovleovich TEGLEV 16–12–1813

Alexei Dmitrieovich TIRKOV 16–12–1813

Yeugeni Ivanovich TISHEVSKI 16–12–1813

Igor Ivanovich TRESKIN 16–12–1813

Alexander Gerssevanovich TSHAVTSHAVADSE 16–12–1813

Anton Maximovich von VIETINGHOFF 16–12–1813

Pavel Fedorovich VILHELMOV 16–12–1813

Josef Fedorovich VISSOZKI 16–12–1813

Alexander Jakovieovich von WEYRAUCH 16–12–1813

ZICKEL (also spelt ZICKEIN) 16–12–1813

Wenzel Philipp von MARSCHALL 18–12–1813

Sergei Vassiliovich SIBIN 18–12–1813

Georg Dubislaf Ludwig von PIRCH 24–12–1813

1814

Alexei Alexandrovich BIBEKOV 1–1–1814

Nikolai Filippovich JEMELIANOV 1–1–1814

Michail Fedorovich NIKITIN 1–1–1814

Andrei Igorovich von VIETINGHOFF 1–1–1814

Ivan Alexandrovich von WISIN 1–1–1814

Karl Schneider Freiherr von ARNO 8–1–1814

Johann Gotthold HECKEL 11–1–1814

Justin Stanislavovich RASTKOVSKI 11–1–1814

Paul von WERNHARDT 14–1–1814

Lars Alger BERGENEREUTZ 11–2–1814

Karl Eduard CARLHEIM-GYLLENSKÖLD 11–2–1814

Gustaf Adolf HJERTA 11–2–1814

Axel Otto Graf MÖRNER 11–2–1814

Matwei Ivanovich JAGODOVSKI 2–3–1814

KARISHEV 2–3–1814

Ivan KULIABKA 2–3–1814

Käpitan Borissovich SHETOCHIN 2–3–1814

Michail Ivanovich TOGAITSHINOV 2–3–1814

PUSIN 3–3–1814

Johann Ivan BRANDT 6–3–1814

Ivan Ivanovich DESKUR (also spelt DESCOURS) 6–3–1814 (first award),
    12–12–1814 (second award)

MAKUCHIN 6–3–1814 (first award), 12–12–1814 (second award)

Ivan Terentieovich POTULOV 6–3–1814 (first award),
    12–12–1814 (second award)

Fedor Nikolaiovich PUSHKAREV 9–3–1814

Count Gustaf Gustafovich ARMFELT 19–3–1814

Pavel Sergieieovich BERNIKOV 19–3–1814

Andrei Vassilieovich BOGDANOVSKI 19–3–1814

Nikolai Jakovleovich BUTKOVSKI 19–3–1814

Ivan Dmitrieovich DMITRIEV 19–3–1814

Alexander Samoilovich FIGNER 19–3–1814

Prince Alexander Sergieieovich GOLIZIN 19–3–1814

Igor Fedorovich von der HOVEN 19–3–1814

Baron Igor Jermolaieovich KLEBEK 19–3–1814

Konstantin Michailovich KOLOTINSKI 19–3–1814

Michail Avramovich KOVRIGIN 19–3–1814

Fedor Ivanovich PANTENIUS 19–3–1814

Gustaf Magnus von RENNENKAMPFF 19–3–1814

Josef Roszner Freiherr von ROSZENEGG 19–3–1814

Andrei Petrovich SHUCHOV 19–3–1814

TOLSTOI 19–3–1814

Johann Friedrich Karl von ALVENSLEBEN 31–3–1814 (with OL)

Alexia Alexieieovich FILIPOV 31–3–1914 (first award),
    12–12–1814 (second award)

Neidhardt von GNEISENAU 31–3–1814

Wilhelm August Anton Karl Freiherr von KAGENECK 31–3–1814

Friedrich Emilius Ferdinand Heinrich von KLEIST 31–3–1814

Ivan Nikolaieovich KOLETSHIZKI 31–3–1814 (first award),
    12–12–1814 (second award)

August Friedrich von MACH 31–3–1814

Jevstafi Charitonovich POKROVSKI 31–3–1814 (first award),
    12–12–1814 (second award)

Karl Georg Albrecht Ernst von HAKE 3–4–1814

Karl Axel Graf von ROSEN 4–4–1814

Franz Josef Freiherr von BEUST 9–4–1814

Prince Freidrich Adalbert von HOHENZOLLERN-HECHINGEN
    9–4–1814

Wilhelm von MUFFLING 9–4–1814 (with OL)

Sir Hudson LOWE 10–4–1814

AFANASSIEV 11–4–1814

ALISSOV 11–4–1814

Pavel Adamovich AMPACH 11–4–1814

Anton Ivanovich ANTONOVSKI 11–4–1814

Michail Ivanovich BAKAIEV II 11–4–1814

Prince Peter Semenovich BARATEIEV II 11–4–1814

Sergei Gerassimovich BATURIN 11–4–1814

Baron Fedor Christoforovich BELLINGHAUSEN 11–4–1814

Jermolai Astafieovich BERGMANN 11–4–1814

Jemelian Ossipovich BIELOGRADSKI 11–4–1814

Peter Michailovich BIKOV III 11–4–1814

Alexander Petrovich BORNOVOLOKOV 11–4–1814

Ivan Ivanovich BRUSLIANSKI 11–4–1814

BULASHOV 11–4–1814

Alexei Ivanovich CHARTSHENKO-DENISSENKO 11–4–1814

Vassili Jelissieovich CHITROVO 11–4–1814

CHOMIAKOV 11–4–1814

Nikolai Alexandrovich CHVOSTOVSKI 11–4–1814

Feodossi Ivanovich DAMITSH 11–4–1814

Dmitri Petrovich DANILOV 11–4–1814

Dmitri Vassilieovich DAVIDOV 11–4–1814

Parfeni Semenovich DEMIANKOV 11–4–1814

Alexander Ivanovich DMITRIEV-MAMONOV 11–4–1814

Michail Dmitrieovich FEDOSSEIEV 11–4–1814

Viktor Alexieieovich FROLOV-BAGRIEIEV 11–4–1814

Karl Gustafovich von GERBEL III 11–4–1814 (first award),
    11–8–1814 (second award)

Fedor Astafieovich GLEITZMANN 11–4–1814

Alexei GOLOSHTSHAPOV 11–4–1814

Baron Jen Baptiste Louis de GOSSARD 11–4–1814

GRUSINOV 11–4–1814

Count Nikolai Nikolaieovich GUDOVICH 11–4–1814

Grigori Ivanovich JANNAU II 11–4–1814

Michail Alexandrovich JERMOLOV 11–4–1814

Peter Nikolaieovich JERMOLOV 11–4–1814

Ivan Sacharovich JERSHOV 11–4–1814

Peter Michailovich JURGENIEV II 11–4–1814

Ivan Vassilieovich KARATSHINSKI 11–4–1814 (first award),
    12–12–1814 (second award)

Ivan Petrovich KARZOV I 11–4–1814

Pavel Stepanovich KARZOV 11–4–1814

Porfiri Sergieieovich KASHINZOV II 11–4–1814

Likurg Lambrovich KATSHONI 11–4–1814

Baron Nikolai Ivanovich von KORFF 11–4–1814

Porfiri Pavlovich KOROBIN III 11–4–1814

Arsenic Jermolaieovich KOROVKIN 11–4–1814

Pavel Matvieieovich KORSSAKOV I 11–4–1814

Lev Ivanovich von KOSCHEMBAHR 11–4–1814

Prince Vladimir Nikolaieovich KOSLOVSKI 11–4–1814

Nikolai Grigorieovich KOSTIN 11–4–1814

Nikolai Ivanovich KOSTIREV 11–4–1814

Sergei Andreieovich KOSTOMAROV 11–4–1814

Leonid Yuriovich KRASINSKI 11–4–1814

Dmitri Ivanovich KREKSHIN 11–4–1814

Dmitri Sergieieovich KRILOV 11–4–1814

Nikolai Ivanovich KRIVZOV 11–4–1814

Vladimir Pavlovich KRUPENIN 11–4–1814

Igor Sergieieovich KURDIUMOV 11–4–1814

Vassili Vassilieovich KUSHIN 11–4–1814

Nikita Petrovich KUSMIN 11–4–1814

LABUTIN 11–4–1814

Nikolai Ivanovich LADIGIN 11–4–1814

Peter Pavlovich LAPPA 11–4–1814

Alexander Jakovieovich LAVEIKA 11–4–1814

LEPECHIN 11–4–1814

Fedor Grigorieovich LEVSHENKO 11–4–1814

Afanassi LICHAREV 11–4–1814

Jevstafi Maximovich LINGREN 11–4–1814

Ivan Ivanovich LOUR 11–4–1814

Alexei Dmitrieovich MEDVIEDEV 11–4–1814

MEKNOB 11–4–1814

Karl Karlovich MELLARD 11–4–1814

Prince Alexander Sergieieovich MENSHIKOV 11–4–1814

Panfemir Christoforovich MOLOSTVOV 11–4–1814

Ivan Nikolaiovich MORDVINOV II 11–4–1814

Ivan Pavlovich MORTSHALOV 11–4–1814

Matvei Matvieieovich MUROMZOV 11–4–1814

Sergei Alexandrovich NAUMOV 11–4–1814

Michail Kusmitsh NIKIFOROV 11–4–1814

NOVIZKI 11–4–1814

OSERSKI 11–4–1814

Vladimir Grigorieovich PATKUL 11–4–1814

Ivan Ivanovich PENSKOI 11–4–1814

Ivan Alexandrovich PIETIN 11–4–1814

Karl Karlovich von PIRCH I 11–4–1814

Wilhelm Antonovich PLESKI 11–4–1814

Peter POTULOV V 11–4–1814

Lavrenti Jakovleovich PROSORKEVICH 11–4–1814

Alexander Dmitrieovich PTEMKIM I 11–4–1814

Fedor Fedorovich RALL III 11–4–1814

RASSOCHIN 11–4–1814

Jakob Andreieiovich READ 11–4–1814

Alfons Gabriel Broglio de REVEL I 11–4–1814

Chali Ivanovich RISVANOVICH 11–4–1814

Matvei Mustafovich ROMANOVSKI II 11–4–1814

Peter Igorovich RUBZOV 11–4–1814

Ivan Danilovich SABLOZKI 11–4–1814

Ivan Grigorieovich SABUDSKI 11–4–1814

Nikolai Ivanovich SAMUIZKI 11–4–1814

Baron Anton Andreieiovich SCHLIPPENBACH 11–4–1814

SHOLOBOV 11–4–1814

Alexander Nikita SINEINKOV 11–4–1814

Michail Nikolaieovich SOCHAZKI 11–4–1814

Karl Otto Wilhelm von STRANDMANN 11–4–1814

Fedor Jermolaieovich STRIABIN 11–4–1814

Konstantin Petrovich van SUCHTELEN 11–4–1814

Ivan Alexandrovich TITOV IV 11–4–1814

Nikolai Michailovich TITOV II 11–4–1814

Vladimir Michailovich TITOV I 11–4–1814

Afanassi Petrovich TIUTSHEV I 11–4–1814

Alexei Petrovich TIUTSHEV II 11–4–1814

Jakob Matvieieovich TRETIAKOV 11–4–1814

Nikolai Gavrilovich TSHAGIN 11–4–1814

Michail Jakoleovich TSHEODAIEV 11–4–1814

Peter Pavloich TSHUMAKOV 11–4–1814

Leo Josef von TUCHOLKA 11–4–1814

Prince Fedor Vladimirovich UKINSIEV 11–4–1814

Michail Andreieovich USHAKOV I 11–4–1814

Nikolai Pavlovich USHAKOV 11–4–1814

Fedor Fedorovich UVAROV 11–4–1814

Pavel Fedorovich VADKOVSKI II 11–4–1814

Ivan Michailovich VIKINSKI 11–4–1814

Jevgraf Stepanovich VISSITSKI 11–4–1814

Ivan Andreieiovich VONLIARSKI 11–4–1814

Ivan Ossipovich von WITTE I 11–4–1814

Saltan Davliet Murat BIEIEV 12–4–1814

Marquis de la Maisonfort Dubois DESCOURS 13–4–1814

Nikonor Vassilieovich JAMINSKI 13–4–1814 (first award),
    3–6–1814 (second award)

Alexei Karpovich KARPOV 13–4–1814

Wilhelm Michailovich LAPPA 13–4–1814

Andrei Andreieiovich LECHNER 13–4–1814

Karl August Ludwig von WEDELL 13–4–1814

Count Vladimir Stepanovich APRAXIN 24–4–1814

Dmitri Jevlampieovich BASHMAKOV 24–4–1814

Alexei Nikolaiovich DIAKOV 24–4–1814

Alexander Petrovich LATSHINOV 24–4–1814

Sergei Petrovich NEKLUDOV 24–4–1814

Franz Florentin Graf VALORY 24–4–1814

Ignaz GOESCHL 25–4–1814

Prince Johann Karl von HOHENZOLLERN-HECHINGEN 25–4–1814

Prince Konstantin Ludwig Karl von LOEWENSTEIN-WERTHEIM-
    ROSENBERG 25–4–1814

Josef von der MARCK 25–4–1814

Johann Heinrich Christian SCHMALTZ 25–4–1814

Albrecht Bresserer von THAISINGEN 25–4–1814

Prince August Maria Maximilian von THURN und TAXIS 25–4–1814

Friedrich TREUBERG 25–4–1814

Alexei Ivanovich MAIOROV 27–4–1814

Karl Ivanovich ALBRECHT II 6–5–1814

Fedor Ivanovich BARTHOLOMAI 6–5–1814

Filipp Antonovich von BISTROM 6–5–1814 (first award),
    13/18–10–1814 (second award)

Marquis Josef Pavlovich de BOISSESSON 6–5–1814

Stephan Alexandrovich CHILKOV 6–5–1814

Danilo Alexandrovich von GERSTENZWEIG 6–5–1814 (first award),
    13/18–10–1814 (second award)

Wilhelm Otto von GLASENAPP II 6–5–1814

JEROPKIN 6–5–1814

Peter Andreieovich KASIN I 6–5–1814

Lev Vassilieovich KLIMOVSKI 6–5–1814

KOCHIUS 6–5–1814

Ivan Gavrilovich KRUGLIKOV 6–5–1814

Prince Zenofont Fedorovich KVITNIZKI 6–5–1814

Karl Christianovich MEIER II 6–5–1814

Alexander Nikiforovich SABORINSKI III 6–5–1814

Semen Nikiforovich SABORINSKI II 6–5–1814

Dmitri Petrovich SELEZKI 6–5–1814

Nikolai Dmitrieovich SKOBELZIN 6–5–1814 (first award),
    8–5–1814 (second award)

Baron Peter Prokofieovich SOLOTOSEVSKI 6–5–1814

Dmitri Alexieieovich STALIPIN (also spelt STOLIPIN) 6–5–1814
    (first award), 13/18–10–1814 (second award)

Karl Gustafovich von STRANDMANN 6–5–1814

Alexander Grigorieovich STROGANOV 6–5–1814

Nikolai Onufrieovich SUCHOSANET III 6–5–1814

Vassili Alexandrovich SUCHOVO-KOBULIN 6–5–1814

Kasimir Ivanovich TSHUDOVSKI 6–5–1814

VASTIANOV (also spelt VASSIANOV) 6–5–1814

Michail Feddieieovich VISHIZKI 6–5–1814 (first award),
    12–5–1814 (second award)

Ivan Afanassieovich VUITSH II 6–5–1814

Ossip Ivanovich YUSHKOV 6–5–1814

Vassili Alexandrovich BIBIKOV 8–5–1814

Alexander Ivanovich BOGDANOV 8–5–1814

Afanassi Fedorovich BURSSAK II 8–5–1814

Friedrich Andreieovich FANSHAVE 8–5–1814

Alexander Fedorovich FUHRMANN 8–5–1814

Ivan Ivanovich GAVRILENKO 8–5–1814

Karl Graf von HESSENSTEIN 8–5–1814

Fedor Semenovich ILOVAISKI XVI 8–5–1814

Vladimir Ivanovich JUSHKOV 8–5–1814

Alexander Michailovich KAMENOV 8–5–1814

Ivan Nikolaiovich KOBIAKOV 8–5–1814

KUNIZKI 8–5–1814

Heinrich Karl Wilhelm KÜPFER 8–5–1814

Alexander Vassilieovich ORIOV 8–5–1814

Ivan Andreieovich PROTOPOPOV 8–5–1814

Peter Andreieovich SASS 8–5–1814 (first award), 29–5–1814
    (second award), 13/18–10–1814 (third award)

Vassili Matvieieovich SHMURIN 8–5–1814

Alexei Fedorovich SHVEDKIN 8–5–1814

Peter Chrestianovich TROUSSON 8–5–1814

Adam Leontieovich VITKOVSKI 8–5–1814 (first award),
    13/18–10–1814 (second award)

Karl Borissovich von BERG 9–5–1814

Thomas Noel HARRIS 9–5–1814

Prince Gustaf Kalixt Biron von KURLAND 9–5–1814 (with OL)

Dmitri Petrovich MEYER 9–5–1814

Paul Jakovieovich von RENNENKAMPFF 9–5–1814

Roman Alexandrovich von SALZA 9–5–1814

Baron Karl Karlovich AudÉ de SION 9–5–1814

Gustaf Gustafovich von SMITTEN 9–5–1814

Igor Fedorovich von SMITTEN 9–5–1814

Vinzent Grimmer von ADELSBACH 11–5–1814

Christian APPEL 11–5–1814

Ludwig August FALLON 11–5–1814

Georg GELBER 11–5–1814

Wenzel HÖRING 11–5–1814

Mecklenburg von KLEEBERG 11–5–1814

Karl Rudolf Graf von der SCHULENBERG 11–5–1814

Count Stefan SZÉCHÉNYI 11–5–1814

Karl Friedrich Freiherr von VIETINGHOF (aka Scheel von
    SCHELLENBERG) 11–5–1814

Fedor Karaczay Graf von WALIE-SZAKA 11–5–1814

Konstantin Moritz Gneomar Graf von WARTENSLEBEN 11–5–1814

Johann Friedrich Ernst Sir Johann de ZERBI 11–5–1814

Alexander Michailovich DIEIEV 12–5–1814

Ivan Anton GUROV 12–5–1814

Peter Danilovich ROMANOV 12–5–1814

Prince Peter TSHERNIEVICH 12–5–1814

Baron Christian von ZWEIBRÜCKEN 12–5–1814

Count Vassili Ivanovich APRAXIN 13–5–1814

Jevgeni Michailovich DLUSKI 13–5–1814

Karl Fedorovich HIPPIUS 13–5–1814 (first award),
    12–12–1814 (second award)

Hippolit Michailovich LADA 13–5–1814

Alexander Ivanovich LISAGUB 13–5–1814

Fedor Karlovich LOEWNTHAL 13–5–1814

Alexander Nikolaieovich LVOV 13–5–1814

Filipp Petrovich MARKEVICH 13–5–1814

Peter Ivanovich PAULI (also spelt PAOLI) 13–5–1814 (first award), 13/18–10–1814 (second award)

Count Jaroslav Stanislavovich POTOCKI 13–5–1814

Andrei Andreieiovich READ V 13–5–1814

Vladimir Nikolaiovich SHENSHIN 13–5–1814

Peter Andreieovich VOIGT (also spelt FOCHT) 13–5–1814 (first award), 13/18–10–1814 (second award)

Baron Alexander von WOLFF 13–5–1814

Lev DOLINSKI 15–5–1814

August Graf von PONINSKI 19–5–1814

BRUMMEL 20–5–1814

Lev Semenovich STUDSINSKI 22–5–1814

Karl Johann Nepomuk Graf CLAM-MARTINITZ 25–5–1814

Karl August Freiherr von SCHARPFFENSTEIN 25–5–1814

Marquis Wilhelm Friedrich Erdmann Ferdinand Forcade de BIAIX 26–5–1814

Jossif Ivanovich BICHALOV 26–5–1814

Marquis de Montpezat Leopold Augustine Jean Joseph d'AINESY 29–5–1814

Ivan Alexieieovich ALEXIEIEV 30–5–1814

MOLTSHANOV (also spelt MULTSHANOV) 30–5–1814

Peter Avramovich TSHERNOSUBOV V 30–5–1814

Kord Friedrich Bernhard Hellmuth von HOBE 31–5–1814 (with OL)

Andreas Ernst KÖHN 31–5–1814 (with OL)

MELNIKOV IV 31–5–1814

Nikolai Grigorieovich MELNIKOV V 31–5–1814

Thomas von OTHEGRAVEN 31–5–1814 (with OL)

Johann Karl Josef von SCHON 31–5–1814 (with OL), (first award), 2–10–1815 (with OL), (second award)

Karl August Heinrich Wilhelm von SCHÜTZ 31–5–1814 (with OL)

Karl August von STUTTERHEIM 31–5–1814

Vollmar Karl Friedrich von CLAUSEWITZ (OL 31–5–1814) (date of first award unclear)

Johann August Friedrich Hiller Freiherr von GAERTRINGEN (OL 31–5–1814) (date of first award unclear)

Friedrich Ernst von LOEBELL (OL 31–5–1814) (date of first award unclear)

Johann Heinrich Otto von SCHMIDT (OL 31–5–1814) (date of first award unclear)

Baron Leonard Albrecht Karl von DELEN 1–6–1814

Ludwig Leopold Gottlieb Herman von BOYEN 3–6–1814 (with OL)

Friedrich Karl Ferdinand von MÜFFLING 3–6–1814 (with OL)

Johann Gustaf Georg von RAUCH (OL 3–6–1814) (date of first award unclear)

Alexander Filippovich von ESSEN 7–6–1814

Alexander Sacharieovich MURAVIEV 7–6–1814

Artamon Sacharieovich MURAVIEV 7–6–1814

Count Sergei Fedorovich ROSTOPHIN 7–6–1814

Jakob Nikolaieovich BROSIN II 11–6–1814

Karl Freidrich Ludwig Graf von KLINCKOWSTRÖM 11–6–1814 (with OL)

Charles WOOD 7/22–6–1814

On 7/22–6–1814 the award was also made to two unknown British officers

Karl Theodor Friedrich Graf von PAPPENHEIM 4/7–7–1814

Ivan Lavrebtieovich von SIEVER 11–8–1814

Baron Peter Ludwig von BUDBERG 14–8–1814

Alexander Nikita AKUTIN 17–8–1814

Apollon Vassilieovich BRESOVSKI 17–8–1814

Adolf Christoforovich BURMEISTER 17–8–1814

Alexander Karlovich de GERVAIS 17–8–1814

Matvei Manuilovich PEIKER 17–8–1814

Michail Stepanovich PERSKI 17–8–1814

Count Heraklius August de POLIGNAC 17–8–1814

Christofor Ossipovich STEGMANN 17–8–1814

Alexander Christianovich STEVEN 17–8–1814

Pavel Alexandrovich UGIUMOV 17–8–1814

Jevdokim Romanovich BURMEISTER 19–8–1814

Peter Vassilieovich DUBELT 20–8–1814

Baron Peter Andreieiovich FREDERIKS 20–8–1814

Grigori Nikolaieovich GLINKA 20–8–1814

Nikolai Petrovich POROCHOVNIKOV 20–8–1814

Pavel Petrovich TSHERKASSOV 20–8–1814

Alexander Dmitrieovich TULUBIEV 20–8–1814

Ivan Petrovich BIBIKOV 22–8–1814

Nikolai Vassilieovich RITSHKOV 22–8–1814

Karl Friedrich Ferdinand von STRANTZ 27–8–1814

Ivan Ivanovich BEDRIAGA 28–8–1814

Ivan Semenovich MIRONOV 28–8–1814

Friedrich Erhard Leopold von RÖDER 7–9–1814 (with OL)

Dmitri Nikolaieovich BOLOGOVSKI 10–9–1814

Wilhelm Fabian von BROZOWSKY 11–10–1814

ABAKUMOV 13/18–10–1814

ADABASHEV 13/18–10–1814

Dmitri Ivanovich ALEXANDROVICH 13/18–10–1814

Alexei Petrovich ALEXIEIEV 13/18–10–1814

Konstantin Stephanovich ANDREIEVSKI 13/18–10–1814

Nikolai Ivanovich ANDRUSSKI 13/18–10–1814

Nikolai Petrovich ANNENKOV 13/18–10–1814

Count Alexander Petrovich APRAXIN 13/18–10–1814

APUSHKIN (also spelt APUCHTIN) 13/18–10–1814

Alexei Fedorovich ARBUSSOV 13/18–10–1814

Baron Karl Karlovich von ARPSHOFEN 13/18–10–1814

Kondrati Kondratieovich BABST 13/18–10–1814

Jakob Ivanovich BACHMANN 13/18–10–1814

Nikanor Nikolaieovich BALKASHIN 13/18–10–1814

Count Alexander Apollonovich de BALMAINE 13/18–10–1814

Pavel Petrovich BARISHNIKOV 13/18–10–1814

Peter Petrovich BARISHNIKOV 13/18–10–1814

Johann BECKER 13/18–10–1814

Peter Ivanovich BERGENSTRALE 13/18–10–1814

Arsenic Jakovieovich BERSILOV 13/18–10–1814

Larion Michailovich BIBIKOV 13/18–10–1814

Jossif Michailovich BICHALOV 13/18–10–1814

Valenti Vassilieovich BLASHIEVSKI 13/18–10–1814

Paul Petrovich BLUM 13/18–10–1814

Vassili Ivanovich BOGDANOVICH 13/18–10–1814

Ivan Pavlovich BOGUSLAVSKI 13/18–10–1814

Ivan Fedorovich BORGRAF 13/18–10–1814

Ernst Ludwig Hans von BOSE 13/18–10–1814

Ivan Dmitrieovich BOVAISKI XII 13/18–10–1814

Ivan Ivanovich BRENNER 13/18–10–1814

Michail Petrovich BRESHINSKI 13/18–10–1814

Peter Michailovich BRESOBRASOV 13/18–10–1814

Anton Valerianovich BRESOVSKI 13/18–10–1814

Dmitri Michailovich BRILKIN 13/18–10–1814

Christofor Alexandrovich von BRINCKEN 13/18–10–1814

Jakob Petrovich BUBLIK 13/18–10–1814

Fedor Vassilieovich von BUDBERG 13/18–10–1814

Peter Vassilieovich BULGARSKI 13/18–10–1814

Christian Nikolaieovich BUSHEN 13/18–10–1814

Semen Jevstafieovich BUSSOV 13/18–10–1814

Ivan Ivanovich CHRAPOVIZKI 13/18–10–1814

Matvei Jevgrafovich CHRAPOVIZKI 13/18–10–1814 (second award),
(date of first award unclear)

Sergei Petrovich CHURSTSHOV 13/18–10–1814

Ivan Ignatieovich DAMBROVSKI 13/18–10–1814

Ivan Petrovich DANNENBERG 13/18–10–1814

Jevdokim Vassilieovich DAVIDOV 13/18–10–1814

Nikolai DAVIDOV 13/18–10–1814

Peter Ivanovich DAVIDOV 13/18–10–1814

Baron Ivan Fedorovich von DELLINGHAUSEN 13/18–10–1814

Andronik Andronikovich DENISSIEVSKI 13/18–10–1814

Karl Fedorovich von DERSCHAU 13/18–10–1814

Peter Nikolaieovich DIAKOV 13/18–10–1814

DIETERICHS (also spelt DIETERIKS) 13/18–10–1814

Peter Leontieovich DITTMAR 13/18–10–1814

Prince Nikolai Andreieovich DOLGORUKI 13/18–10–1814

Roman Antonovich DOMBROVSKI 13/18–10–1814

Karp DROBISHEVSKI 13/18–10–1814

Adam Jakoleovich DSITSHKANEZ 13/18–10–1814

Akim Vassilieovich DUVANOV 13/18–10–1814

Kosma Michailovich EISMONT 13/18–10–1814

Alexander Ivanovich EMME 13/18–10–1814

Ferdinand Friedrich Wilhelm von FABECKY 13/18–10–1814

Grigori Andreieovich FANSHAVE 13/18–10–1814

FEDOROV 13/18–10–1814

Gustaf Fedorovich von FRICKS 13/18–10–1814

Pavel Nikolaieovich GAGIN 13/18–10–1814

Fedor Semenovich GAIEVSKI 13/18–10–1814

Andrei Petrovich GALAGAN 13/18–10–1814

Alexander Sacharieovich GARICHVOSTOV 13/18–10–1814

Alexander Semenovich GERASSIMOV 13/18–10–1814 (with OL)

Vassili Vassilieovich GERBEL 13/18–10–1814

Michail Gerassimovich GOIARIN 13/18–10–1814

Prince Andrei Michailovich GOLIZIN I 13/18–10–1814

Prince Ivan Alexieieovich GOLIZIN 13/18–10–1814

Prince Michail Michailovich GOLIZIN II 13/18–10–1814

Prince Pavel Alexieieovich GOLIZIN 13/18–10–1814

Prince Vassili Sergieieovich GOLIZIN 13/18–10–1814

Prince Vladimir GOLIZIN 13/18–10–1814

GONTSHAROV 13/18–10–1814

Jakob Fedorovich GORDIEIEV 13/18–10–1814

Peter Alexieieovich GRATSHOV 13/18–10–1814

Pavel Semenovich GRAVE 13/18–10–1814

Peter Fedorovich GRIGORIEV 13/18–10–1814

GROMOV 13/18–10–1814

Pavel Nikolaieovich HBENER 13/18–10–1814

Heinrich August von HELDORF 13/18–10–1814

Alexander Jakovieovich HELWIG 13/18–10–1814

Otto von HUHN 13/18–10–1814

Otto Fedorovich von HUHN 13/18–10–1814

Sergei Alexandrovich ISLENIEV 13/18–10–1814

Nikolai Grigorieovich ISSIUMOV 13/18–10–1814

Ivan Antonovich JAROSLAVZEV 13/18–10–1814

Grigori Ivanovich JEFIMOVICH 13/18–10–1814

Alexander Dmitrieovich JERMAKOV 13/18–10–1814

Ivan Sacharieovich JERSHOV 13/18–10–1814

Andrei Alexandrovich JESIMOVICH 13/18–10–1814 (second award),
(date of first award unclear)

Dmitri Semenovich JESSAKOV 13/18–10–1814

Jevstafi JEVSTAFIEOVICH 13/18–10–1814

Alexander Bogdanovich von KAHLEN I 13/18–10–1814

Paul Bogdanovich von KAHLEN II 13/18–10–1814

Nikolai Igorovich KALATSHEVSKI 13/18–10–1814

Alexander Dmitrieovich KARAOULOV 13/18–10–1814

Dmitri KARAOULOV I 13/18–10–1814

Nikolai Dmitrieovich KARAOULOV 13/18–10–1814

Akim Akimovich KARPOV V 13/18–10–1814

Ivan Nikolaieovich KARTAMISHEV 13/18–10–1814

Kosma Ivanovich KASHA 13/18–10–1814

Alexander Ivanovich KASHINZOV 13/18–10–1814

Nikita Prochorovich KASHPEROV 13/18–10–1814

Gennadi Ivanovich KASNAKOV 13/18–10–1814

Prince Alexei Ivanovich KASTROV II 13/18–10–1814

KATASHEV 13/18–10–1814

KELDERMANN 13/18–10–1814

Alexander Karlovich KELLNER 13/18–10–1814

Otto Karl Diedrich Graf von KEYSERLINGK 13/18–10–1814

Fedor KIREREVSKI 13/18–10–1814

Dmitri Igorovich KISHINSKI 13/18–10–1814

Vassili Michailovich KISHKIN 13/18–10–1814

Peter Alexieieovich KLADISHTSHEV 13/18–10–1814

Fedor Borissovich KLEIN 13/18–10–1814

Peter von KLEIST 13/18–10–1814

Peter Fedorovich KNIASEV 13/18–10–1814

Vassili Fedorovich KNOBEL 13/18–10–1814

Pontus Voldemar von KNORRING 13/18–10–1814

KOILENSKI 13/18–10–1814

Stepan Ivanovich KOLOGRIVOV 13/18–10–1814

Pavel Andreieovich KOLSAKOV 13/18–10–1814

Franz Ivanovich KOMPAN 13/18–10–1814

Gavril Ilish KONOVKIN 13/18–10–1814

Vassili Ivanovich KOSHKIN 13/18–10–1814

Josef Wilhelm Graf von KOSKÜLL 13/18–10–1814

Baron Peter Ivanovich von KOSKÜLL 13/18–10–1814

Semen Grigorieovich KRASNOKUTSKI 13/18–10–1814

Ossip Ivanovich KRAUSE 13/18–10–1814

Alexander Alexieieovich KRILOV 13/18–10–1814

Semen Jossifovich KRITSHINSKI 13/18–10–1814

Alexander Jakovleovich KRIVSKI 13/18–10–1814

Alexander Ivanovich KRIVZOV 13/18–10–1814

Jefim Nikitit KRIZIN 13/18–10–1814

Peter Antonovich von KRÜDENER 13/18–10–1814

Theodor Ernst von KRUMMES 13/18–10–1814

Danilo Antonovich KUBITOVICH 13/18–10–1814

Vladimir Grigorieovich KURSHEVSKI 13/18–10–1814

Fedor KUTEINIKOV II 13/18–10–1814

Vassili Nikolaieovich LADOMIRSKI 13/18–10–1814

Nikolai Petrovich LAITUCHIN 13/18–10–1814

Peter Petrovich LATSHINOV 13/18–10–1814 (with OL)

Ossip Vassilieovich LEONTOVIH 13/18–10–1814

Artemi Danilovich LEVOSHKA 13/18–10–1814

Ivan Petrovich LISSANEVICH 13/18–10–1814

LISSANOVSKI 13/18–10–1814

Ivan Vassilieovich LITVINOV 13/18–10–1814

Prince Boris Alexandrovich LOBANOV-ROSTOVSKI 13/18–10–1814

Roman Alexandrovich LOHMANN 13/18–10–1814

Prince Pavel Petrovich LOPUCHIN 13/18–10–1814

Ivan LOVIEKO 13/18–10–1814

Panteleimon Semenovich LUKITSH 13/18–10–1814

Dmitri Michailovich LVOV 13/18–10–1814

Ivan Semenovich MAGDENKO I 13/18–10–1814

Count Rudolf Ossipovich de MAISTRE 13/18–10–1814

Silvester Sigismundovich MALINOVSKI 13/18–10–1814

Ivan Averianovich MAMONOV 13/18–10–1814

Nikolai Jakovleovich MANDRIKA 13/18–10–1814

Matvei Ivanovich MANUILOV 13/18–10–1814

Narkiss Pavlovich MARIANOVICH 13/18–10–1814

Andrei Ivanovich MARKEVITSH (also spelt MARKOVITSH)
    13/18–10–1814

Danilo Jakovlieovich MARTIANOV 13/18–10–1814

Pavel Petrovich MARTINOV 13/18–10–1814

Ivan Jefimovich MASKE (also spelt MASSKA) 13/18–10–1814

Alexander Petrovich MASSIOV 13/18–10–1814

Fedor Timofieovich MASSLENIZKI 13/18–10–1814

Baron Vassili Ivanovich von MEDEM 13/18–10–1814

Paton de MEIERAN 13/18–10–1814

Pavel Moissieieovich MELIKOV 13/18–10–1814 (second award),
    (date of first award unclear)

Michail MELNIKOV 13/18–10–1814

Michail Ivanovich MELNIKOV 13/18–10–1814

Karl Demianovich von MERLIN 13/18–10–1814

Wichard Georg Wilhelm Ludwig von MEYERINCK 13/18–10–1814
    (award later rescinded and replaced with the Prussian Iron Cross Second
    Class)

Nikolai Davidovich MIAKININ 13/18–10–1814

Ivan Ossipovich MILEIKA 13/18–10–1814

Vladimir Perfilieovich MOLOSTVOV 13/18–10–1814

Michail Markovich MORSHIN 13/18–10–1814

Filipp Denissieovich MOSHENSKI 13/18–10–1814

MÜLLER 13/18–10–1814

Alexander Matvieieovich MUROMZOV 13/18–10–1814

Michail Nikolaieovich MUSSIN-PUSHKIN 13/18–10–1814

Andrei Andreieiovich NABEL 13/18–10–1814

NAGATKIN 13/18–10–1814

Franz Grigorieovich NARVOISH 13/18–10–1814

Ivan Ivanovich NBEIELOV II 13/18–10–1814

NELIDOV 13/18–10–1814

Peter Alexieieovich NIELOV 13/18–10–1814

Vladimir Ivanovich NIKOLEV 13/18–10–1814

Alexander Ivanovich NISTROM 13/18–10–1814

Nikita Ivanovich NOVIKOV 13/18–10–1814

Stepan OGORELIZ 13/18–10–1814

Gavril Semenovich OKUNIEV 13/18–10–1814

Ossip Danilovich OLSHEVSKI 13/18–10–1814

Alexander Dmitrieovich OLSUVIEV 13/18–10–1814

Ivan Albrechtovich ORANSKI 13/18–10–1814

Vassili Jakovilovich OVANDER 13/18–10–1814

Count Ivan Petrovich von der PAHLEN 13/18–10–1814

Michail Jakovleovich PALIZIN 13/18–10–1814

Vladimir Ivanovich PALIZIN 13/18–10–1814

Nikolai Petrovich von PANKRATIEV 13/18–10–1814

Fedor Sergieieovich PANUTIN 13/18–10–1814

Apollon Andreieovich PARFAZKI 13/18–10–1814

Friedrich von PATKUL 13/18–10–1814

Dorofei Jemelianovich PAVLENKO 13/18–10–1814

Grigori PAVLOV 13/18–10–1814

Pavel Artemieovich PAVLOV 13/18–10–1814

Pavel Ivanovich PESTEL 13/18–10–1814

Jakob Ivanovich PETERSON 13/18–10–1814

Andrei Petrovich PETROVICH 13/18–10–1814

Andrei Andreieovich PETROVSKI 13/18–10–1814

Nikolai Ivanovich PETROVSKI-MURAVSKI 13/18–10–1814

Yuri Vassilieovich PETRULIN 13/18–10–1814

Vassili Gavrilovich PIATKIN 13/18–10–1814

Ivan Christoforovich PILCHOVSKI 13/18–10–1814

Vassili Afanasieovich PILIUGIN 13/18–10–1814

Ivan Andreieovich PIMANOV 13/18–10–1814

Semen Ossipovich ROKSHANIN 13/18–10–1814

Narkiss POMERANSKI 13/18–10–1814

Alexander Jemelianovich POPOV 13/18–10–1814

Ivan Vassilieovich POSDIEIEV (also spelt PODSHIDAIEV)
    13/18–10–1814

Alexander Michailovich POTEMKIN 13/18–10–1814

Jakob Alexieieovich POTEMKIN 13/18–10–1814 (second award),
    (date of first award unclear)

Doctor Georg Heinrich von POTT 13/18–10–1814

Nikolai Ivanovich PRIASHEVSKI 13/18–10–1814 (first award),
    12–12–1814 (second award)

Tichon Fedorovich PROKOFIEV 13/18–10–1814

Andrei Alexandrovich PUETLING 13/18–10–1814

Karl Karlovich PUSIN 13/18–10–1814

PUSIREVSKI 13/18–10–1814

Pavel Sergeieiovich PUSTSHIN 13/18–10–1814

Jakob Nikolaieovich RADITSH 13/18–10–1814

Vassili Fedorovich RALL IV 13/18–10–1814

Karl Karlovich RAMM 13/18–10–1814

Nikolai Andreieovich READ 13/18–10–1814

REBRIKOV III 13/18–10–1814

REDRIKOV 13/18–10–1814

Boris Borissovich von REHBINDER 13/18–10–1814

Ivan Ivanovich REICH 13/18–10–1814

Avram Avramovich REICHEL 13/18–10–1814

Nikolai Jakovleovich REPNINSKI 13/18–10–1814

Erhard Romanovich von REUTERN 13/18–10–1814

Baron Otto Filippovich von RÖNNE 13/18–10–1814

Fedor Grigorieovich ROSALION-SOSHALSKI 13/18–10–1814

Baron Peter Fedorovich von ROSEN 13/18–10–1814

Ludwig Christianovich ROTH 13/18–10–1814

Pavel Alexieieovich RSHEVSKI 13/18–10–1814

Konstantin Ivanovich RUDNIZKI 13/18–10–1814

Dmitri Michailovich RUSSANOV 13/18–10–1814

Pavel Ivanovich SABLIN 13/18–10–1814

Jakob Vassilieovich SACHARSHEVSKI 13/18–10–1814

Anton SADLUZKI 13/18–10–1814

Voin Dmitrieovich SADONSKI 13/18–10–1814

Fedor Andreieovich SALOV 13/18–10–1814

Baron Karl Alexandrovich von SALZA 13/18–10–1814

Akim Petrovich SAMBURSKI 13/18–10–1814

Sergei Vassilieovich SAMSONOV 13/18–10–1814 (first award), 12–12–1814 (second award)

Karl Andreieovich de SAUVEPLAN 13/18–10–1814

Ludwig Adolf Graf von SAYN-WITTGENSTEIN 13/18–10–1814

Wilhelm Franzovich SCHARENBERG 13/18–10–1814

Gustaf Ivanovich SCHEFFLER 13/18–10–1814

Fedor Martinovich SCHEIN 13/18–10–1814

Fedor Karlovich SCHIERMANN 13/18–10–1814

Karl Karlovich SCHIERMANN 13/18–10–1814

Jakob Vassilieovich von SCHILLING 13/18–10–1814

Alexander Cnrestianovich SCHMIDT 13/18–10–1814

Christofor Karlovich SCHOTT 13/18–10–1814

Grigori Ivanovich SCHUBERT 13/18–10–1814

SELESNIEV 13/18–10–1814

SELIVANOV 13/18–10–1814

Michail Petrovich SELLIENIEZKI 13/18–10–1814

Danilo SEMENOV 13/18–10–1814

Prince Nikolai Alexandrovich SHACHMATOV 13/18–10–1814

Jakob Ivanovich SHAMSHEV 13/18–10–1814

Ivan Vassilieovich SHATALOV 13/18–10–1814

Dmitri Nikolaieovich SHELECHOV 13/18–10–1814

Nikolai SHEMONIN 13/18–10–1814

Apollon Stephanovich SHEMSHUSHNIKOV 13/18–10–1814

Karl SHENNE 13/18–10–1814

SHEVIAKOV 13/18–10–1814

SHIBAIEV 13/18–10–1814

Nicolai Nikolaieovich SHILIACHTIN 13/18–10–1814

Peter Ivanovich SHIPOV 13/18–10–1814

Sergei Pavlovich SHIPOV 13/18–1814

Pavel Sergieieovich SHISHKIN 13/18–10–1814

Peter Ivanovich SHISHKOV (also spelt SHISHKIN) 13/18–10–1814

Timofei Andreieovich SHMAROV 13/18–10–1814

Peter Aganassieovich SHOSHIN 13/18–10–1814

Vassili Pavlovich SHTSHERBOV 13/18–10–1814

Galaktion Stepanovich SHUKOVSKI 13/18–10–1814

Michail Stephanovich SHUKOVSKI 13/18–10–1814

Dmitri Ivanovich SHULGIN 13/18–10–1814

Peter SHULGIN 13/18–10–1814

SHUMOVSKI 13/18–10–1814

Alexander Ivanovich SIVAI 13/18–10–1814

Ivan Nikititsh SKOBELEV 13/18–10–1814

Alexander SMOLIANINOV 13/18–10–1814

Christofor Fedorovich SOLDAEN 13/18–10–1814

Ignati Moisseieovich SOLOGUB 13/18–10–1814

Grigori Karlovich SONN 13/18–10–1814

Alexei Matvieieovich SPIRIDOV 13/18–10–1814

Baron Fedor Maximovich von STACKELBERG 13/18–10–1814

Vladimir Vassilieovich von STACKELBERG 13/18–10–1814

Alexander Fedorovich STAEL 13/18–10–1814

Andrei Antonovich STAHN 13/18–10–1814

Matvei STEPANOV 13/18–10–1814

STEPANOV 13/18–10–1814

Karl von STEPHANI 13/18–10–1814

Fedor Alexieieovich von STRANDMANN 13/18–10–1814

Alexander Sergeieiovich STREMOUCHOV 13/18–10–1814

Nikolai Karlovich von STÜRLER 13/18–10–1814

Paul Petrovich van SUCHTELEN 13/18–10–1814

Sergei Pavlovich SUMAROKOV 13/18–10–1814

Vassili Vassilieovich SUSHKOV 13/18–10–1814

Nikolai Michailovich SVIAGIN 13/18–10–1814

TANNAUER 13/18–10–1814

Ossip Fedorovich TARASHKEVICH 13/18–10–1814

Pavel Petrovich TARBEIEV 13/18–10–1814

Baron Anton von TAUBE 13/18–10–1814

Leonti Antonovich TERMIN 13/18–10–1814

Ivan Franzovich TERPIELIVSKI 13/18–10–1814

Jevgeni Ossipovich TERPIELIVSKI 13/18–10–1814

THAL (also spelt THALEN) 13/18–10–1814

Fedor Andreieiovich TICHANOV 13/18–10–1814

Pavel Petrovich TIMOFEIEV 13/18–10–1814

Vassili Grigorieovich TISHIN 13/18–10–1814

Count Andon Demianovich TISHKIEVICH 13/18–10–1814

Alexei Igorovich TITOV 13/18–10–1814

Prince Serbedshab TIUMENEV 13/18–10–1814

Afanassi Jemelianovich TOLMATSHEV 13/18–10–1814

Ivan Andreieovich TOLSDORFF 13/18–10–1814

Count Alexander Dmitrieovich TOLSTOI 13/18–10–1814 (first award), 14–10–1814 (second award)

Count TOLSTOI 13/18–10–1814

Andrei Stepanovich TOMILOVSKI 13/18–10–1814

Alexander Lvovich TRISHATNI 13/18–10–1814

Prince Sergei Petrovich TRUBEZKOI I 13/18–10–1814

Prince Yuri Petrovich TRUBEZKOI 13/18–10–1814

Vladimir Nikolaiovich TSHAGIN 13/18–10–1814

Michail Petrovich TSHEKALOV 13/18–10–1814

Ivan Jefimovich TSHEMESSOV 13/18–10–1814 (with OL)

Peter Nikititsh TSHERNAIEV 13/18–10–1814

Tsherni-Subov TSHERNOSUBOV 13/18–10–1814

Nikolai Stephanovich TSHERTORISHSKI 13/18–10–1814

Vassili Nikolaieovich TSHERTORISHSKI 13/18–10–1814

Pavel Apollonovich TSHERTOV 13/18–10–1814

Matvei Nikolaieovich TSHICHATSHEV 13/18–10–1814

Andreian Nikolaieovich TSHOGLOKOV 13/18–10–1814

Michail Danilovich TSHURAKOVSKI 13/18–10–1814

Dorimedont Titovich TULUBIEV 13/18–10–1814

Prince Sergei Dmitrieovich URUSSOV 13/18–10–1814

Fedor Alexandrovich UVAROV 13/18–10–1814

Fedor Semenovich UVAROV 13/18–10–1814

Ivan Fedorovich VADKOVSKI I 13/18–10–1814

Nikolai Vassilieovich VASSILTSHIKOV 13/18–10–1814 (second award),
     (date of first award unclear)

Peter Alexandrovich VELENIN 13/18–10–1814

Ivan Franzovich VILTSHINSKI 13/18–10–1814

Michail VLASSOV 13/18–10–1814

Prince Sergei Grigorieovich VOLKONSKI 13/18–10–1814

Nikolai Apollonovich VOLKOV 13/18–10–1814

Ivan Arianovich VORONIEZ 13/18–10–1814

Nikolai Faddieieovich VOROPANOV 13/18–10–1814

Ivan Gustafovich VULFFERT 13/18–10–1814

Alexander Jakovleovich WACHSMUTH 13/18–10–1814

Ludwig Andreieovich von WRANGEL 13/18–10–1814

Alexander Fedorovich WÜRST 13/18–10–1814

ZIRENIEV 13/18–10–1814

Gustaf Magnus ADLERCREUTZ 11–11–1814

Wilhelm Friedrich von HAMMERSTEIN-EQUORD 11–11–1814

Georg Freiherr von SCHEITHER 11–11–1814

Erik Georg ULFSPAREE 11–11–1814

Franz von WEKS 11–11–1814

Fedor Andreieovich ALADIN 12–12–1814

Peter Ivanovich ALBRECHT 12–12–1814

Pavel Vassilieovich ALFERIEV 12–12–1814

ALFIMOV 12–12–1814

ASOVSKI 12–12–1814

Stepan BAGAIEVSKOV 12–12–1814

Lev Lvovich BAROKOV 12–12–1814

Konstantin Michailovich BESGIN 12–12–1814

BOGULTEROV 12–12–1814

Johann BRANDT 12–12–1814

BRAUN 12–12–1814

Alexei Dementieovich BRESIN 12–12–1814

Christofor von BREWERN 12–12–1814

Nikolai Bogdanovich BRONEVSKI 12–12–1814

Fedor Vassilieovich BULGAKOV 12–12–1814

Fedor Fedorovich BURMEISTER 12–12–1814

Anton Ossipovich CHMIELIEVSKI 12–12–1814

Vassili Stepanovich CHRAPATSHOV 12–12–1814

Samuli Peter Andreieovich DANNENBERG 12–12–1814

Leopold Kusmit DEROSHINKI 12–12–1814

Nikolai Ivanovich DOBRISHIN 12–12–1814

Pavel Franzovich DOMBROVSKI 12–12–1814

Josef Freiherr von DROSTE zu VISCHERING 12–12–1814

Grigori Antonovich DSHESHELEI 12–12–1814

Peter Sergeieiovich DUBROVIN 12–12–1814

Fedor Alexandrovich JEROPKIN 12–12–1814

Karl August Varnhagen von ENSE 12–12–1814

FAHLENBERG 12–12–1814

FISCHER 12–12–1814

FOKIN 12–12–1814

Karl Petrovich GORSKI 12–12–1814

Sergei Nikolaieovich GREKOV 12–12–1814

Fedor Ivanovich GRIGOROV 12–12–1814

Ernst von HERBERT 12–12–1814

Ivan Martinovich HINGLIAT 12–12–1814

Igor Christoforovich von der HOVEN 12–12–1814

Baron von HOYM 12–12–1814

Vassili Jakovlieovich HUBERTI 12–12–1814

Baron Gustaf Gustafovich von IGELSTROEM 12–12–1814

ILJIN 12–12–1814

ISEDMIROV 12–12–1814

Peter Michailovich ISKRIZKI 12–12–1814

Igor Sacharieovich IVANOV III 12–12–1814 (second award),
    (date of first award unclear)

IVASHKIN 12–12–1814

Moissei Avramovich JAKIMACH 12–12–1814

Nikolai Andreieovich JELAGIN 12–12–1814

JERMOLAIEV 12–12–1814

Vassili Jakovlieovich KALINOVSKI 12–12–1814

Ivan Michailovich KAPZEVICH 12–12–1814

Ivan Stanislavovich KARTSHEVSKI 12–12–1814

Peter Fedorovich KAUFMANN 12–12–1814

Semen Ivanovich KINDIAKOV 12–12–1814

Ivan Ivdokimovich KIOV 12–12–1814

Vassili Danilovich KNISHNIKOV 12–12–1814

Vassili Ivanovich KOLIUBAKIN 12–12–1814

Nikolai Ivanovich KORF (also spelt KORSH) 12–12–1814

Ivan Stepanovich KOROVIN 12–12–1814

Vassili Ivanovich KOSHIN 12–12–1814

Josef Ignatieovich KUHN 12–12–1814

Alexander Ivanovich KUPFER 12–12–1814

LACHMANN 12–12–1814

Nikolai Ivanovich LAPTIEV 12–12–1814

Justin Vassilieovich LEVANDOVSKI 12–12–1814

Alexander Jakolieovich LIATKOVSKI 12–12–1814

Nikolai Fedorovich LISHIN 12–12–1814 (second award),
  (date of first award unclear)

Roman Karlovich Freytag von LORINGHOVEN 12–12–1814

Alexander Sergieieovich LOSHKAREV 12–12–1814 (second award),
  (date of first award unclear)

Nikolai Loginovich MANSEI 12–12–1814

von MANTEUFFEL 12–12–1814

Michail Nikolaieovich MAZNEV 12–12–1814

Jossif Stepanovich MENSHINSKI 12–12–1814

Nikolai MICHAILOSKI 12–12–1814

Kosma Ivanovich MORKOVNOKOV 12–12–1814

Stepan Stepanovich NATARA I 12–12–1814

NATARA II 12–12–1814

Andrei Alexieieovich NOVOPOLIEZ 12–12–1814

OSMOLOVSKI 12–12–1814

Saveli Alexieieovich OSSIPOVICH 12–12–1814

Franz Kasimirovich OSTRESHKOVSKI 12–12–1814

Grigori Dmitrieovich PESHTSHANSKI 12–12–1814

Alexander Petrovich POSSIET 12–12–1814

POSSUDOVSKI 12–12–1814

Nikolai Ivanovich PREISS (also spelt PRIESS) 31–3–1814 (first award),
  12–12–1814 (second award)

Alexander Fedorovich PRUDNIKOV 12–12–1814

Karl Ivanovich RICHTER 12–12–1814

Filadelf Kyrillovich RINDIN 12–12–1814

Alexander Vassilieovich ROGOVSKI 12–12–1814

Baron Andrei Fedorovich von ROSEN 12–12–1814

Baron Otto Fedorovich von ROSEN 12–12–1814

Fedor Igorovich ROSENSTEIN 12–12–1814

Ivan Pavlovich RUDAKOV 12–12–1814

Peter SAFIANOV 12–12–1814

Alexei Dmitrieovich SAMKOVSKI 12–12–1814

Karl Vassilieovich von SANDEN-PESKOVICH 12–12–1814

Karl Leontieovich SCHULINIUS 12–12–1814

Jakob SCHULTZ 12–12–1814

Grigori Alexieieovich SELIVANOV 12–12–1814

Ludwig Michailovich SHAFRANSKI 12–12–1814

David SHAGLEVSKI 12–12–1814

Michail Vassilieovich SHISHMAREV 12–12–1814

SIKORSKI 12–12–1814

Fedor Lvovich SKARDOVI-RINGTON 12–12–1814

SLIEPZOV 12–12–1814

Grigori Dementieovich SLIUNIAIEV 12–12–1814

Alexei Pavlovich SLOEZKI 12–12–1814

Stepan Gerassimovich SOBOLEVSKI 12–12–1814

Xavier Petrovich SOKOLVSKI 12–12–1814

Martin Michailovich STACHOVSKI 12–12–1814

STEPANOV 12–12–1814

Ivan Fedorovich van der STRUF 12–12–1814

Ossip Ivanovich SULIMA 12–12–1814

Michail Stepanovich SVIDA 12–12–1814

TEMIROV (also spelt TIMIROV) 12–12–1814

TEPLOV 12–12–1814

Alexei Michailovich TICHOZKI 12–12–1814

Bogdon Karlovich von TIESENHAUSEN 12–12–1814

Prince Karl Anselm von THURN und TAXIS 12–12–1814

Ossip Grigorieovich TREGUBOV 12–12–1814

Michail TSHAPLIN 12–12–1814

Platon Gavrilovich TULENINOV 12–12–1814

Arseni Semenovich TULUBIEV 12–12–1814

Lev Antonovich TURGENIEV 12–12–1814

Adam Stanislavovich VARLOVSKI 12–12–1814

Michail Vassilieovich VASSILIEV 12–12–1814

Ivan Lukitsch VELENTI 12–12–1814

Platon Vassilieovich VERBOVSKI 12–12–1814

Andrei Petrovich VIRUBOV 12–12–1814

Stanislav Ossipovich VISHNIAKOVSKI 12–12–1814

Vassili Silovich VOLKOV 12–12–1814

Semen Ivanovich VOLODIMIROV 12–12–1814

Ernst Heinrich Adolf von PFUEL 28–12–1814 (OL 31–12–1831)

1815

Theodor Werner Christian von BELOW 1–1–1815

Ludwig TOMPSON 1–1–1815

Fedor Bogdanovich FALK 12–3–1815

Alexander Ivanovich TIMRODT 12–3–1815

BRUNNER 5–4–1815

von GROTHUSS 5–4–1815

Ivan Peter Eduard von LOEWENSTERN 5–4–1815

Vassili Jakovlieovich MIKULIN 5–4–1815

Vladimir Grigorieovich NOVOSSILZOV 5–4–1815

Anton Freiherr von FAHENBERG 4–5–1815

Count Elias Almázy von ZSADÁNY und TÖRÖK-SZ MIKLÓS 25–5–1815

Karl KLOTZSCH 10–6–1815

Friedrich Wilhelm Bogislav von LEMKE 19–6–1815

Heinrich Adolf Eduard von THILE II 24–6–1815

Peter Lavrovich SUKOVKIN 7–8–1815

Count Alexander Nikolaieovich PANIN 15–8–1815

Michail Petrovich RODSIANKO 15–8–1815

Paul Sergieieovich SHKURIN 15–8–1815

Matvei Kyrillovich KIRPITSHEV 19–8–1815

Vladimir Petrovich KOSLAINOV 19–8–1815

Ivan Ivanovich TARASSOV 19–8–1815

Count Ivan Matvieieovich PLATOV 7–9–1815

Leonti Vassilieovich DUBELT 25–9–1815

Baron Ludwig Ivanovich von SEDDLER 25–9–1815

August Ferdinand von ARNAULD de la PERIÈRE 2–10–1815 (with OL)

Wilhelm Friedrich Karl August von BARDELEBEN 2–10–1815

Karl August Ludwig von BENNING 2–10–1815

Ludwig BOEDICKER 2–10–1815

Johann Christian August von BOEHLER 2–10–1815 (with OL)

Ludwig Friedrich Hans Wilhelm von BORSTELL 2–10–1815 (with OL)

Johann Karl Ludwig BRAUN 2–10–1815 (with OL)

Wilhelm Heinrich Karl Ludwig von DITFURTH 2–10–1815 (with OL)

Karl Ludwig Siegmund von ENGELHART 2–10–1815 (with OL)

Ludwig von ESCHWEGE 2–10–1815

Johann Konrad von FLIES 2–10–1815

Ernst August Moritz von FROELICH 2–10–1815 (with OL)

Wilhelm HÜTTEROD 2–10–1815

Christian Friedrich Wilhelm von JAGOW 2–10–1815 (with OL)

Heinrich Eugen Freiherr von KELLER 2–10–1815 (with OL)

Friedrich Wilhelm von LOSSBERG 2–10–1815

August Ludwig Ernst von MASHALL 2–10–1815

Friedrich Wilhelm von MÜNCH 2–10–1815

Stanislaus von OPPENKOWSKY 2–10–1815 (with OL)

Otto Karl Lorenz von PIRCH 2–10–1815 (with OL)

Johann Ernst SCHEFFER 2–10–1815

Heinrich Tobias SCHMIDT 2–10–1815

Ernst Friedrich SCHOEDDE 2–10–1815

Arnold von SCHUTTER 2–10–1815 (with OL)

Karl Friedrich von SELASINSKY 2–10–1815 (with OL)

Albrecht von SONNEBERG 2–10–1815

Karl Moritz von STEIN 2–10–1815

Karl Friedrich Franziscus von STEINMETZ 2–10–1815

August Leopold von STUTTERHEIM 2–10–1815 (with OL)

Wilhelm Gustaf Friedrich WARDENBURG 2–10–1815

Heinrich Karl von WIEDBURG 2–10–1815

Engel Ludwig Stach von GOLTZHEIM (OL 2–10–1815)
(date of first award unclear)

August George Friedrich Magnus von HEDEMANN (OL 2–10–1815)
(date of first award unclear)

Ludwig Friedrich Heinrich von HOLLEBEN (OL 2–10–1815)
(date of first award unclear)

Karl Thilo Ludwig von KRAFFT (OL 2–10–1815)
(date of first award unclear)

Karl Heinrich Christian Ludwig von ROHR (OL 2–10–1815)
(date of first award unclear)

Johann Joachim Friedrich von SYDOW (OL 2–10–1815)
(date of first award unclear)

Nikolai Nikolaieovich PUSTSHIN 3–10–1815

Franz von LEISTNER 15–10–1815

Nikolai Ivanovich von DAHLEN 7–11–1815

Feofilakt Alexieieovich GLUCHOV 7–11–1815

Richard DICKINSON 9–11–1815 (with OL)

Sir Henry HARDING 9–11–1815

1816

Friedrich August Karl Ludwig von der MARWITZ 14–1–1816 (with OL)

Johann George von BERENHORST 2–5–1816

Josef Simonyi Freiherr von VITETZVÁR 2–5–1816

Georg Christian Fromhold WOSSIDIO 18–6–1816

Prince Adam Karl Wilhelm Stanislaus Eugen Paul von WÜRTTEMBERG
18–6–1816

Hieronymus Michaelis Ignatius von GRODZKI 23–10–1816

August Friedrich Albrecht von KALCKREUTH 23–10–1816

Nikolai Jesimovich KLEVESAHL 23–10–1816

Christian Wilhelm STIEMER 23–10–1816

Otto Wilhelm Karl Friedrich von TORNOW 23–10–1816

August Friedrich Wilhelm von WULFFEN 23–10–1816

1817

Count Charles Louis Prosper CHÉRISEY 30–3–1817

Baron Vassil Igorich von RÖNNE 30–3–1817

Konstantin Alexieieovich TOKAREV 19–6–1817

Josef Gentsy de GENTS 13–8–1817

Count August de la ROCHEJAQUELEIN 26–8–1817

Peter Romanovich von SCHEEL 2–10–1817

1818

Joachim Gottfried von BRANDENSTEIN 15/18–1–1818

Sir Felton Elwil Bathurst HERVEY 15/18–1–1818

Adolf Heinrich HEYDENREICH 15/18–1–1818

1819

Peter Petrovich TRUBEZKOI early 1819 (exact date unknown)

Peter Savovich FIRSSOV 2–7–1819

Alexander Ivanovich HERMANN 16–9–1819

Paul Adolfovich Freiherr von MOLTKE 1–11–1819

1820

Georg August Graf zu YSENBURG-PHILIPPSEICH 7–8–1820

1821

August Graf BELLEGARDE 26–7–1821

Johann Hrabovsky von HRABOVA 26–7–1821

Moritz Freiherr von SAHLHAUSEN 26–7–1821

1824

Christof Johann Ferdinand Alexander ALBERT 23–1–1824

Vladimir Michailovich MORDVINOV 18–4–1824

Grigori Michailovich BESOBRASOV 5–5–1824

Ossip Ignatieovich DUTSHINSKI 5–5–1824

Karl Karlovich von ESSEN 5–5–1824

Johann FREIGANG 5–5–1824

Prince GAGARIN 5–5–1824

GÜNZEL I 5–5–1824

Karl Vassilieovich HARDER 5–5–1824

Alexander Andreieovich JACHONTOV 5–5–1824

Igor Dmitrieovich MILEANT 5–5–1824

Kornili Issaieovich MOLOKOV 5–5–1824

Captain Karl Ivanovich MÜLLER 5–5–1824

Vassili Sergieieovich NOROV 5–5–1824

Konstantin Pavlovich OFROSSIMOV 5–5–1824

Nikolai Ossipovich POGORSKI-LINKEVICH 5–5–1824

REICHARD (also spelt REICHART) 5–5–1824

Konstantin Alexieieovich RSHEVSKI 5–5–1824

SELIVANOV I 5–5–1824

Peter Alexandrovich SVIETSHIN 5–5–1824

Vassili Ivanovich TICHMENEV 5–5–1824

Count Peter Fedorovich von BUXHÖWDEN 18–9–1824

Alexei Danilovich GREKOV VII 18–9–1824

Nikolai Nikolaieovich RETKIN (also spelt REDKIN) 18–9–1824

SEMENOV 18–9–1824

Kyrill Chrestianovich SHELE II 18–9–1824

1825

Fedor Fedorovich MÜLLER 12–1–1825

Michail Igorovich KIREIEV 23–11–1825

Xaver Petrovich Freiherr von SCHANZENBACH 23–11–1825

Nikolai TRIZONSKI 23–11–1825

Count Ivan Ossipovich von WITTE 23–11–1825

1826

Ivan Vikentieovich LOSSOVSKI 22–12–1826

Evgeni Andreieovich READ 22–12–1826

1828

August Ludwig Ferdinand Graf von NOSTITZ 5–11–1828 (with OL)

Wilhelm Ulrich von THUN 16–12–1828

Louis Auguste Bernard MOLIERE 17–12–1828

Karl Theodor Freiherr von REITZENSTEIN 17–12–1828

Karl Gustaf Ernst von KÜSTER 30–12–1828

1830

Ignaz Heinrich von CLER 13–12–1830

1831

Karl von SEYDLITZ und KURSBACH 11–10–1831

1832

Karl Ossipovich Gilein von GEMBITZ 17–2–1832

Fedor Fedorovich HAVERLAND I 17–2–1832

Gustaf von KLUGEN III 17–2–1832

Baron Georg Otto Wilhelm von MEYENDORF 17–2–1832

Michail Ivanovich TSHEVAKINSKI 17–2–1832

Sir Francis Bond HEAD 18–10–1832

Ivan Kusmitsh GORTALOV 15–12–1832

1839

Feldmarschall Hellmuth Karl Bernard Graf von MOLTKE
29–11–1839 (first award), (OL 17–2–1871), 19–1–1873 (second
award), (P 24–5–1874), (GCS 8–3–1879), (C 29–11–1889 – this was
a special award with diamonds)

Traugott Wilhelm Heinrich von MÜHLBACH 29–11–1839

1840

Archduke Friedrich Ferdinand Leopold of AUSTRIA 30–11–1840

1845

Marquis Gabriel du Pac de BADENS et SOMBRELLE
22–5–1845 (with Crown). The award was made for action in 1792.

1846

Albrecht Wilhelm Graf von der GROEBEN 18–12–1846

Prince Friedrich Wilhelm Waldemar of PRUSSIA 18–12–1846

Prince Wilhelm Friedrich Karl of PRUSSIA 18–12–1846 (with OL)

Count Oriola Eduard Ernst Lobo da SILVERIA 18–12–1846

1848

Eduard Ludwig Wilhelm von BONN 1–9–1848

Prince (aka The Red Prince) Friedrich Karl Nikolaus of PRUSSIA
16–9–1848 (OL 27–2–1864), (GCS 20–9–1866), (OL 2–9–1873)

Johann Karl Wolf Dietrich von MÖLLENDORF 18–9–1848

Friedrich Gustaf Graf von WALDERSEE 18–9–1848

Eduard Freidrich Leopold d'Artis de BEQUIGNOLLES 19–9–1848

Hugh HALKETT 19–9–1848

Prince Freidrich Wilhelm Paul Ferdinand Ludwig August RADIZWILL
19–9–1848

Theodor Karl Daniel von ROMMEL 19–9–1848

Karl Friedrich von STEINMETZ 19–9–1848 (first award),
16–6–1871 (second award)

August Wilhelm Ernst von STOCKHAUSEN 19–9–1848

Friedrich Adolf WIESNER 19–9–1848

Prince Friedrich Emil of SCHLESWIG-HOLSTEIN-SONDERBURG-
AUGUSTENBURG 14–10–1848

August Heinrich von BRANDT 29–11–1848

Leopold Friedrich Ferdinand Heinrich von WEDELL 29–11–1848

1849

Archduke Albrecht Friedrich Rudolf of AUSTRIA 10–4–1849

Prince Albert Friedrich August Anton Ferdinand Josef Crown Prince of
SAXONY 21–7–1849 (OL 6–12–1870)

Friedrich Wilhelm August KIRCHFELDT 27–7–1849

Prince of Prussia Friedrich Wilhelm Ludwig WILHELM I 27–7–1849
(OL 4–8–1866), (GCS 11–11–1866)

August Friedrich Heinrich von PFUHL 31–7–1849

Karl Ludwig Wilhelm Ernst von PRITTWITZ 9–8–1849

Friedrich Adolf von WILLISEN 16–8–1849

Grand Duke Konstantin Nikolaieovich of RUSSIA 17–8–1849

Duke Ernst August Karl Johannes Leopold Alexander Eduard of SAXE-COBURG-GOTHA 11–9–1849

Georg Wilhelm Friedrich Brunsich Edler von BRUN 20–9–1849

1850

Gottlieb Wilhelm GROSS 19–3–1850

Carlo Cesare Filangieri Prince of SATRIANO and Duke of TAORMINA 19–3–1850

1854

Bernhard Wilhelm von KLINCKOWSTRÖM 8–8–1854 (with Crown). The award was made for action in 1796.

1859

Prince Alexander Ludwig Christian Georg Friedrich Emil of HESS and the RHINE 3–11–1859

1861

Maria Leopold Franz d'Assisi of the KINGDOM of the Two SICILIES 20–2–1861

1864

Karl Wilhelm Ludwig Freiherr von der GABLENZ 27–2–1864

Prince Friedrich Karl Nikolaus of PRUSSIA 27–2–1864

Duke Wilhelm Nikolaus of WÜRTTEMBERG 22–3–1864

Gustaf Albert von MANSTEIN 21–4–1864

Eduard Gustaf Ludwig von RAVEN 21–4–1864

Oberst Karl Konstantin Albrecht Leonhardt von BLUMENTHAL 22–4–1864 (OL 17–9–1866), (B 22–4–1898)

Louis Max Napoleon COLOMIER 22–4–1864

Friedrich Karl Ernst Eduard Vogel von FALCKENSTEIN 22–4–1864

Gustaf Eduard HINDERSIN 22–4–1864

August Ferdinand von MERTENS 22–4–1864 (first award), 24–3–1871 (second award)

Richard Emil von BERGMANN 30–5–1864

Friedrich Wilhelm Heinrich Ernst von BEEREN 7–6–1864 (very rare posthumous award)

Georg Wilhelm Ferdinand Gustaf BEKUHRS 7–6–1864

Arnold Gottfried BENDEMANN 7–6–1864

August Emil Alexander von BERGER 7–6–1864

Baron Karl Gustaf Wilhelm von BUDDENBROCK 7–6–1864

Philipp Christian Karl Wilhelm August Freiherr von CANSTEIN 7–6–1864

Karl Bernard von CONTA 7–6–1864

Karl Friedrich Wilhelm Leopold DAUN 7–6–1864

Diederich Franz Ferdinand Maria Johann von DEVIVERE 7–6–1864

Karl Gustaf Alfred Wilhelm von DOERING 7–6–1864

Alphons Wilhelm Georg Heinrich Girodz von GAUDI 7–6–1864

Wilhelm Adolf Heinrich von GERSDORFF 7–6–1864

Ernst Matthias Andreas von HARTMANN 7–6–1864

Julius Bruno HEBLER 7–6–1864

Eduard Julius Ernst HUNDT 7–6–1864

Adolf Karl Hermann KERLEN 7–6–1864

Karl Friedrich von KETTLER 7–6–1864

Ludwig Wilhelm Martin von KORTH 7–6–1864

Christian Karl Gerdus Alfred von KROHN 7–6–1864

Stanislaus Paul Eduard von LESZCZYNSKI 7–6–1864 (OL 5–2–1871)

Eduard Julius Ludwig von LEWINSKI 7–6–1864

Gustaf Eduard Karl Friedrich LOEBBECKE 7–6–1864

Johann Karl Eduard Fragstein von NEIMSDORFF 7–6–1864

Georg Karl Konstantin Freiherr von PUTTKAMER 7–6–1864

Karl von REINHARD 7–6–1864

Karl Berthold Siegismund RIPPENTROP 7–6–1864

Eduard Ludwig von SPEIS 7–6–1864

Heinrich Maximilian von TRESKOW 7–6–1864

Karl Eberhard Herwarth von BITTENFELD 29–6–1864

August Karl Friedrich Christian von GROEBEN 3–7–1864

Julius Heinrich August Edwin von ROEDER 3–7–1864

Friedrich Wilhelm Herman Karl von BROCKHUSEN 14–8–1864

Eduard Kuno von der GOLTZ 14–8–1864

Julius Emil Eugen Ludwig Graf von HACKE 14–8–1864

Graf Leopold von GONDRECOURT 18–8–1864

1865

Friedrich Wilhelm Rembert Graf von BERG 18–1–1865 (with Crown).
The award was made for action in 1815.

1866

Hugo von KIRCHBACH 20–9–1866 (OL 16–2–1871)

Konstantin Reimar von ALVENSLEBEN 17–6–1866 (OL 31–12–1870)

Crown Prince Friedrich Wilhelm Nikolaus FRIEDRICH III 29–6–1866
(OL 3–8–1873), (GCS 20–9–1866), (OL 2–9–1873)

Oberst August Wilhelm Alexander von PAPE 17–9–1866 (OL 22–3–1872)

Friedrich Wilhelm Ludwig von WITTICH 20–9–1866 (OL 5–12–1870)

1867

Theodor Rudolf Hermann Bloch von BLOTTNITZ 15–1–1867

Hans Wilhelm CHORUS 15–1–1867

Ewald Gotthold Hugo GALLU 15–1–1867

1869

Emperor Alexander II of RUSSIA 8–12–1869 (OL 8–12–1871),
(GCS 24–4–1878)

1870

Albert Theodor Emil von ROON 28–10–1870

Rudolf Otto von BUDRITZKI 1–11–1870

Herman Heinrich Theodor von TRESCKOW 5–12–1870 (first award),
16–6–1871 (second award)

*Friedrich Franz Erstherzog von MECKLENBURG-SCHWERIN (OL 5–12–1870)
(date of first award unclear)*

*Friedrich Wilhelm Karl Oskar Freiherr von WRANGEL (OL 5–12–1870)
(date of first award unclear)*

Prince Friedrich August Georg Ludwig Wilhelm of SAXONY 6–12–1870

Ludwig Samson Arthur Freiherr von und der TANN-RATHSAMHAUSEN
22–12–1870

Karl Rochus Edwin von MANTEUFFEL (OL 24–12–1870)
(date of first award unclear)

Prince Friedrich Heindrich Albrecht of PRUSSIA (OL 31–12–1870)
(date of first award unclear)

Konstans Bernhard von VOIGTS-RHETZ (OL 31–12–1870)
(date of first award unclear)

Richard Georg von WEDELL (OL 31–12–1870)
(date of first award unclear)

1871

Arnold Karl Georg von KAMEKE (OL 2–1–1871)
(date of first award unclear)

Georg Ferdinand von BENTHEIM 6–I–1871

Ferdinand Rudolf von KUMMER (OL 12–1–1871)
(date of first award unclear)

Karl Friedrich Wilhelm Leopold August von WERDER (OL 17–1–1871)
(date of first award unclear)

Heinrich Elie Karl von BLUMENTHAL 18–I–1871

Georg Leo von CAPRIVI 18–I–1871

Wilhelm Friedrich Eduard Heinrich Alexander Freiherr von
FALKENHAUSEN 18–I–1871

Moritz Freiherr von der GOLTZ 18–I–1871

Julius Wilhelm KÖRBER 18–I–1871

Ferdinand Heinrich Wilhelm SANNOW 18–I–1871

Julius Karl Philipp Werner von VOIGTS-RHETZ 18–I–1871

Karl Gustaf Leopold Freiherr von BUDDENBROCK (OL 18–1–1871)
(date of first award unclear)

Louis Ferdinand Wolf Anton von STELPNAGEL (OL 18–1–1871)
(date of first award unclear)

Gustaf Wilhelm Friedrich von STIEHLE (OL 18–1–1871)
(date of first award unclear)

Georg Otto von WULFFEN (OL 18–1–1871)
(date of first award unclear)

Christof Gottlieb Albert Freiherr von BARNEKOW (OL 20–1–1871)
(date of first award unclear)

78

Heinrich Karl Ludwig Adolf von GLÜMER 5–2–1871

Wilhelm Herman Ludwig Alexander Karl Graf von WARTENSLEBEN
    5–2–1817 (C 19–I–1873)

Eduard Friedrich von FRANSECKY (OL 5–2–1871)
    (date of first award unclear)

Ernst Karl Oskar von SPERLING (OL 5–2–1871)
    (date of first award unclear)

Adolf Friedrich Heindrich Alexander von ZASTROW (OL 5–2–1871)
    (date of first award unclear)

Karl Ewald von SCHMIDT 7–2–1871

Karl Gustaf von SANDRART 16–2–1871

Friedrich Johann Eduard Christof von SCHMIDT 16–2–1871

Prince Kraft Karl August Eduard Friedrich zu HOHENLOHE-
    INGELFINGEN 17–2–1871

Hans Ludwig Udo von TRESCKOW 17–2–1871

Louis Oskar von BOCK 24–2–1871

Wilhelm Theodor Karl Jobst von BOECKING 24–2–1871

Major Karl Friedrich Ferdinand Julius BUMKE 24–2–1871

Albert Gidion Alexander Hellmuth von MERMERTY 24–2–1871

Otto Julius Wilhelm Maximilian von STRUBBERG 24–2–1871

Ernst Engelbert Oskar Viktor von der BURG (OL 24–2–1871)
    (date of first award unclear)

Karl Friedrich Wilhelm von WITZENDORFF (OL 24–2–1871)
    (date of first award unclear)

Gustaf Herman von ALVENSLEBEN 28–2–1871

Friedrich Gustaf von FLATOW 28–2–1871

Friedrich Wilhelm Ludwig Karl Grand Duke of HESSE and by the RHINE
    28–2–1871

Peter Friedrich Ludwig LEHMANN 28–2–1871

Anton Wilhelm Karl von L'ESTOCQ 28–2–1871

Kurt Ludwig Adalbert von SCHWERIN 28–2–1871

George Heinrich Karl Freiherr von PUTTKAMER 28–2–1871

Ludwig Otto Lukas von CRANACH (OL 28–2–1871)
  (date of first award unclear)

Karl Friedrich Alexander von DIRINGSHOFEN (OL 28–2–1871)
  (date of first award unclear)

Friedrich Wilhelm Alexander von KRAATZ-KOSCHLAU (OL 28–2–1871)
  (date of first award unclear)

Ernst Matthias Andreas von HARTMAN 3–3–1871

Eduard Julius Ludwig August von LEWINSKI 3–3–1871

Generalleutnant Ernst Wilhelm Moritz Otto Schuler Freiherr von SENDEN
  3–3–1871

Wilhelm Karl Albert du TROSSEL 3–3–1871

Friedrich Wilhelm von WYONA 3–3–1871

Theophil Eugen Anton von PODBIELSKI 5–3–1871

Generalleutnant Prince Friedrich Wilhelm Nikolaus Albrecht of PRUSSIA
  10–3–1871 (with OL)

Rudolf Franz Wilhelm von HELDEN-SARNOWSKI 12–6–1871

Karl Ludwig Freiherr von SCHLOTHEIM 15–6–1871

Gustaf von ALVENSLEBEN 16–6–1871

Prince Friedrich August Eberhard of WÜRTTEMBERG 16–6–1871

Friedrich Leopold Karl Alexander Freiherr von der BECKE 28–11–1871

Paul Peter Emil von WYONA 28–11–1871

Hans Adolf Julius von BELOW 2–12–1871

Grand Duke Michail Nikolaieovich of RUSSIA 8–12–1871 (first award),
  18–11–1877 (second award)

Grand Duke Nikolai Nikolaieovich of RUSSIA 8–12–1871 (first award),
  28–11–1877 (second award)

1872

General der Infanterie Jakob Freiherr von HARTMANN 1–3–1872

Justus Karl Wilhelm Albert Friedrich Emil von DRESKY 22–3–1872

Crown Prince Humbert of ITALY 29–5–1872

King Victor Emanuel of ITALY 29–5–1872

1873

Karl Bernhard Herman von BRANDENSTEIN 19–1–1873

Karl Wilhelm von der ESCH 19–1–1873

Otto Karl Georg von FÖRSTER 19–1–1873

Heinrich Paul GEISSLER 19–1–1873

Walter Philipp Werner von GOTTBERG 19–1–1873

Gottlieb Ferdinand Albert Alexis Graf von HAESLER
(aka 'Der Alte Haeseler') 19–1–1873 (OL 22–3–1915)

Alfred August Louis Wilhelm von LEWINSKI 19–1–1873

Josef Maximilian Fridolin von MAILLINGER 19–1–1873

Wilhelm von MASSOW 19–1–1873

Emil Georg NEUMEISTER 19–1–1873

Eduard von PESTEL 19–1–1873

Louis Karl Wilhelm Friedrich Levin von ROTHMALER 19–1–1873

Hans Rudolf Ferdinand von SCHACHTMEYER 19–1–1873

Friedrich Ernst Ferdinand von SCHELIHA 19–1–1873

Karl Heinrich Rudolf von WECHMAR 19–1–1873

1877

Kasimir JULIANOVICH 23/25–9–1877

Friedrich Wilhelm Albert Viktor von LIGNITZ 25–9–1877

Grand Duke Alexander Alexandrovich, Heir to the Thorn of RUSSIA
28–11–1877

Grand Duke Vladimir Alexandrovich of RUSSIA 28–11–1877

Prince Karl Eitel Friedrich Zephyrin Ludwig of RUMANIA 18–12–1877

1878

Grigori Nikonorovich KURLOV 14–4–1878

The following ten awards were made by Special Arrangement:

Josef Vladimirovich HURKO (also spelt GURKO) 24–4–1878

Prince Alexander Konstabtinovich IMERENTINSKI 24–4–1878

Ivan Davidovich LASAREV 24–4–1878

Count Michail Tarielovich LORIS-MELIKOV 24–4–1878

Count Dmitri Alexieieovich MILIUTIN 24–4–1878

Arthur Adamovich NEPOKPOITSHIZKI 24–4–1878

Fedor Fedorovich RADEZKI 24–4–1878

Michail Dmitrieovich SKOBELEV II 24–4–1878

Prince Dmitri Ivanovich SVIATOPOLK-MIRSKI 24–4–1878

Arsas Artemeiovich TERGUKASSOV 24–4–1878

1882

Duke of Connaught Prince Arthur Wilhelm Patrick Albert of GREAT
BRITAIN 17–11–1882

1884

Prince Otto Eduard Leopold von BISMARCK 1–9–1884 (with OL),
(P 1896)

1887

Prince Heinrich Ludwig Wilhelm Adalbert Waldemar Alexander of HESSE
and by the RHINE 7–7–1887

1894

Friedrich Rabot Freiherr von SCHELE 20–11–1894

1895

Prince Ludwig 'Wilhelm' August of BADEN 18–12–1895

1896

Prince Friedrich August Georg Ludwig Wilhelm Maximilian Karl Maria
Nepomuk Baptist Xaver Romans of SAXONY 8–3–1896

1900

Wilhelm Andreas Jakob Emil von LANS 24–6–1900

Anton Georg Ludwig Alfred Graf von SODEN 20–9–1900

Fritz Theodor KREMKOW 27–11–1900

1901

Arthur Sigismund von FÖRSTER 28–5–1901

Alfred Ludwig Heinrich Karl Graf von WALDERSEE 30–7–1901

1902

Admiral Ernst Adolf Julius Guido von USEDOM 5–4–1902 (OL 23–8–1915)

1903

Gunboat SMS *ILTIS* 27–1–1903.
   This award was to recognise the bravery of her entire crew.

1905

Maresuke Kiten NOGI 10–1–1905 (first award to a Japanese)

Anatoli Michailovich von STOESSEL 10–1–1905

Erich Viktor Karl August FRANKE 2–11–1905

Karl Theodor Johann MEISTER 2–11–1905

Adrian Dietrich Lothar von TROTHA 2–11–1905

Roll of Honour: a complete chronological list of all *Pour le Mérite* holders, 1914–1918

The following is a complete chronological list of all First World War *Pour le Mérite* holders. Where two or more have been awarded for the same day, I have put them in order of rank, if known. By virtue of rank they are considered *Primus inter Pares*, 'first among equals'. If the rank is the same, I have put them in alphabetical order. Each entry starts with the rank, then the name; surnames are in CAPITALS. This will be followed in some cases by their position or command and then the date of the award. Where this is followed by another date in brackets, it is the date of the award of the Oak Leaves. If the Oak Leaves were awarded at the same time as the *Pour le Mérite* it will be shown thus (with OL), and the Peace Class thus (P). If two or more have been awarded on the same date then they are listed in rank order; if the rank is the same, they will be in alphabetical order. Names in **bold** are from the German (Army or Naval) Air Service and have their full stories told in the main text. Not included in this list are those who shot down the required number of enemy aircraft but were not actually awarded the *Pour le Mérite*, although their stories are told in the main text. Their names can be found in the alphabetical list in Chapter 8.

1914

General der Infanterie Otto von EMMICH 7–8–1914 (OL 14–5–1915)

Generalmajor Erich LUDENDORFF 22–8–1914 (OL 23–2–1915)

Generalfeldmarschall Franz Joseph I of AUSTRIA 27–8–1914 (with OL)

Generalfeldmarschall Paul von HINDENBURG 2–9–1914 (OL 23–2–1915)

General der Infanterie Hans von ZWEHL 8–9–1914 (OL 17–10–1917)

Leutnant Otto von der LINDE 18–9–1914

Hans Hartwig von BESELER 10–10–1914 (OL 20–8–1915)

Kapitänleutnant Otto WEDDIGEN (*U–9*) 24–10–1914

General der Infanterie Remus von WOYRSCH 25–10–1914

General August von MACKENSEN 27–11–1914 (OL 3–6–1915)

Generalleutnant Karl LITZMANN 29–11–1914 (OL 18–8–1915)

Generalleutnant Kurt von MORGEN 1–12–1914 (OL 11–12–1916)

General der Infanterie Reinhard von SCHEFFER-BOYADEL 2–12–1914

1915

General der Infanterie Bruno von MUDRA 13–1–1915 (OL 17–10–1916)

General der Infanterie Ewald von LOCHOW 14–1–1915 (OL 13–11–1915)

General der Infanterie Fritz von BELOW 16–2–1915 (OL 11–8–1916)

General der Infanterie Otto von BELOW 16–2–1915 (OL 27–4–1917)

General der Infanterie Erich von FALKENHAYN 16–2–1915
(OL 3–6–1915)

Generalleutnant Robert KOSCH 20–2–1915 (OL 27–11–1915)

General der Kavallerie Georg von der MARWITZ 7–3–1915
(OL 14–5–1915)

Generaloberst Karl von EINEM (aka von ROTHMALER) 16–3–1915
(OL 17–10–1916)

General der Infanterie Julius RIEMANN 16–3–1915

Generalleutnant Paul FLECK 16–3–1915

Oberst Prince Eitel Friedrich of PRUSSIA 22–3–1915 (OL 14–5–1915)

Generaloberst Alexander von KLUCK 28–3–1915

Karl Wilhelm Paul von BÜLOW 4–4–1915

Kaiser WILHELM II 12–5–1915 (with OL)

Generalfeldmarschall Archduke Friedrich, Duke of TESCHEN 12–5–1915
(OL 4–1–1917)

Feldmarschall Erstherzog FRIEDRICH (Austro-Hungarian Army)
12–5–1915 (OL 4–1–1918)

Generaloberst Franz CONRAD von HÖTZENDORF (Austro-Hungarian
Army) 12–5–1915 (OL 26–1–1917)

General der Infanterie Hermann von FRANÇOIS 14–5–1915
(OL 27–7–1917)

General der Infanterie Alexander von LINSINGEN 14–5–1915
    (OL 3–7–1915)

General der Infanterie Karl von PLETTENBERG 14–5–1915

Oberst Hans von SEEKT 14–5–1915

General der Infanterie Ernst II, Herzog von SAXONY ALTENBURG
    30–5–1915

Generalleutnant Paul Ritter von KNEUSSL 3–6–1915 (OL 11–1–1917)

Kapitänleutnant Otto HERSING (*U–21*) 5–6–1915

Generalmajor Alfred ZIETHEN 14–6–1915

General der Infanterie Eberhard von CLAER 29–6–1915

Generaloberst Felix Graf von BOTHMER 7–7–1915 (OL 25–7–1917)

General der Infanterie Friedrich von GEROK 7–7–1915

Generalmajor Paulus von STOLZMANN 7–7–1915

General der Kavallerie Götz Freiherr von KÖNIG 23–7–1915

General der Artillerie Max von GALLWITZ 24–7–1915 (OL 28–9–1915)

Generalleutnant Adolf WILD von HOLENBORN 2–8–1915

Feldmarschall Prince Leopold of BAVARIA 5–8–1915 (OL 25–7–1917)

General der Infanterie Helmuth von MOLTKE 7–8–1915

Grossadmiral Alfred von TIRPITZ 10–8–1915

Generaloberst Hermann von EICHHORN 18–8–1915 (OL 28–09–1915)

Crown Prince Rupprecht of BAVARIA 22–8–1915 (OL 20–12–1916)

Feldmarschall Duke Albrecht of WÜRTTEMBERG 22–8–1915

General der Infanterie Wilhelm, Crown Prince of the German Empire and of
    PRUSSIA 22–8–1915 (OL 8–9–1916)

General Hermann von STRANTZ 22–8–1915

Generaloberst Ludwig von FALKENHAUSEN 23–8–1915
    (OL 15–4–1916)

General der Infanterie Max von FABECK 23–8–1915

Generalleutnant Damed ENVER-PASCHA (Turkish Army) 23–8–1915
    (OL 10–1–1916)

General der Infanterie Hans Emil Alexander GAEDE 25–8–1915

Generaloberst Josias von HEERINGEN 28–8–1915 (OL 28–8–1916)

General der Kavallerie Eugen von FALKENHAYN 28–8–1915
    (OL 13–11–1915)

Generalleutnant Max HOFMANN 28–8–1915 (OL 5–7–1918)

Generalleutnant Artur Arz von STRAUSSENBURG (Austro-Hungarian
    Army) 28–8–1915 (OL 6–8–1917)

General der Artillerie Friedrich von SCHOLTZ 3–9–1915

Leutnant Karl WILLWEBER 3–9–1915

Generalmajor Wilhelm GROENER 11–9–1915

Generalmajor Gerhard TAPPEN 11–9–1915

General der Infanterie Kuno von STEUBEN 13–10–1915

Generalleutnant Constantin SCHMIDT von KNOBELSDORF 17–10–1915

Admiral Ludwig von SCHRÖDER 20–10–1915 (OL 23–12–1917)

General der Infanterie Arnold von WINCKLER 27–11–1915

Hermann Baron Kövess von KÖVESSHAZA (Austro-Hungarian Army)
    4–12–1915 (OL 26–3–1918)

1916

General der Kavallerie Otto LIMAN von SANDERS-PASCHA 10–1–1916
    (with OL)

General der Infanterie Kurt von PRITZELWITZ 12–1–1916

Hauptmann Oswald BOELCKE 12–1–1916

Oberleutnant Max IMMELMANN 12–1–1916

Generalleutnant Nikolaus Todorow JEKOW (Bulgarian Army) 18–1–1916

Korvettenkapitän Nikolas Burggraf und Count of DOHNA-SCHLODIEN
    (Cruiser *MÖWE*) 7–3–1916

General der Infanterie Hans von GURETZKY-CORNITZ 9–3–1916

Oberleutnant Cordt von BRANDIS 14–3–1916

Hauptmann Hans-Joachim HAUPT 16–3–1916

Kapitänleutnant Otto STEINBRINCK (*UB–18*) 29–3–1916

Hauptmann Hans-Joachim BUDDECKE 14–4–1916

Generalfeldmarschall Charles I of AUSTRIA 20–5–1916 (OL 6–12–1916)

Feldmarschall Archduke Eugen of AUSTRIA 23–5–1916 (OL 3–11–1917)

Admiral Franz von HIPPER 5–6–1916

Admiral Reinhand SCHEER 5–6–1916 (OL 1–2–1918)

Admiral Adolf von TROTHA 5–6–1916

Leutnant Kurt RACKOW 7–6–1916

Leutnant Kurt WINTGENS 1–7–1916

Leutnant Max Ritter von MULZER 8–7–1916

Leutnant Otto PARSCHAU 10–7–1916

Leutnant der Reserve Wilhelm FRANKL 12–7–1916

Leutnant Walter HÖHNDORF 20–7–1916

Oberleutnant Ernst Freiherr von ALTHAUS 21–7–1916

Oberst Karl HOEFER 23–7–1916 (OL 14–4–1918)

Hauptmann Konrad KALAU von HOFE 23–7–1916

Grossadmiral Prince Heinrich of PRUSSIA 1–8–1916 (OL 24–1–1918)

General der Infanterie Konrad von GOSSLER 10–8–1916

General der Infanterie Friedrich Bertram SIXT von ARMIN 10–8–1916

General der Artillerie Hans von KIRCHEN 11–8–1916

General der Infanterie Ferdinand von QUAST 11–8–1916 (OL 10–4–1918)

Kapitänleutnant Walther FORSTMANN (*U–39*) 12–8–1916

General der Kavallerie Friedrich von BERNHARDI 20–8–1916
    (OL 15–5–1918)

General der Infanterie Oskar Ritter von XYLANDER 20–8–1916

Oberst Wilhelm HEYE 20–8–1916 (OL 3–4–1918)

General der Infanterie Max von BOEHM 24–8–1916 (OL 20–5–1917)

Generalleutnant Walther von LÜTTWITZ 24–8–1916 (OL 24–3–1918)

General der Infanterie Berthold von DEIMLING 28–8–1916

General der Infanterie Erich von GRÜNDELL 28–8–1916

General der Infanterie Otto Freiherr von HÜGEL 28–8–1916

General der Infanterie Hugo von KATHEN 28–8–1916 (OL 27–8–1917)

General der Artillerie Richard von SCHUBERT 28–8–1916

Generalleutnant Hermann von KUHL 28–8–1916 (OL 20–12–1916),
    (P 1924)

Generalleutnant Emil LLSE 28–8–1916

General der Infanterie Karl d'ELSA 1–9–1916

General der Kavallerie Maximilian von LAFFERT 1–9–1916

General der Infanterie Theodor Freiherr von WATTER 1–9–1916

Generalleutnant Hermann von STEIN 1–9–1916

Generalleutnant Konrad KRAFFT von DELLMENSINGEN 7–9–1916
  (OL 11–12–1916)

King Ferdinand I of BULGARIA 8–9–1916 (with OL)

Oberstleutnant August von GOETZEN 11–9–1916

General der Infanterie Karl von FASBENDER 13–9–1916

General der Infanterie Günther von PANNEWITZ 13–9–1916

Schellendorff Bernhard von BRONSART 16–9–1916

General der Kavallerie Wolf Freiherr von MARSCHALL und
  ALTENGOTTERN 21–9–1916 (OL 16–5–1918)

Oberst Emil HELL 21–9–1916 (OL 11–1–1918)

Oberst Georg JOHOW 21–9–1916

Oberst Friedrich Karl von LOSSBERG 21–9–1916 (OL 24–4–1917)

Oberstleutnant Oskar SCHWERK 21–9–1916

Generalleutnant Otto von STEETTEN 22–9–1916

Oberst Gottfried MARKQUARD 27–9–1916

General der Infanterie Dedo von SCHENCK 2–10–1916

General der Kavallerie Ludwig Freiherr von GEBSATTEL 4–10–1916

General der Artillerie Hans von GRONAU 4–10–1916 (OL 6–8–1918)

Generalfeldmarschall Eduard von BÖHM-ERMOLLI 7–10–1916
  (OL 1–6–1917)

General der Infanterie Johannes von EBEN 7–10–1916 (OL 8–6–1917)

Oberst Max HOFFMANN 7–10–1916 (OL 25–7–1917)

Generalleutnant Alfred von BÖCKMANN 8–10–1916 (OL 1–6–1917)

Kapitänleutnant Lothar von ARNAULD de la PERIÈRE (*U–35*)
  11–10–1916

Generalleutnant Richard von CONTA 15–10–1916 (OL 26–3–1918)

Generalleutnant Otto von GARNIER 17–10–1916

Admiral Wilhelm SOUCHON 29–10–1916

Oberst Paul von LETTOW-VORBECK 4–11–1916 (OL 10–10–1917)

Leutnant der Reserve Gustav LEFFERS 5–11–1916

Leutnant der Reserve Albert DOSSENBACH 11–11–1916

Oberleutnant Hans BERR 4–12–1916

Generaloberst Ludwig III of BAVARIA 8–12–1916

Generalleutnant Viktor KÜHME 11–12–1916

Generalleutnant Eberhard Graf von SCHMETTOW 11–12–1916

Generalleutnant Hermann von STAAB 11–12–1916

Oberst Hans HESSE 11–12–1916

Major Georg WETZELL 11–12–1916

Oberstleutnant Max BAUER 19–12–1916 (OL 28–3–1918)

Crown Prince of Bayern RUPPRECHT 20–12–1916

Kapitänleutnant Max VALENTINER (*U–38*) 26–12–1916

1917

Kapitänleutnant Hans WALTHER (*U–52*) 9–1–1917

Rittmeister Manfred Freiherr von RICHTHOFEN 12–1–1917

General der Artillerie Richard von BERENDT 14–1–1917
    (OL 24–11–1917)

Grossadmiral Henning von HOLTZENDORFF 22–3–1917
    (OL 1–2–1918)

Feldmarschall Archduke Joseph August of AUSTRIA 30–3–1917
    (OL 26–3–1918)

Generaloberst Erstherzog JOSEPH (Austro-Hungarian Army) 30–3–1917
    (OL 26–3–1918)

**General der Kavallerie Ernst von HOEPPNER (Chief of the Air Service)
    8–4–1917**

**Oberst Hermann THOMSEN (later von der LEITH-THOMSEN)
    (Chief of Staff of the Air Service) 8–4–1917**

Leutnant der Reserve Werner VOSS 8–4–1917

General der Infanterie Albano von JACOBI 12–4–1917

Oberleutnant Fritz Otto BERNERT 23–4–1917

Oberst Friedrich Graf von der SCHULENBURG 24–4–1917
    (OL 23–3–1918)

General der Infanterie Georg WICHURA 26–4–1917

Generalleutnant Carl DIEFFENBACH 26–4–1917

Generalleutnant Eberhard von HOFACKER 26–4–1917 (OL 24–11–1917)

Generalleutnant Otto von MOSER 26–4–1917

Leutnant Karl Emil SCHÄFER 26–4–1917

General der Infanterie Walter REINHARDT 30–4–1917

Generalleutnant Karl Ritter von WENNIGER 1–5–1917

Oberstleutnant Georg BRUCHMÜLLER 1–5–1917 (OL 26–3–1918)

Generalmajor Karl von LEWINSKI 2–5–1917

Major Adolf STEINWACHS 2–5–1917

Leutnant Kurt WOLFF 4–5–1917

Generalleutnant Hermann Ritter von BURKHARDT 12–5–1917

General der Infanterie Otto von PLÜSTOW 12–5–1917

Major Wilhelm LINCKE 12–5–1917

Leutnant Lothar Freiherr von RICHTHOFEN 14–5–1917

Leutnant der Reserve Heinrich GONTERMANN 14–5–1917

General der Infanterie Magnus von EDERHARDT 20–5–1917
    (OL 25–9–1917)

General der Infanterie Horst Edler von der PLANITZ 20–5–1917

Generalmajor Heinrich von MAUR 20–5–1917

Oberst Martin Freiherr von OLDERSHAUSEN 20–5–1917

Oberstleutnant Wilhelm von GOERNE 20–5–1917 (OL 26–8–1918)

Oberstleutnant Ernst SCHÜTZ 20–5–1917

Oberstleutnant Georg SICK 20–5–1917

Major Richard MOELLER 20–5–1917

Generaloberst Erstherzog EUGENE (Austro-Hungarian Army) 23–5–1917
    (OL 3–11–1917)

General der Infanterie Eduard von LIEBERT 6–6–1917

Major Robert von KLÜBER 14–6–1917

Hauptmann Ernst von BRANDENBURG 14–6–1917

Leutnant Karl ALLMENRÖDER 14–6–1917

General der Infanterie Oskar von EHRENTHAL 15–6–1917

Oberstleutnant George von OVEN 24–7–1917

Oberstleutnant Hans Ritter von HEMMER 25–7–1917

Major Rudolf FRANTZ 25–7–1917

General der Infanterie Franz Freiherr von SODEN 27–7–1917

Generalmajor Karl Freiherr von BARDORFF (Austro-Hungarian Army)
    27–7–1917

Oberst Max-Friedrich von SCHLECHTENDAL 27–7–1917

Oberstleutnant Hans PREUSKER 27–7–1917

Oberstleutnant Hans SCHMID 27–7–1917

General der Infanterie Adolph von CARLOWITZ 29–7–1917
    (OL 25–5–1918)

Oberstleutnant Hermann von BALCKE 29–7–1917

Kapitänleutnant Walther SCHWIEGER (*U–88*) 30–7–1917

Major Wilhelm HAGEDORN 30–7–1917

Oberleutnant Paul Freiherr von PECHMANN 31–7–1917

Oberleutnant Adolf Ritter von TUTSCHEK 3–8–1917

Generalleutnant Rudolf von BORRIES 4–8–1917

Generalleutnant Günther von ETZEL 4–8–1917 (OL 26–10–1918)

Oberstleutnant Willi von KLEWITZ 6–8–1917

Oberstleutnant Albrecht von THAER 6–8–1917

Oberleutnant Eduard Ritter von DOSTLER 6–8–1917

Oberleutnant Heino von HEIMBURG (*UC–22*) 11–8–1917

General der Infanterie Eduard von BELOW 18–8–1917

Generalleutnant Georg FUCHS 18–8–1917

Generalleutnant Hermann Freiherr von STEIN 20–8–1917

Fregattenkapitän Peter STRASSER 20–8–1917

Oberstleutnant Reinhold SALTZWEDEL (*UC–71*) 20–8–1917

Generalmajor Wilhelm MECKEL 26–8–1917

Major Heinrich Freiherr von HADELN 26–8–1917

General der Infanterie Günther Graf von KIRCHBACH 27–8–1917

Generalleutnant Albert von BERRER 27–8–1917

Generalmajor Hasso von WEDEL 27–8–1917

Oberstleutnant Wilhelm REINHARD 27–8–1917

Major Siegfried Graf zu EULENBURG-WICKEN 27–8–1917
  (OL 4–9–1918)

Oberst Curt Freiherr von WÄNGENHEIM 3–9–1917

Leutnant Max Ritter von MÜLLER 3–9–1917

Generalleutnant Achmed DJEMAL-PASCHA (Turkish Army) 4–9–1917

Oberst Friedrich Freiherr Kress von KRESSENSTEIN 4–9–1917

Generalleutnant Martin CHALES de BEAULIEU 5–9–1917

General der Infanterie Oskar von HUTIER 6–9–1917 (OL 23–3–1918)

Generalleutnant Ludwig von ESTORFF 6–9–1917

Generalleutnant Otto Ritter von RAUCHENBERGER 6–9–1917
  (OL 19–10–1918)

Generalmajor Traugott von SAUBERZWEIG 6–9–1917

Generalleutnant Hugo Elstermann von ELSTER 22–9–1917

Oberst Richard HENTSCH 23–9–1917

Generalmajor Georg MAERCKER 1–10–1917 (OL 3–5–1918)

Kapitänleutnant Rudolf KLEINE 4–10–1917

Oberstleutnant Heinrich SCHMEDES 5–10–1917

Generaloberst Eduard von BOEHM-ERMOLLI (Austro-Hungarian Army)
  7–10–1917 (OL 27–7–1918)

General der Infanterie Ernst von BACMEISTER 8–10–1917

Generalmajor Felix LANGER 8–10–1917 (OL 7–11–1918)

Oberst Karl Graf von der SCHULENBURG-WOLFSBURG 8–10–1917

Oberstleutnant Franz von BEHR 8–10–1917

Oberstleutnant Wilhelm von THADDEN 8–10–1917

Major Ferdinand HEROLD 8–10–1917

Leutnant Walter von BÜLOW-BOTHKAMP 8–10–1917

Oberstleutnant Konrad KRAEHE 8–10–1917 (OL 15–8–1918)

Generalmajor Arnold LEQUIS 11–10–1917 (OL 5–12–1917)

Generalmajor Theodor TEETZMANN 11–10–1917

Oberleutnant Rudolf BERTHOLD 12–10–1917

Oberstleutnant Gottfried EDELBÜTTEL 12–10–1917

General der Infanterie Georgi Stojanow TODOROW (Bulgarian Army)
14–10–1917

Korvettenkapitän Karl BARTENBACH (U-Boat Flotilla Chief) 27–10–1917

Leutnant Walther SCHNIEBER 27–10–1917

Vizeadmiral Erhardt SCHMIDT 31–10–1917

Admiral Paul BEHNKE 31–10–1917

Generalleutnant Siegfried Freiherr von ENDE 31–10–1917

Oberstleutnant Ernst Freiherr von FORSTNER 31–10–1917
(OL 17–6–1918)

Konteradmiral Magnus von LEVETZOW 31–10–1917

Major Walter Freiherr von SCHLEINITZ 31–10–1917

Major Ludwig Wilhelm Freiherr von WILLISEN 1–11–1917

General der Infanterie Moriz von LYNCKER 2–11–1917

Generaloberst Svetozar Boroëvić von BOJNA (Austro-Hungarian Army)
3–11–1917

Generalmajor Alfred Freiherr von WALDSTÄTTEN (Austro-Hungarian
Army) 3–11–1917

Generalleutnant Egon Graf von SCHMETTOW 4–11–1917

Oberstleutnant Kurt FISCHER 4–11–1917

Major Alfred von VOLLARD-BOCKELBERG 4–11–1917

Kapitänleutnant Hans ADAMS (*U–82*) 6–11–1917

Generalmajor Hermann von DRESLER und SCHARFENSTEIN
8–11–1917

Generalmajor Arthur von GABAIN 8–11–1917 (OL 17–4–1918)

Generalmajor Arthur Freiherr von LÜTTWITZ 8–11–1917

Major Franz HEINRIGS 8–11–1917

Oberst Erich von TSCHISCHWITZ 9–11–1917

General der Infanterie Alfred KRAUSS (Austro-Hungarian Army)
12–11–1917

Generalleutnant Heinrich von HOFMANN 12–11–1917 (OL 18–9–1918)

Kapitänleutnant Robert MORAHT (*U–64*) 12–11–1917

Oberstleutnant Ernst FRAHNERT 14–11–1917

Oberst Willi MATTHIAS 22–11–1917

Leutnant der Reserve Kurt WÜSTHOFF 22–11–1917

Generalmajor Ernst von BELOW 24–11–1917 (OL 13–10–1918)

Generalleutnant Christoph Ritter von KIEFHABER 24–11–1917

Generalmajor Hans von BELOW 24–11–1917

Generalmajor Rudolph HAMMER 24–11–1917

Oberst Boleslaus von KUCZKOWSKI 24–11–1917

Oberstleutnant Wilhelm Graf von GLUSZEWSKI-KWILECKI 24–11–1917

Major Karl von KEISER 24–11–1917

Major Karl von RETTBERG 24–11–1917

Hauptmann Viktor BANGERT 24–11–1917

Hauptmann Wilhelm von GAZEN 24–11–1917

Hauptmann Wolff von GRAEFFENDORFF 24–11–1917

Leutnant der Reserve Erwin BÖHME 24–11–1917

Oberst Leo von PACZYNSKI-TENCIN 25–11–1917

Major Tuft Friedrich von SEELHORST 26–11–1917

Oberst Armin KOENEMANN 28–11–1917

Oberstleutnant Markus STACHOW 28–11–1917

Major Hans BESELER 28–11–1917

Hauptmann Horst von WOLFF 28–11–1917

Oberstleutnant Max ZUNEHMER 29–11–1917

Leutnant Hans KLEIN 2–12–1917

Oberst Hans von HEYNIK 3–12–1917

Fregattenkapitän Hugo von ROSENBERO 4–12–1917

Hauptmann Alfred KELLER 4–12–1917

Leutnant der Reserve Julius BUCKLER 4–12–1917

Oberleutnant Eduard Ritter von SCHLEICH 4–12–1917

Hauptmann Eduard WITTCKIND 4–12–1917

Leutnant Ferdinand SCHÖRNER 5–12–1917

Generalmajor Ludwig Ritter von TUTSCHEK 8–12–1917

Oberstleutnant Hermann REINICKE 8–12–1917

Major Theodor SPROESSER 10–12–1917

Oberleutnant Erwin ROMMEL 10–12–1917

Kapitänleutnant zur See Friedrich CHRISTIANSEN 11–12–1917

Kapitänleutnant Hans ROSE (*U–53*) 20–12–1917

Kapitänleutnant Otto WÜNSCHE (*U–97*) 20–12–1917

Generalleutnant Arthur von LINDEQUIST 23–12–1917 (OL 7–11–1918)

Generalleutnant Oskar Freiherr von WATTER 23–12–1917

Generalleutnant Richard WELLMANN 23–12–1917

Oberst Erich Freiherr von OLDERSHAUSEN 23–12–1917
    (OL 26–3–1918)

Oberstleutnant Otto HASSE 23–12–1917 (OL 12–5–1918)

Oberstleutnant Richard von PAWELFZ 23–12–1917

Major Erich KREBS 23–12–1917

Major Karl Ritter von PRAGER 23–12–1917

Major Max STAPFF 23–12–1917

Major Hans von VOSS 23–12–1917

Hauptmann Erich SCHOLTZ 23–12–1917

Oberleutnant Hermann FRICKE 23–12–1917

Oberleutnant Hans HOWALT (*UB–40*) 23–12–1917

Leutnant der Reserve Heinrich BONGARTZ 23–12–1917

Leutnant Hans-Georg HORN 23–12–1917

Korvettenkapitän Waldemar KOPHAMEL (*U–151*) 29–12–1917

1918

Oberst Fritz von SELLE 6–1–1918

Oberst Friedrich von TAYSEN 6–1–1918

Oberstleutnant Hans von SYDOW 6–1–1918

Admiral Eduard von CAPELLE 9–1–1918

Generalleutnant Manfred Freiherr von RICHTHOFEN 18–1–1918

Generalmajor Siegfried von la CHEVALLERIE 20–1–1918
    (OL 5–10–1918)

Major Walter von DELIUS 20–1–1918

Major Hans KLOEBE 20–1–1918

Oberstleutnant Otto TESCHNER 22–1–1918

Hauptmann Gustav STOFFLETH 22–1–1918

Kapitänleutnant Max VIEBEG (*UB–80*) 30–1–1918

Oberstleutnant Friedrich Franz von HUTH 31–1–1918

Hauptmann Reinhard SEILER 31–1–1918

Leutnant Hans MARKMANN 12–2–1918

Fregattenkapitän Karl August NERGER (Raider *WOLF*) 24–2–1918

Kapitänleutnant Hans-Joachim von MELLENTHIN (*UB–49*) 25–2–1918

Oberstleutnant Wolfgang STEINBAUER (*UB–48*) 3–3–1918

Korvettenkapitän Oskar HEINECKE (Torpedo Boat Flotilla Chief) 5–3–1918

Major Friedrich BRINCKMANN 6–3–1918

Generalleutnant William BALCKE 9–3–1918

Hauptmann Bruno LOERZER 12–3–1918

Kapitänleutnant Otto SCHULTZE (*U–63*) 18–3–1918

Fregattenkapitän Karl von MÜLLER (Cruiser *EMDEN*) 19–3–1918

Major Ernst von BILA 23–3–1918

Generaloberst Hans von PLESSEN 24–3–1918

Admiral Georg Alexander von MÜLLER 24–3–1918

Generalleutnant Horst Ritter und Edler von OETINGER 26–3–1918

Oberstleutnant Kurt Freiherr von LUPIN 26–3–1918

Oberstleutnant Viktor KELLER 27–3–1918

Oberst Hermann Ritter MERTZ von QUIRNHEIM 28–3–1918

Major Hans von DRIGALSKI 28–3–1918

Major Friedrich von KRIEGSHEIM 28–3–1918

Generalleutnant Wilhelm von DÜCKER 29–3–1918

Oberleutnant Heinrich Claudius KROLL 29–3–1918

Kapitänleutnant Ralph WENNIGER (*UB–55*) 30–3–1918

Oberst Paul KRAUSE 1–4–1918

Oberstleutnant Georg DORNDORF 1–4–1918

Oberstleutnant Peter SCHEUNEMANN 1–4–1918

Major Fedor von BOCK 1–4–1918

Major Eduard von WESTHOVEN 1–4–1918

Oberstleutnant Hermann DRECHSEL 3–4–1918

Oberstleutnant Friedrich Freiherr von ESEBECK 3–4–1918

Generalmajor Heindrich SCHEÜCH 8–4–1918

Generalmajor Ernst von WRISBERG 8–4–1918

Major Karl von HAGEN 8–4–1918

General der Infanterie Friedrich von GONTARD 9–4–1918 (OL 4–8–1918)

Generalleutnant Viktor ALBRECHT 9–4–1918

Generalleutnant Kurt von dem BORNE 9–4–1918 (OL 7–11–1918)

Generalleutnant Walter von HÜLSEN 9–4–1918

Generalmajor Wilhelm von GRODDECK 9–4–1918

Generalmajor Bernhard Finck Graf von FINCKENSTEIN 9–4–1918

Kapitänleutnant Horst Freiherr Treusch von BUTTLAR-BRANDENFELS 9–4–1918

Major Hubert HEYM 9–4–1918

Major Berend ROOSEN 9–4–1918

Oberleutnant Ernst UDET 9–4–1918

Oberst Hermann Ritter von LENZ 10–4–1918

Hauptmann Kuno-Hans von BOTH 10–4–1918

Leutnant Emil TREBING 14–4–1918

Generalleutnant Nikolaus Ritter von ENDRES 17–4–1918 (OL 4–8–1918)

Generalleutnant Erich FREYER 17–4–1918

Generalmajor Karl BERGER 17–4–1918

Generalmajor Dietrich von ROEDER 17–4–1918

Generalmajor Paul TIEDE 17–4–1918

Hauptmann Achim von ARNIM 17–4–1918

Oberst Siegfried RODIG 21–4–1918

Oberstleutnant Richard von KEISER 21–4–1918

Major Curt von BEERFELDE 21–4–1918

Major Cordt Freiherr von BRANDIS 21–4–1918

Major Alexander COMMICHAU 21–4–1918

Major Wilhelm von DITFURTH 21–4–1918

Major Paul KLETTE 21–4–1918 (OL 26–8–1918)

Major Kurt von KLÜFER 21–4–1918

Major Otto KOCH 21–4–1918

Major Friedrich von MIASKOWSKI 21–4–1918

Major Axel von PLATEN 21–4–1918

Major Walter von UNRUH 21–4–1918

Hauptmann Walter CASPARI 21–4–1918

Hauptmann Martin GOESCH 21–4–1918

Hauptmann Karl von PLEHEW 21–4–1918

Hauptmann Armin REICHENBACH 21–4–1918

Hauptmann Ernst SCHAUMBURG 21–4–1918

Hauptmann Gustav Adolf von WULFFEN 21–4–1918

Generaloberst Elimar von CRANACH 22–4–1918

Generalleutnant Georg von SCHÜSSLER 22–4–1918

Generalleutnant Karl von STUMPFF 22–4–1918

Generalmajor Johannes von BRUSSE 22–4–1918

Generalmajor Axel von PERESDORFF 22–4–1918

Oberstleutnant Kurt von DEWIISS 22–4–1918

Oberstleutnant Hans Eberhard von RIESENTHAL 22–4–1918

Major Ulrich von GERMAR 22–4–1918

Major Julius von LANGSDORFF 22–4–1918

Major Otto RUHNAU 22–4–1918

Hauptmann George SOLDAN 22–4–1918

Oberst Wilhelm HUNDRICH 23–4–1918

Hauptmann Ferdinand BRISKEN 23–4–1918

Oberleutnant Carl MENCKHOFF 23–4–1918

Kapitänleutnant Carl Siegfried Ritter von GEORG (*U–101*) 24–4–1918

Korvettenkapitän Gustav SIESS (*U–33*) 24–4–1918

Oberleutnant Johannes LOHS (*UB–57*) 24–4–1918

Generalleutnant Viktor DALLMER 26–4–1918 (OL 8–6–1918)

Generalleutnant Ludwig SIEGER 27–4–1918

Generalleutnant Paul GRÜNERT 3–5–1918

Oberst Hans von WERDER 3–5–1918

Oberstleutnant Carl MERKEL 3–5–1918

Oberst Georg FROTSCHER 5–5–1918

Kapitänleutnant Erwin WASSNER (*UB–59*) 5–5–1918

Major Helmuth BOHM 5–5–1918

Major Friedrich von PIRSCHER 5–5–1918

Oberstleutnant Ernst von HOHNHORST 6–5–1918

Major Lothar FRITSCH 6–5–1918

Major Philipp SANDER 6–5–1918

Oberstleutnant Erich BÖHME 7–5–1918

Major Erwin von COLLANI 7–5–1918

Major Alexander von FALKENHAUSEN 7–5–1918

General der Infanterie Georg Freiherr von GAYL 8–5–1918

Generalmajor Walter von BERGMANN 8–5–1918

Generalmajor Kurt Freiherr Prinz von BUCHAU 11–5–1918

Generalmajor Rüdiger von der GOLTZ 15–5–1918

Oberst Otto Freiherr von BRANDENSTEIN 15–5–1918

Generalmajor Prince Franz of BAVARIA 16–5–1918

Oberstleutnant Robert BÜRKNER 16–5–1918

Major Wilhelm HUMSER 16–5–1918

Hauptmann Rudolf TEICHMANN 18–5–1918

Hauptmann Hermann KÖHL 20–5–1918

Major Wilhelm SCHNIEWINDT 21–5–1918

Hauptmann Sieghard von SALDERN 21–5–1918

Oberst Franz von EPP 29–5–1918

Kapitänleutnant Andreas MICHELSEN (Commander-in-Chief of U-Boats)
31–5–1918

Oberleutnant Erich LÖWENHARDT 31–5–1918

Leutnant Fritz PÜTTER 31–5–1918

Major Schellendorff Walter Siegfried von BRONSART 2–6–1918

Major Georg KAULBACH 2–6–1918

Oberleutnant Hermann Wilhelm GÖRING 2–6–1918

Leutnant der Landwehr Friedrich NIELEBOCK 2–6–1918

Major Werner von BLOMBERG 3–6–1918

Hauptmann Kurt von OESTERREICH 5–6–1918

Oberstleutnant Wilhelm von HASSY 6–6–1918

Leutnant der Reserve Rudolph Otto WINDISCH 6–6–1918

Ernst-Karl von KRETSCHMANN 8–6–1918

Leutnant Wilhelm Paul SCHREIBER 8–6–1918

Major Kurt von GREIFF 9–6–1918

Oberst Detlof Graf von SCHWERIN 12–6–1918

Generalleutnant Karl von BORRIES 13–6–1918

Generalmajor Otto Freiherr von DIEPENBROICK-GRÜTER 13–6–1918

Generalmajor Walter von HAXTHAUSEN 13–6–1918

Hauptmann Karl von FREYHOLD 14–6–1918

Hauptmann Siegfried HAENICKE 14–6–1918

Generalleutnant Robert LOEB 17–6–1918

Major Albrecht STEPPUHN 17–6–1918

Hauptmann Ludwig Freiherr von PREUSCHEN von und zu LIEBENSTEIN
17–6–1918

Generalmajor Wilhelm von DOMMES 18–6–1918

Oberstleutnant Wilhelm FAUPEL 18–6–1918 (OL 4–8–1918)

Oberst Walther Dietrich von WITZLEBEN 23–6–1918

Oberstleutnant Julius von STOEKLERN zu GRÜNHOLZEK 23–6–1918

Hauptmann Waldemar BERKA 23–6–1918

Oberleutnant Hans von RAVENSTEIN 23–6–1918

Leutnant Robert HIERONYMUS 23–6–1918

Leutnant Hans KIRSCHSTEIN 24–6–1918

Generalleutnant Roderich von SCHOELER 30–6–1918

Oberst Udo von FISCHER 30–6–1918

Major Josef BISCHOFF 30–6–1918

Major Karl FRIEDERICI 30–6–1918

Major Albrecht Freiherr von ROTBERG 30–6–1918

Major Felix SCHELLE 30–6–1918

Leutnant Karl RUTHENBURG 30–6–1918

Leutnant Emil THUY 30–6–1918

Kapitänleutnant Wilhelm MARSCHALL (*UB–105*) 4–7–1918

Oberstleutnant Max LUDWIG 5–7–1918

Oberstleutnant Hans von TROILO 5–7–1918

Major Hans-Heydan von FRANKENBERG und LUDWIGSDORF 5–7–1918

Major Karl von KIETZELL 5–7–1918

Major Engelbert von MORSBACH 5–7–1918

Major Ernst GRUSON 6–7–1918

Major Arthur PIKARDI 6–7–1918

Hauptmann Wilhelm PREUSSER 6–7–1918

Leutnant der Reserve Peter RIEPER 7–7–1918

Generalleutnant Georg von ENGELBRECHTEN 8–7–1918

Leutnant der Reserve Fritz RUMEY 10–7–1918

Hauptmann Walter TRENCK 15–7–1918

Oberstleutnant Paul KIENITZ 16–7–1918

Major Ernst Adolph Alphons Freiherr von SCHIMMELMANN 16–7–1918

Leutnant Josef Carl Peter JACOBS 18–7–1918

Major Rudolf LANGE 21–7–1918

Generalleutnant Antol Graf von BREDOW 23–7–1918

Oberleutnant Otto KISSENBERTH 24–7–1918

Oberstleutnant Friedrich Ritter von BOGENDÖRFER 31–7–1918

Oberstleutnant Friedrich Ritter von HAACK 4–8–1918

Oberstleutnant Adolff HERRGOTT 4–8–1918

Major Erich GUDOWIUS 4–8–1918

Major Erich KEWISCH 4–8–1918

Major Robert MATTIASS 4–8–1918

Major Rudolf SCHNIEWINDT 4–8–1918

Major Edwin von STÜLPNAGEL 4–8–1918

Oberleutnant zur See Gotthard SACHSENBERG 5–8–1918

Major Josef BARTH 9–8–1918

Hauptmann Franz WALZ 9–8–1918

Oberstleutnant Richard d'ALTON-RAUCH 15–8–1918

Oberstleutnant Moritz ROTHENBÜCHER 15–8–1918

Major Maximilian von KNOCH 15–8–1918

Major Ferdinand MÜLLER 15–8–1918

Major Rudolf MÜLLER 15–8–1918

Major Martin OTTO 15–8–1918

Major Fritz Freiherr von WEDEKIND 15–8–1918

Leutnant der Reserve Joseph VELTJENS 16–8–1918

Kapitänleutnant Paul HUNDIUS (*UB-103*) 18–8–1918

Kapitänleutnant Wilhelm WERNER (*U-55*) 18–8–1918

Major Wilhelm HAUPT 18–8–1918

Rittmeister Karl BOLLE 21–8–1918

General der Infanterie Alfred von LARISCH 25–8–1918

Major Alois CARACCIOLA-DELBRÜCK 25–8–1918

Major Georg von HARDER 25–8–1918

Oberstleutnant Hermann von BRANDENSTEIN 27–8–1918

Major Arnold von DETTEN 27–8–1918

Major Emil von SCHNIZER 27–8–1918

Hauptmann Otto PLATH 27–8–1918

Hauptmann Karl von WENCKSTERN 27–8–1918

Oberst Leopold Freiherr von LEDEBUR 29–8–1918

Oberst Friedrich von LUCK und WITTEN 29–8–1918

Oberstleutnant Wolff von STUTTERHEIM 29–8–1918

Leutnant Friedrich-Wilhelm DERNEN 29–8–1918

Generalleutnant Carl BRIESE 30–8–1918

Major Kurt Moritz von QUEDNOW 30–8–1918

Hauptmann Kurt KÜHME 30–8–1918

Hauptmann Siegfried RUNGE 30–8–1918

Generalmajor Theodor RENNER 1–9–1918

Major Georg von KRANOLD 1–9–1918

Hauptmann Otto GABCKE 1–9–1918

Oberleutnant zur See Theodor OSTERKAMP 2–9–1918

Generalleutnant Albert Hermann von FRITSCH 3–9–1918

Major Werner SCHERING 3–9–1918

Generalleutnant Albert von MUTIUS 4–9–1918

Oberstleutnant Franz Graf von MAGNIS 4–9–1918

Major Erich BRÜCKNER 4–9–1918

Major Gerhard von LÖBBECKE 7–9–1918

Oberleutnant Friedrich Ritter von RÖTH 8–9–1918

Oberstleutnant Ludwig HAUSS 11–9–1918

Hauptmann Max von MERTENS 11–9–1918

Major Friedrich BECKER 17–9–1918

Major Heinrich von BÜNAU 17–9–1918

Major Otto MÜLLER 17–9–1918

Generalmajor Wilhelm RIBBENTROP 18–9–1918

Major Georg Freiherr von dem BUSSCHE-HADDENHAUSEN 18–9–1918

Major Hans Peter van VAERNEWYCK 18–9–1918

Leutnant Ernst JÜNGER 18–9–1918 (the last living recipient; he died in 1998)

Generalleutnant Friedrich von FRIEDEBURG 20–9–1918

Generalmajor Rudolf von HORN 21–9–1918

General der Infanterie Adolf von OVEN 22–9–1918

Major Ernst Graf YORCK von WARTENBURG 23–9–1918

Hauptmann Kurt von BRANDENSTEIN 26–9–1918

Leutnant Otto KÖNNECKE 26–9–1918

Generalmajor Carl NEHBEL 30–9–1918

Oberstleutnant Eckhand LOEBEN 30–9–1918

Hauptmann Rudolf LÜTERS 30–9–1918

Leutnant der Reserve Walter BLUME 30–9–1918

Leutnant der Reserve Wilhelm GRIEBSCH 30–9–1918

Oberleutnant Daniel GERTH 1–10–1918

Hauptmann Leo LEONHARDY 2–10–1918

Kapitänleutnant Kurt HARTWIG (*U-63*) 3–10–1918

Generalleutnant Detlew VETT 4–10–1918

Generalmajor Georg POHLMANN 4–10–1918

Oberstleutnant Franz Freiherr von EDELSHEIM 4–10–1918

Major Walter SCHULTZ 4–10–1918

Hauptmann Stanislaus BEHRENDT 4–10–1918

Hauptmann Ernst BUSCH 4–10–1918

General der Kavallerie Hans KRUG von NIDDA 7–10–1918

Oberstleutnant Horst von METZSCH 7–10–1918

Generalleutnant Alfred von KLEIST 8–10–1918

Oberstleutnant Oskar von HAHNKE 8–10–1918

Oberstleutnant Theodor von WEBER 8–10–1918

Oberleutnant Robert Ritter von GREIM 8–10–1918

Major Fritz WULFF 8–10–1918

General der Infanterie Arnold Ritter von MÖHL 9–10–1918

Generalmajor Ludwig BRESSLER 9–10–1918

Generalmajor Ernst KABISCH 9–10–1918

Major Tido von BREDERLOW 9–10–1918

Major Wilhelm PFAEHLER 9–10–1918

Hauptmann Felix von BERNUTH 9–10–1918

Hauptmann Otto LANCELLE 9–10–1918

Hauptmann Karl SEIDEL 9–10–1918

Hauptmann Hermann WILCK 9–10–1918

Oberstleutnant Rudolph POPELKA (Austro-Hungarian Army) 11–10–1918

Generalmajor Friedrich KUNDT 12–10–1918

Generalmajor Hans von der ESCH 13–10–1918

Oberst Karl PAULUS 13–10–1918

Major Franz-Karl von BOCK 13–10–1918

Hauptmann Jürgen von GRONE 13–10–1918

Hauptmann Heinrich KIRCHHEIM 13–10–1918

Oberleutnant Erich HOMBURG 13–10–1918

Oberleutnant Albert MÜLLER-KAHLE 13–10–1918

Generalmajor Eduard KREUTER 14–10–1918

Major Max CLAUSIUS 15–10–1918

Hauptmann August von TIPPELSTIRCH 15–10–1918

Major Georg von GÖTZ 17–10–1918

Major Hans SEHMSDORFF 17–10–1918

General der Artillerie Adolf FRANKE 18–10–1918

Major Paul BADER 20–10–1918

Generalmajor Ernst von UECHTRITZ und STEINKIRCH 21–10–1918

Major Albrecht Graf von STOSCH 21–10–1918

Oberleutnant Heinrich BRINKORD 21–10–1918

Generalleutnant Ernst von OVEN 25–10–1918

Generalmajor Johannes von DASSEL 25–10–1918

Generalmajor Georg MÜHRY 25–10–1918

Oberstleutnant Hermann RUDOLPH 25–10–1918

Major Walter ARENS 25–10–1918

Major Schellendorff Hans von BRONSART 25–10–1918

Major Leopold MILISCH 25–10–1918

Major Albert SCHOEN 25–10–1918

Oberleutnant Oskar Freiherr von BOENIGK 25–10–1918

Leutnant Franz BÜCHNER 25–10–1918

Leutnant der Reserve Arthur LAUMANN 25–10–1918

King Boris III of BULGARIA 26–10–1918

Generalleutnant Wilhelm von PUTTKAMER 26–10–1918

Generalmajor Rudolf DÄNNER 26–10–1918

Major Johann Ritter von SCHMIDTLER 26–10–1918

Leutnant Oliver Freiherr von BEAULIEU-MARCONNAY 26–10–1918

Oberst Albert HEUCK 28–10–1918

Major Hans PETRI 28–10–1918

Oberleutnant Edgar JOSENHANSS 28–10–1918

Leutnant Fritz RÜMMELEIN 28–10–1918

Generalmajor Wilhelm KAUPERT 29–10–1918

Major Siegfried WOLTERSDORF 29–10–1918

Major Clemens PFAFFEROTT 30–10–1918

Major Hermann WÜLFING 30–10–1918

Hauptmann Heinrich STRACK 30–10–1918

Oberstleutnant Ralph von EGIDY 31–10–1918

Major Ernst HAMMACHER 31–10–1918

Generalleutnant Emil WALDORF 1–11–1918

Oberst Gustav von OPPEN 1–11–1918

Oberstleutnant Fritjof Freiherr von HAMMERSTEIN-GESMOLD
    1–11–1918

Hauptmann Hans SOTTORF 1–11–1918

Leutnant Karl THOM 1–11–1918

Oberstleutnant Hans von GROTHE 2–11–1918

Leutnant Paul BAÜMER 2–11–1918

Major Benno PFLUGRADT 3–11–1918

General der Kavallerie Friedrich Wilhelm von HETZBERG 4–11–1918

Generalleutnant Rudolf RUSCHE 4–11–1918

Generalmajor Hans Freiherr von HAMMERSTEIN-GESMOLD 6–11–1918

Oberstleutnant Adolf SCHWAB 6–11–1918

Major Friedrich BRUNS 6–11–1918

Major Gustav DAMMANN 6–11–1918

Major Hans-Heinrich von KAHLDEN 6–11–1918

Major Wilhelm OSIANDER 6–11–1918

Major Franz de RAINVILLE 6–11–1918

Major Ernst von SCHÖNFELDT 6–11–1918

Major Otto STOBBE 6–11–1918

Hauptmann Theodor GROEPPE 6–11–1918

Generalmajor Siegfried von HELD 7–11–1918

Oberst Armand von ALBERTI 8–11–1918

Oberst Maximilian Freiherr von REITZENSTEIN 8–11–1918

Oberstleutnant Ernst KAETHER 8–11–1918

Major Erich GAERTNER 8–11–1918

Hauptmann Wilhelm Edler von GRAEVE 8–11–1918

Hauptmann Karl HANSEN 8–11–1918

Hauptmann Emil Berthold MEYER 8–11–1918

Leutnant Ulrich NECKEL 8–11–1918

Leutnant Carl DEGELOW 9–11–1918

CHAPTER 5

Campaigns of the *Pour le Mérite*

Leutnant Karl ALLMENRÖDER 'Karlcken' (30 victories)

The son of a Lutheran pastor, Karl Allmenröder was born in the small town of Wald on 3 May 1896. His strict upbringing was instrumental in his decision to become a doctor, but his studies were interrupted by the outbreak of war. He enlisted in Field Regiment Nr 62 and after training was posted to Field Regiment Nr 20, but within months he returned to the 62nd. He saw active service in Poland and was awarded the Iron Cross 2nd Class in March 1915, and received a commission on the 30th. He was awarded the Friedrich August Cross 1st Class in August.

By this time his brother Willi had enlisted and together the brothers applied for the German Army Air Service, being accepted on 29 March 1916. On completion of their training at the Flying School at Halberstadt, they were posted to *Flieger Abteilung* (FA) 227 and in November to *Jasta* 11. This *Jasta* was led by Manfred von Richthofen and was to become the second highest scoring *Jasta* in the German Army Air Service.

Allmenröder scored his first victory on 16 February 1917 when he shot down a BE2c from 16 Squadron. By the end of March he had shot down another four aircraft and had been awarded the Iron Cross 1st Class. April started with a victory over a BE2 of 13 Squadron, near Lens. On 25, 26 and 27 April he shot down three aircraft on three consecutive days, bringing his total to nine. His triumph was only marred by the news that his brother, who had scored two victories, had been shot down and severely wounded; he was later invalided out of the Air Service.

In May, another thirteen victories, including three doubles on the 13th, 24th and 25th, brought his score to twenty-two. In June he shot down one on the 3rd, two on the 4th and another one on the 5th, bringing his tally to twenty-six. On 6 June he was awarded the Knight's Cross of the Royal Hohenzollern House Order and on 14 June 1917 he was awarded the *Pour le Mérite*. Four more aircraft fell to him on 18, 24, 25 and 26 June. The last one, a Nieuport Scout flown by Gerald Nash, an ace with seven victories, was his thirtieth and final victory. The next day, 27 June 1917, at 9.45am his patrol was attacked by British fighters over Zillebeke and his aircraft was shot down, killing him instantly. Allmenröder was just 21 years old. He is buried in the Evangelical Cemetery in Wald, Germany, but there is no longer a headstone.

He was posthumously awarded the Oldenburg Friedrich August Cross 1st and 2nd Class and the Bayern Militar Kronen Order 4th Class.

Oberleutnant Ernst Freiherr von ALTHAUS 'Hussar Althaus' (9 victories)

The son of the adjutant to the Duke of Saxe-Coburg-Gotha, Ernst Althaus was born in Coburg, Bavaria, on 19 March 1890. He joined the 1st Royal Saxon Hussar Regiment Nr 18 at the age of 16 as an ensign, and was promoted to Leutnant in 1911.

When war broke out in 1914 his regiment was immediately sent into action. Althaus was awarded the Saxon Knight's Cross to the Order of St Heinrich and the Iron Cross 2nd Class on 27 January 1915, for action in a number of clashes with the enemy. However, he was set on flying and on 4 April 1915 was transferred to the Air Service; on completion of his training, he was promoted to Oberleutnant on 6 August and became known as 'Hussar Althaus' in the Air Service.

Althaus was posted to FA23 on 20 September and from there to *Kek* Vaux (later to become part of *Jasta* 4) and scored his first victory on 3 December when he shot down a BE2c of 13 Squadron west of Roye. His next victory was a French Voisin of *Escadrille* VB101 on 2 February 1916, followed by another BE2c on 26 February. On 19 March his tally was raised to four when he shot down a Caudron GIV and on 30 April, while on patrol over St Mihiel, he shot down number five, a French Farman. Wounded in the leg during a dog-fight at about this time, Ernst was taken to hospital for treatment and while there he met a nurse whom he later married. When he returned to his unit he was told he had been awarded the Iron Cross 1st Class and the Knight's Cross with Swords of the Royal Hohenzollern House Order. On 21 July 1916 he was awarded the *Pour le Mérite*, and shot down number eight the next day. On 4 March 1917 he was again wounded in combat. While he was in hospital, his unit became part of *Jasta* 4.

After recuperation he was posted to *Jasta* 14, but soon afterwards was picked by Manfred von Richthofen to take command of *Jasta* 10. Here he flew an Albatros DV with the initials of his nickname 'HA' painted in Morse code – five dots and a dash – on a deep chrome yellow or orange/red fuselage. His last confirmed victory came on 24 July 1917 when he shot down a Sopwith Camel of 70 Squadron. One month later his eyesight started to fail and he relinquished command to Werner Voss. Althaus was given command of *Jastaschule* 11 for a time but his eyesight continued to get worse, and he was returned to army duties, commanding an infantry company in the Verdun sector. He was captured by the US Army on 15 October 1918 and imprisoned in a POW camp until the end of September 1919. As well as his nine confirmed victories, he also had eight unconfirmed.

After the war he entered the legal profession and become a barrister, but went blind in 1937. Despite this, he continued to study law and during the Second World War was appointed Director of the County Court in Berlin. In 1945 he worked for a short time as an interpreter for the Allies. After a short illness he died on 29 November 1946. His other decorations include the Saxon Ernestine House Order, Knight 2nd Class with Swords, the Brunswick War Merit Cross 2nd Class and the Hesse Honour Decoration for Bravery.

Leutnant Paul BAÜMER 'The Iron Eagle' (43 victories)

Paul Baümer was born in Duisberg-Ruhrart on 11 May 1986 and spent much of his childhood fascinated by the Zeppelins that flew from near his home. His first job was as a dental assistant and one of the patients was a pilot, who persuaded him to take up flying. Baümer joined his local flying club, paying for his own lessons. His first flight ended with him landing in a tree! However, he persisted, finally obtaining his flying licence. On the outbreak of war he tried to enlist as a navy airman but was turned down; the reason for this is not known. Instead he volunteered for Infantry Regiment Nr 70 at Saarbrucken, and after training he saw action at St Quentin. Early in 1915 he was posted to XXI Army Corps on the Russian Front, being severely wounded in the left arm.

During his recovery Baümer applied for a transfer to the German Army Air Service, but was again turned down. He then heard about vacancies for technicians in the Army Air Service and, using his experience as a dental assistant, persuaded the authorities to accept him. At the beginning of 1916 he was accepted for general duties in the German Army Air Service and posted to Dobritz. Within a short time he had persuaded his commanding officer to look at his previous flying experience and put him forward for flying training. Baümer qualified with ease and in October 1916 was posted to *Armee Flugpark* Nr 1 as a ferry pilot and flight instructor. His talents were soon recognised and he was promoted to Gefreiter on 19 February 1917 and posted on 26 March to *Flieger Abteilung* 7; three days later he was promoted again, this time to Unteroffizier.

On 15 May he was awarded the Iron Cross 2nd Class and within days was sent for fighter training. On completion of this he was posted to *Jasta* 2 (Boelcke) and two days later to *Jasta* 5. On 12, 13 and 15 July he scored his first three victories when he shot down three observation balloons, and for this he was awarded the Iron Cross 1st Class. Baümer was posted back to *Jasta* 2 in August 1917, shooting down three aircraft in September and nine more in November, including doubles on the 6th and 8th; three more in December raised his tally to eighteen by the end of 1917.

On 12 February 1918, in recognition of his bravery, he was awarded the Gold Military Service Cross. For his nineteeth victory he shot down a Sopwith Camel over Zonnebeke on 9 March, and was rewarded with a commission to Leutnant on 10 April. His twentieth (and *Jasta* 2's 200th), twenty-first and twenty-second victories – a Sopwith Camel and two RE8s – were all shot down on 23 March. On 29 May he suffered an injured jaw while trying to land a badly shot up Pfalz DVIII on a new airfield in the near dark; this was to put him out of action until September. When he returned to *Jasta* 2 in September he was immediately given the nickname *Der Eiserne Adler* ('The Iron Eagle') after being awarded the Silver Wound Badge. During September 1918 he shot down sixteen enemy aircraft, including three each on the 21st and 29th, and a double on the 24th. By the end of the month he had increased his total to thirty-eight, including shooting down eight Allied aircraft in less than a week. Luck stayed with him as he was one of the few pilots of the First World War to survive a parachute jump from a burning aircraft. In October he shot down another five, with another double on the 4th, bringing his total to forty-three. His last victory was over Captain Lyn Campbell (a seven victory ace) and Second Lieutenant W. Hodgkinson.

The *Pour le Mérite* was awarded on 2 November 1918, making him one of only five recipients of both the *Pour le Mérite* and the Golden Military Cross. For a short time after the war he worked for Blohm & Voss in Hamburg, but could not settle and returned to his dental studies. He was still a keen flyer, taking part in aerobatic competitions, before starting his own aircraft company – Baümer Aero GmbH – in Hamburg. His designers were the Guether brothers, who later became famous working with the Ernst Heinkel design team. On 15 July 1927, while testing the Rohrbach Rofix all metal-cantilever monoplane during an aerobatic display over Copenhagen, his aircraft stalled and spun into the waters of the Ore Sound. His body was recovered and buried at Ohesdorf, near Hamburg, Germany.

Leutnant Oliver Freiherr von BEAULIEU-MARCONNAY 'Bauli' (25 victories)

The son of a Prussian army captain, Oliver Beaulieu-Marconnay was born in Berlin on 14 September 1898. He was brought up at Hochschule in the typical military fashion of the day, and in 1915, at the age of 17, he joined up as a cadet. Enlisting into his father's regiment, Prussian Dragoon Regiment Nr 4, he was almost immediately in action. By July 1916, after fighting in the Rokitno Swamps, he had been awarded the Iron Cross 1st and 2nd Class and been promoted to Leutnant.

Early in the spring of 1917 he applied for a transfer into the German Army

Air Service and was accepted. He passed out in November and on 1 December 1917 was posted to *Jasta* 18, then moved to *Jasta* 15 on 20 March. Under the leadership of his CO, Joseph Veltjens, he shot down his first aircraft on 28 May 1918, an AR2 over Soissons. 'Bauli', as he became known, followed this by shooting down a DH4 of 27 Squadron and an SE5a of 32 Squadron on 6 June. By the end of June his tally stood at eight, comprising three Sopwith Camels, an SE5a and another DH4. On 9 August he shot down a Sopwith Camel and a Spad II in just 15 minutes, and followed this up by shooting down another three enemy aircraft, on the 11th, 16th and 21st, bringing his total to thirteen by the end of August.

On 2 September 1918, at just 19 years of age, he was given command of *Jasta* 19. By the end of September he had raised his tally to twenty-one, including doubles on the 13th and 16th. In the first two weeks of October he shot down another four aircraft. On 10 October, the day of his twenty-fifth victory, he was on patrol in his favourite aircraft, a Fokker DVII with an interlocking 4D (4th Dragoons) painted on a blue fuselage, when he was caught in crossfire from one of his own *Jasta* and was severely wounded in the upper thigh. He managed to crash-land and was rushed to hospital. When the authorities learned of his injuries, they quickly awarded him the coveted *Pour le Mérite*, and he was told of the award as he lay dying. At 20 he was the youngest recipient of the *Pour le Mérite* during the First World War.

He died on 26 October 1918, and is buried in the Invaliden Friedhof, Scharnhorst Strasse, Berlin.

Oberleutnant Fritz BERNERT 'Otto' (27 victories)

The son of a Burgermeister, Fritz Bernert was born in Ratibor, Upper Silesia, on 6 March 1893. After finishing school, he enlisted into Infantry Regiment Nr 173 as a cadet and was commissioned Leutnant just after the outbreak of war. His regiment was in the thick of the fighting and in November 1914 he was wounded, and received the Iron Cross 2nd Class for his bravery. Returning to duty, he was lightly wounded twice more, then in December he was struck by a bayonet in the left arm which severed the main nerve, leaving him with limited mobility. Deemed unfit for further combat, he applied to join the German Army Air Service as an observer.

Somehow Bernert passed the medical, and in February 1915 he was sent for training. On graduating, he was posted to FFA27 and for the next six months carried out reconnaissance and scouting duties. Then in July he was posted to FFA71. By now he was looking to fly, and applied for pilot training; he was accepted in November and sent to *Jastaschule*. Again he was able to conceal the limited mobility of his arm and at the end of March 1916 was posted to *Kek* Vaux, where on 17 April he shot down a Nieuport fighter. In late August he was posted to *Jasta* 4 and on 6 September scored his second victory when he shot down a Caudron while on patrol over Dompierre. Another Nieuport followed on 11 September over Allenes. He had raised his tally to seven by the end of November, bringing down three in one day, two DH2s and an FE8 on the 9th.

In February 1917 Bernert was posted to *Jasta* 2 and was awarded the Iron Cross 1st Class, the Saxon Albert Order, Knight 2nd Class with Swords and the Knight's Cross with Swords of the Royal Hohenzollern House Order. His first victory with *Jasta* 2 was a Sopwith shot down while on patrol over Ecourt-Mory and at the end of March he brought down a BE2d, bringing his tally to nine. Starting on 1 April he shot down four aircraft in three days, and throughout April he continued to score almost daily. On 23 April 1917 he was awarded the *Pour le Mérite* and to celebrate he shot down five aircraft on the 24th: a Sopwith 1½ Strutter from 70 Squadron, three BE2s from 9 Squadron and a DH4 from 55 Squadron, all within 20 minutes, a record in itself. On 1 May Bernert was given command of *Jasta* 6, with his score now standing at twenty-four. He added three more by the end of May, before taking command of *Jasta* 2 on 9 June 1917.

On 18 August Bernert was wounded again and on his release from hospital was deemed unfit to fly and was assigned to the office of the Inspector of the Flying Service with the rank of Oberleutnant. He was one of only three German pilots known to wear glasses.

He died in his home town of Ratibor from Spanish flu on 18 October 1918.

Oberleutnant Hans BERR (10 victories)

The son of the President of the Braunschweig High Postal Administration, Hans Berr was born on 20 May 1890. Berr always wanted to be a soldier and volunteered for the 4th Magdeburg Reserve Regiment of Light Infantry. At 18 he was commissioned as a Leutnant. When war broke out he was serving in the 7th Light Reserve Infantry Regiment and was soon in action on the Western Front; he was wounded on 6 September 1914 and was awarded the Iron Cross 2nd Class. Berr was promoted to Oberleutnant on 27 January 1915, but by now he wanted to fly, like so many other young aristocrats.

Berr applied to join the German Army Air Service on 3 March 1915 and was trained as an observer. After several months on reconnaissance missions he applied for pilot training. He was posted to the *Jastaschule* at Metz; on graduation he was sent to *Kek* Avillers to fly Fokker EIII Eindeckers.

Berr opened his account on 8 March 1916 when he shot down a Nieuport of *Escadrille* MS3 over Verdun. One week later he shot down a Caudron, also over Verdun. On 21 August, despite having only two victories to his credit, he was appointed to the command of *Jasta* 5, based at Bechamp in the 5th Army area. With the command came the award of the Bavarian Military Merit Order 4th Class with Swords and the Brunswick War Merit Cross. *Jasta* 5 had been flying

Fokker EIII Eindeckers, but was now equipped with Albatros and Halberstadt DIIs.

On 7 October Berr shot down a Caudron, and a BE2b from 34 Squadron, both over Combles. Between 20 and 26 October he added four more to his tally, two FE2s, a Morane Parasol and a balloon. Now with eight confirmed victories he was awarded the Hanseatic Cross, the Ruess War Merit Cross and the Honour Cross 3rd Class with Swords. At some point he was also awarded the Iron Cross 1st Class. He scored his ninth victory on 1 November and his tenth and last victory on the 3rd, and on 4 December he was awarded Germany's highest honour, the *Pour le Mérite*. (This was before the High Command doubled the required number of victories from eight to sixteen.)

On 6 April 1917 *Jasta* 5, led by Berr, engaged 57 Squadron over Noyelles. In the heat of battle Vizefeldwebel Paul Hoppe had just moved in behind a Vickers Gunbus when Berr came swooping in from the right and crashed into him. Both aircraft plunged to the ground. Hoppe and Berr were killed.

Oberleutnant Rudolf BERTHOLD 'The Iron Knight' (44 victories)

The son of a Franconian Forester, Rudolf Berthold was born on 24 March 1891 at Ditterswind, near Bamberg in northern Bavaria. In 1910, at the age of 19, he volunteered for the army and was assigned to Brandenburg Infantry Regiment Nr 20. The humdrum life of a peacetime soldier was not for him, so he learned to fly at a private flying club. On 26 September 1913 he gained his flying licence, and asked to be transferred to the newly formed German Army Air Service. At the outbreak of war Berthold was posted to FFA23 for training as an observer in Halberstadt two-seaters and by the end of 1914 he had been awarded the Iron Cross 2nd Class and promoted to Feldwebel for his part in a number of reconnaissance missions.

In 1915 Berthold carried out a large number of reconnaissance missions and was awarded the Iron Cross 1st Class in the autumn of that year. Subsequently he asked for a transfer to a fighter unit. He was sent to *Jastaschule* in December 1915 and then posted to *Kek* Vaux on graduation. Flying a single-seat Fokker, on 2 February 1916 he opened his tally by shooting down a Voisin over Chaulnes. By the end of April he had shot down four more and was awarded the *Bayerisch Kriegsverdienst Orden* IV Class, the Knight's Cross of St Heinrich's Order and the Saxon Knight's Cross of the Military St Henry Order. On 25 April he crash-landed his Pfalz EIV and suffered severe injuries, although he returned to his unit before his injuries were properly healed and was promoted to Leutnant. This was the first of several wounds and injuries he was to suffer, but they rarely kept him from the front for long; indeed, he became famous for returning to his unit before recovering completely from his injuries.

In August 1916 Berthold was given command of *Jasta* 4 after forming it from

Kek Vaux, and was awarded the Knight's Cross with Swords of the Royal Hohenzollern House Order on 27 August. On 14 October 1916 he handed *Jasta* 4 over to Hans-Joachim Buddecke and took command of *Jasta* 14. It was not until 24 March 1917 that he scored his next victory, shooting down a Farman from *Escadrille* F7. In May his patrol was attacked by British aircraft and Berthold was shot down; his aircraft crashed within the German lines and he was pulled from the wreckage with a fractured skull, and broken nose, pelvis and thigh. After just two months in hospital he again discharged himself and returned to his unit. On 12 August he was given command of *Jasta* 18 and promoted to Oberleutnant, and on the 21st he shot down a Spad, raising his tally to thirteen. In September Berthold shot down fourteen enemy aircraft, including doubles on the 4th and 16th, bringing his total to twenty-seven, including Captain Alwayne Loyd of 32 Squadron, an ace with six victories. On 2 October he shot down his twenty-eighth, a DH4 from 57 Squadron. On 10 October 1917 his right arm was shattered by a bullet during a dog-fight with British aircraft. He was awarded the *Pour le Mérite* in hospital on 12 October (some sources say it was awarded in 1916, but most agree it was 1917) and promoted to Hauptmann. Once again he discharged himself and returned to his unit. However, he would not score again until May 1918.

Berthold was given command of *Jagdgeschwader* Nr 2 in March 1918, and took with him nearly all the best pilots from *Jasta* 14, exchanging them with the pilots from *Jasta* 15. Over the next four months he would shoot down another fourteen enemy aircraft, including six in June. Then on 10 August 1918 he was flying his Fokker DVII with red nose and blue fuselage, and a 'winded sword' painted on the side, when his patrol encountered a British patrol of DH4s. Berthold shot down two of the enemy aircraft, in the process colliding with one of them, which was credited as his forty-fourth victory. However, his Fokker was badly damaged; his desperate struggle to keep it in the air was in vain, and he crashed into a house. Although he survived, this accident ended his combat career.

By the time Berthold was released from hospital the war was over, and in 1919 he joined the *Freikorps*. His unit, the *Eiserne Schar* ('Iron Horde'), fought during the postwar German revolution. On 15 March 1920 he was attacked and beaten by rioters in Harburg, and it is said he was strangled to death with the ribbon of his *Pour le Mérite* – a tragic end. He is buried in the Invaliden Friedhof, Scharnhorst Strasse, Berlin. His original headstone was inscribed: 'Honoured by his enemies – slain by his German brethren.' However, this has since been destroyed and replaced by a less impressive headstone.

Leutnant der Reserve Walter BLUME (28 victories)

Walter Blume was born in the village of Hirschberg near the Silesian Mountains on 10 January 1896. He took up a tool-making apprenticeship on graduating from school in 1911. When the war broke out he enlisted into Silesian *Jaeger* Battalion Nr 5, which was soon posted to East Prussia. Within a few months Blume had been severely wounded in action near Lyck. After recovering in hospital, he applied to transfer to the newly formed German Army Air Service.

With his application approved, he reported to the Flying Reserve Unit at Grossenhain on 30 June 1915 and was then posted to the Flying School at Leipzig-Mockau. After graduating, he was assigned to the Research and Exercise Field West Unit near St Quentin on the Western Front. Two months later he was posted to Army Aeroplane Park A at Strassburg to await a posting. On 18 June 1916 Blume was assigned to FFA65 as a reconnaissance pilot, then a month later to FA(A)280. He quickly distinguished himself and was awarded the Iron Cross 2nd Class on 24 July and promoted to Vizefeldwebel on 23 August. He continued in this role, being commissioned Leutnant der Reserve on 31 January 1917.

At the beginning of March he was selected by Bruno Loerzer and Hermann Göring to be one of the pilots to form *Jasta* 26. After a month's conversion and tactical training, the *Jasta* was assigned to the St Quentin area and soon became involved in heavy fighting. On 10 May Blume opened his score by shooting down a DH4 from 55 Squadron over Gouzeaucourt. By the end of November he had raised his tally to six and been awarded the Iron Cross 1st Class. During a patrol on 29 November 1917 he encountered some Bristol fighters from 48 Squadron, and was hit in the chest. Fighting to keep control of his badly damaged aircraft and drifting into unconsciousness, he managed to bring his aircraft back to his base. Critically wounded, he would take three months to recover.

Blume returned to the front on 5 March 1918 to command *Jasta* 9 in the Champagne sector. He was back in the thick of the fighting with a vengeance, and on 21 April shot down a Spad over Chiry-Ourscamps, taking his tally to seven. During the next three months he shot down ten more aircraft, bringing his score to seventeen. On 6 August he shot down a Spad over Bazoches for victory number eighteen and was awarded the Knight's Cross with Swords of the Royal Hohenzollern House Order the next day. By the end of September his tally was twenty-six and he was awarded the *Pour le Mérite* on 30 September 1918. His twenty-seventh victory (and *Jasta* 9's 100th), came on 2 October. Blume's final victory came on 28 October 1918, shooting down a Sopwith Camel of 209 Squadron over Remaucourt.

After the end of the war Blume returned home to complete his engineering studies and finish his degree. He then became a designer for the Arado and Albatros aviation companies and was responsible for contributing to many of the designs of the aircraft used in the Second World War. After that war he helped to build jet aircraft, and was taken by the Russians to help with their jets.

Walter Blume died on 27 May 1964.

Hauptmann Oswald BOELCKE (40 victories)

The son of a schoolteacher, Oswald Boelcke was born in Giebichenstein in Saxony on 19 May 1891. He was one of six children, whose father made sure all his children were educated to their full potential. After leaving school, Boelcke decided on a military career, much to his father's displeasure. In March 1911 he joined the Prussian Cadet Corps and was posted to *Telegrapher* Battalion Nr 3 at Koblenz. From there he was sent to the War School at Metz for officer training.

After graduating, he applied for a transfer to the German Army Air Service, being accepted for pilot training. He was posted to the flying school in Halberstadt, and completed his training in early October 1914. Oswald was first assigned to Trier and two weeks later to FA13 near Montmedy, where his elder brother Wilhelm was stationed as an observer. Naturally the brothers became a team, flying reconnaissance missions over the Argonne sector. Oswald was awarded the Iron Cross 2nd Class the same month for his work in flying reconnaissance missions.

On 4 February 1915 Boelcke was awarded the Iron Cross 1st Class and continued flying reconnaissance missions until April. In May he was transferred to FA62 and on 4 July, while flying an LVG CI with Leutnant Heinz von Wuhlisch as observer, he shot down his first enemy aircraft, a Morane Parasol, over Valenciennes. Such was his passion for attacking enemy aircraft that his commander transferred him to the single-seat Fokker EIII Eindecker. In early July Oswald saved the life of a 14-year-old French schoolboy and was awarded the Life Saving Medal, although some of the local villagers wanted him to receive the Legion d'Honneur. His second victory came on 19 August 1915 when he shot down a Bristol biplane. While stationed at Douai he met Max Immelmann, and each learned from the other. By the end of 1915 he had scored four more times and been awarded the Knight's Cross with Swords of the Royal Hohenzollern House Order.

During the first two weeks of January Boelcke shot down three more Allied aircraft, bringing his tally to nine, and for this he was awarded the *Pour le Mérite* on 12 January 1916, the same day as Max Immelmann. He steadily increased his tally and by the end of June 1916 he had shot down nineteen aircraft. He was now a household name in Germany, and the High Command sent him on a public relations tour of Vienna, Budapest, Belgrade and Turkey. This gave him time to think about the way air combat was progressing and he wrote a paper for submission to the High Command, called *Air Fighting Tactics*. It was to become the bible for German pilots.

At the end of July Boelcke was recalled from Turkey, given command of *Jasta* 2 and promoted to Hauptmann. He decided to pick his own pilots for his *Jasta*, and among those he selected were Max Müller, Erwin Böhme and Manfred von Richthofen. He scored his twentieth victory on 2 September when he shot down a DH2 from 37 Squadron, and by the end of the month had brought down

The Blue Max

Leutnant Karl
ALLMENRÖDER.

Oberleutnant Ernst Freiherr
von ALTHAUS.

Leutnant Paul
BAÜMER.

Leutnant Oliver Freiherr von
BEAULIEU-MARCONNAY.

Oberleutnant Fritz
BERNERT.

Oberleutnant Hans
BERR.

Oberleutnant Rudolf
BERTHOLD.

Leutnant der Reserve Walter
BLUME.

Hauptmann Oswald
BOELCKE.

Oberleutnant Oskar Freiherr
von BOENIGK.

Leutnant der Reserve Erwin
BÖHME.

Rittmeister Karl
BOLLE.

Leutnant der Reserve Heinrich
BONGARTZ.

Hauptmann Ernst von
BRANDENBURG.

Leutnant Franz
BÜCHNER.

Leutnant der Reserve Julius
BUCKLER.

Hauptmann Hans-Joachim
BUDDECKE.

Leutnant Walter von
BÜLOW-BOTHKAMP.

Kapitänleutnant Horst Freiherr
Treusch von BUTTLAR-
BRANDENFELS.

Kapitänleutnant zur See
Friedrich CHRISTIANSEN.

Leutnant Carl
DEGELOW.

Leutnant der Reserve Albert
DOSSENBACH.

Oberleutnant Eduard Ritter
von DOSTLER.

Leutnant der Reserve Wilhelm
FRANKL.

Oberleutnant Hermann
FRICKE.

Leutnant der Reserve Heinrich
GONTERMANN.

Oberleutnant Hermann
GÖRING.

Oberleutnant Robert Ritter
von GREIM.

Leutnant der Reserve Wilhelm
GRIEBSCH.

Hauptmann Jürgen von
GRONE.

General der Kavallerie Ernst
von HOEPPNER.

Leutnant Walter
HÖHNDORF.

Oberleutnant Erich
HOMBURG.

Leutnant Hans-Georg
HORN.

Oberleutnant Max
IMMELMANN.

Leutnant Josef
JACOBS.

Hauptmann Alfred
KELLER.

Leutnant Hans
KIRSCHSTEIN.

Oberleutnant Otto
KISSENBERTH

Leutnant Hans
KLEIN.

Kapitänleutnant Rudolf
KLEINE.

Hauptmann Hermann
KÖHL.

Leutnant Otto
KÖNNECKE.

Oberleutnant Heinrich
KROLL.

Leutnant der Reserve Arthur
LAUMANN.

Leutnant der Reserve Gustav
LEFFERS.

Oberst Hermann von der
LEITH-THOMSEN.

Hauptmann Leo
LEONHARDY.

Hauptmann Bruno
LOERZER.

Oberleutnant Erich
LÖWENHARDT.

Oberleutnant Carl
MENCKHOFF.

Leutnant Max Ritter von
MÜLLER.

Oberleutnant Albert
MÜLLER-KAHLE.

Leutnant Max Ritter von
MULZER.

Leutnant Ulrich
NECKEL.

Leutnant der Landwehr
Friedrich NIELEBOCK.

Oberleutnant zur See Theodor
OSTERKAMP.

Leutnant Otto
PARSCHAU.

Oberleutnant Paul Freiherr von
PECHMANN.

Leutnant Fritz
PÜTTER.

Leutnant der Reserve Peter
RIEPER.

Oberleutnant Friedrich Ritter
von RÖTH.

Leutnant der Reserve Fritz
RUMEY.

Leutnant Lothar Freiherr von
RICHTHOFEN.

Rittmeister Manfred Freiherr von
RICHTHOFEN.

Oberleutnant zur See Gotthard
SACHSENBERG.

Leutnant Karl
SCHÄFER.

Oberleutnant Eduard Ritter
von SCHLEICH.

Leutnant Wilhelm
SCHREIBER.

Fregattenkapitän Peter
STRASSER.

Leutnant Karl
THOM.

Leutnant Emil
THUY.

Oberleutnant Adolf Ritter von
TUTSCHEK.

Oberleutnant Ernst
UDET.

Leutnant der Reserve Joseph
VELTJENS.

Leutnant der Reserve Werner
VOSS.

Hauptmann Franz
WALZ.

Leutnant der Reserve Rudolph
WINDISCH.

Leutnant Kurt
WINTGENS.

Leutnant Kurt
WOLFF.

Leutnant der Reserve Kurt
WÜSTHOFF

The men who missed out on the *Pour le Mérite*

Leutnant Hans Ritter von
ADAM.

Oberleutnant Eduard
AUFFARTH.

Leutnant Hermann
BECKER.

Oberleutnant Hans
BETHGE.

Leutnant Paul
BILLIK.

Leutnant Gustav
DÖRR.

Leutnant Rudolph von
FREDEN.

Leutnant Friedrich
FRIEDRICHS.

Leutnant Hermann
FROMMHERZ.

Leutnant Otto
FRUHNER.

Leutnant Walter
GOTTSCH.

Leutnant Georg von
HANTELMANN.

Vizefeldwebel Oskar
HENNRICH.

Leutnant Fritz
HOHN.

Leutnant Joseph
MAI.

Leutnant Georg
MEYER.

Leutnant Max
NÄTHER.

Leutnant Karl
ODEBRETT.

Leutnant Hans
PIPPART.

Leutnant Werner
PREUSS.

Hauptmann Wilhelm
REINHARD.

Oberleutnant Otto
SCHMIDT.

another nine enemy aircraft, including two doubles on the 14th and 15th. *Jasta* 2 was becoming one of the most feared in the German Army Air Service. By 26 October Boelke had shot down another eleven aircraft, including another two doubles on the 16th and 22nd, bringing his total to forty.

On 28 October 1916, while flying with von Richthofen and Böhme, they came upon seven DH2s from 24 Squadron and dived to the attack. Boelcke and Böhme were chasing a British fighter, but just as they were closing in for the kill, another British fighter being chased by von Richthofen cut across in front of them. Böhme's undercarriage wheel touched Boelcke's upper left wing, causing damage to his wing and aileron. Böhme managed to control his aircraft but Boelcke's top wing broke away and his Fokker crashed to the ground, killing him instantly.

He is buried in Ehren Cemetery, Heidestrasse, Dessau, Germany.

Oberleutnant Oskar Freiherr von BOENIGK (26 victories)

The son of an army officer, Oskar Boenigk was born on 25 August 1893 in Siegersdorf, Silesia. Following the family tradition, he became an army cadet at 11 years of age and on 22 March 1912 was commissioned Leutnant in the Konig Friedrich III Grenadier Regiment. By the outbreak of war he was a platoon leader and his regiment was soon in action. In October 1914, during the battle of Longwy, he was badly wounded in the chest, spending several months in hospital. On his return to his regiment in the spring of 1915 he was awarded the Iron Cross 2nd Class for bravery at Longwy. Boenigk was soon back in action and was wounded again; after recovering, he fought at the Loretto Heights and Arras. Towards the end of 1915 he applied for a transfer to the Army Air Service; he was accepted and posted to FEA7 in December. In March 1916, after completing his training, Boenigk was posted to *Kampfstaffel* 19, part of KG4.

He spent the next four months on reconnaissance missions and was then posted to *Kampfstaffel* 32. In January 1917 he applied for pilot training and was sent to *Jastaschule*; graduating on 24 June, he was sent to *Jasta* 4. On 20 July 1917 he opened his account by shooting down a Sopwith Camel while on patrol over Tenbrielen. His next victory came a week later over Moorslede when he shot down another Sopwith Camel from 70 Squadron. By the end of September he had shot down another three enemy aircraft, and was awarded the Iron Cross 1st Class. On 21 October he was given command of *Jasta* 21. By the end of 1917 his score stood at six.

Command responsibility and the easing of hostilities meant that in the next six months he did not shoot down any more aircraft. Then in June he shot down a Breguet XIV, three balloons and two Spads, bringing his total to twelve. By the end of August Boenigk's tally had reached twenty-one, including four more balloons. He was awarded the Knight's Cross with Swords of the Royal Hohenzollern House Order on 14 August. On 31 August 1918 he was given command of JG2 and promoted to Oberleutnant. In September JG2 was moved to St Mihiel to oppose the American forces there, and by the end of the month Boenigk had increased his tally to twenty-six. At the beginning of October he was awarded the Saxon Albert Order 2nd Class with Swords, the Prussian Order of St John, Knight of Honour and the Saxon-Ernestine House Order, Knight 2nd Class with Swords, allowing him to use the title 'Freiherr von', and then on 25 October 1918 he was awarded Germany's highest honour, the *Pour le Mérite*. At the end of the war he served during the revolution with distinction.

During the Second World War he served in the Luftwaffe as commander of various airfields and then as an area commander, reaching the rank of Generalmajor. He was taken prisoner by the Russians in May 1945 and died in a prison camp on 30 January 1946. He has no known grave.

Leutnant der Reserve Erwin BÖHME (24 victories)

Erwin Böhme was born on 29 July 1879 in Holzminden on the Weser. After leaving school he went to study engineering at the technical college in Dortmund. He then went to work first in Elberfeld and then Zurich, before leaving for East Africa. It was while supervising the construction of a cable-car between Usambara and the New Hornow Heights that he learnt to fly. Erwin returned to Germany just as war broke out, and enlisted into a *Jäger* regiment. In the spring of 1915, at 35 years of age, he volunteered for flying with the German Army Air Service and was accepted; he was trained as an instructor.

In June 1916 he applied for a transfer to a front-line *Jasta* and at the end of July was sent to *Jasta* 10, part of *Kagohl* 2, on the Eastern Front, commanded by Oswald Boelcke's elder brother Wilhelm. Böhme scored his first victory by shooting down a Nieuport XII over Radzyse on 2 August 1916; this victory is often omitted from his score for some reason. He also had two unconfirmed victories at this time. When Oswald Boelcke was in the process of forming *Jasta* 2, he came to visit *Jasta* 10 and was introduced to Böhme; the two men quickly became friends and Boelcke invited Böhme to join his new unit. On 17 September 1916 Böhme scored his first victory with his new unit, a Sopwith 1½ Strutter from 70 Squadron, over Hervilly, for which he was awarded the Iron Cross 2nd Class.

On 28 October 1916, with Böhme's tally now at five, Boelcke and Böhme were chasing a British DH2; just as they were closing in for the kill, another British fighter being hotly pursued by von Richthofen, cut across in front of them. Boelcke and Böhme tried to take evasive action but collided. Böhme managed to control his aircraft but Boelcke's Fokker was badly damaged and crashed to the ground, killing him instantly. Böhme was devastated and blamed himself, but a board of enquiry cleared him. By the end of 1916 he had shot down another three enemy aircraft, bringing his total to eight. On 7 January 1917 he shot down a DH2 from 32 Squadron over Beugny. Then on 4 February he brought down two enemy aircraft in one day, a DH2 from 32 Squadron flown by Captain W.G.S. Curphy MC, a five victory ace, and a BE2c from 15 Squadron. Curphy was wounded in the head and forced to land inside British lines.

Böhme's luck ran out on 11 February when he was wounded during a dog-fight with a Sopwith 1½ Strutter; he managed to get back to his airfield but was in hospital for a month. Although already awarded the Iron Cross 1st Class, while in hospital he was awarded the Knight's Cross with Sword of the Royal Hohenzollern House Order on 12 March.

On his release from hospital at the end of March he was first given the post of instructor, and then, on 2 July, was posted as commander to *Jasta* 29. He shot down one enemy aircraft on 14 July before being posted back to *Jasta* 2 as its commander. He was wounded again on 10 August; while attacking a two-seater he was shot up by a Sopwith Camel. Injuries to his hand kept him at his deck for a month. He scored two more victories in September and six in October, bringing his tally to twenty-one. On 6 November 1917 he shot down a Sopwith Camel from 65 Squadron, followed by a Nieuport fighter from No. 1 Belgian *Escadrille* on 20 November, bringing his score to twenty-three, and on 24 November he was awarded the *Pour le Mérite*. On 29 November 1917, while on patrol over Zonnebeke, he was engaged by enemy aircraft from 10 Squadron. He shot down a Sopwith Camel, but seconds later was killed by fire from an AWFK VIII 'Big Ack', his aircraft crashing behind British lines. Although awarded the *Pour le Mérite*, he never got to wear it: it was lying unopened on his desk awaiting his return.

He was buried by the British with full military honours at Keerselaarhook. After the war his body was reinterred at Hinter den Linden, but his grave has since been lost.

Rittmeister Karl BOLLE (36 victories)

The son of an academic, Karl Bolle was born on 20 June 1893 in Berlin. In 1912 he went to Oxford University to study economics. Just before war broke out he returned to Germany and joined the 7th von Seydlitz Kurassier Regiment, being commissioned Leutnant, and almost immediately his regiment was fighting on the Western Front. At the beginning of 1915 the regiment was moved to the Russian Front, fighting in Poland and Courland. By the end of 1915 Bolle had been awarded the Iron Cross 2nd Class. He applied for a transfer to the German Army Air Service; his application was accepted and in February 1916 he was posted to Valenciennes for training.

His training completed, he was sent to KG4 in July 1916 as a reconnaissance pilot. After several months on scouting and reconnaissance duties Bolle was posted to *Kampfstaffel* 23 at the end of 1916, having by then been awarded the Wurttemburg Freidrich Order, Knight 2nd Class with Swords. His observer was Lothar von Richthofen, and throughout 1916 they carried out many dangerous missions together. In October Bolle was badly wounded, but on his return he found that the application he had sent in some time previously for a transfer to single-seat fighters had been accepted and at the beginning of 1917 he was posted to *Jastaschule*.

After graduating in July, Bolle was posted to *Jasta* 28, and on 8 August opened his tally by shooting down a DH4 from 57 Squadron while on patrol over Kachtem. His second victory came over Seclin on 21 August when he shot down a Martinsyde G100 from 27 Squadron. It was some time before he scored again, this time downing a Sopwith Camel from 65 Squadron on 18 December 1917. He started the New Year by shooting down another Sopwith Camel from 65 Squadron on 29 January 1918, and the next day he brought down a DH4 from 5 Squadron, bringing his total to five. On 20 February he was given command of *Jasta* 2 and promoted to Oberleutnant. He spent the first two months behind a desk and did not score again until 3 April, when he shot down a DH9 over Frezenberg. On 25 April he brought down another Sopwith Camel.

Over the next three months he raised his tally to twenty-eight, scoring five times in May, seven in June and nine in July. He was promoted to Rittmeister at the beginning of August and awarded the Order of Max Joseph, the Mecklenburg Military Cross of Merit with Swords and the Knight's Cross with Swords of the Royal Hohenzollern House Order. On 21 August 1918 he was awarded the *Pour le Mérite*. By the end of the war he had shot down a total of thirty-six enemy aircraft.

After the Armistice he served in a cavalry regiment of the Reichswehr, and then became a liaison officer with the inter-Allied Aviation Monitoring Commission. Later he became an instructor. In the 1920s he was appointed Director of the German Transportation Flying School. Within ten years he was in charge of all pilot training in Germany, and Göring chose him to be a special adviser within the service. During the Second World War he was a special adviser to the Luftwaffe, a post he held until the end of the war.

Karl Bolle died in Berlin on 9 October 1955.

Leutnant der Reserve Heinrich BONGARTZ (33 victories)

Heinrich Bongartz, the son of a schoolteacher, was born on 31 January 1892 in Gelsenkirchen, Westphalia. After leaving school, he followed the family tradition and went to college to become a teacher. But when war broke out he volunteered to fight, joining Infantry Regiment Nr 16 and later Reserve Infantry Regiment Nr 13 with the rank of Sturmoffizier. The regiment was sent to Verdun and was involved in very heavy fighting throughout 1915. In March 1916 he was awarded the Iron Cross 2nd Class and commissioned Leutnant. By the autumn of 1916 his application for the German Army Air Service had been accepted, and he was posted first to FA5, then to *Kagohl* 5 as a reconnaissance pilot. At the beginning of 1917 Heinrich was posted to *Kasta* 27, and then in April 1917 he was posted to *Jasta* 36.

He opened his score within days when he shot down a Spad VII from *Escadrille* 31 over Viry. By the end of January 1917 he had added another three to his tally, and was awarded the Iron Cross 1st Class. Then on 13 July, with his total at eleven, including five balloons, he was wounded for the first of five times. This put him out of action for two months. On his return to front-line duty he shot down a Sopwith Triplane on 26 September, over Houthult Forest. At the end of the month he was given command of *Jasta* 36. During October he shot down nine more, including three on the 31st, bringing his tally to twenty, and was then awarded the Knight's Cross with Swords of the Royal Hohenzollern House Order. He brought down another six in November and two in December before being awarded the *Pour le Mérite* on 23 December.

On 29 January 1918 he shot down a Sopwith Camel over Poelkapelle; two more in February and three in March brought his tally to thirty-three. He is also said to have had nine unconfirmed victories. He was wounded again on 29 March and 25 April, but on 29 April 1918, while on patrol over Kemmel Hill, he ran into fighters from 74 Squadron and was brought down by Captain C.B. Glynn for his first victory. Bongartz was shot in the head, the bullet passing through his left temple, eye and nose. He was taken unconscious to hospital, but his eye could not be saved and this ended his flying career. Later he took over as Director of the Aeroplane Inspectorate at Aldershorf, a post he held until the end of the war, and then he helped to deactivate the German Army Air Service.

During the revolution he fought against the Spartacists, left-wingers who formed the German Communist Party. Once again he was badly wounded, this time in the leg, finishing his military career. But he could not stay away from aviation and he became Director of *Luftreederen*, German Air Trade. In January 1921 he was involved in a crash and was seriously injured, but recovered within the year.

Bongartz died from a heart attack on 23 January 1946.

Hauptmann Ernst von BRANDENBURG

Ernst von Brandenburg was born in Westphalia on 4 June 1883. After leaving school he volunteered for the army as a cadet, joining the 6th West Prussian Infantry Regiment Nr 149 in Schneidemuhl. In 1911 he was assigned to the Research Institute for the Aviation System to look into the merits of military aviation. By the outbreak of war he was the regimental adjutant with the rank of Oberleutnant, and his regiment was soon in action on the Western Front. During his first year in action he was awarded the Iron Cross 2nd Class but was also wounded so severely that he was declared unfit for trench warfare. On 1 November 1915 he applied for the German Army Air Service and was accepted

After training as an observer in the spring of 1916, Brandenburg was assigned to a reconnaissance unit attached to the infantry. He carried out many missions, for which he was awarded the Iron Cross 1st Class and the Knight's Cross of the Royal Hohenzollern House Order. Then on 10 January 1917 General Hoeppner asked him to form a bomber squadron for the express purpose of bombing England, particularly London. The problems likely to be encountered on such a raid were many, including the unreliability of the available bombers and the weather. *Kagohl* 3, also known as the 'England *Geschwader*', was duly formed and intense training begin. The Gotha bombers did not have sufficient fuel capacity for the round trip so auxiliary tanks had to be fitted. The three-man crews were given extra thick clothes and the bombers were equipped with oxygen which the men could suck from, although most crews said they would have preferred cognac. The 14,000ft bombing altitude gave the bombers a great deal of protection as no Allied fighter at that time could reach that height.

Although attached to the Fourth Army, *Kagohl* 3 operated independently and received orders from OHL. By June 1917 the squadron was ready, but the British weather intervened, twice, but at 10am on 13 June eighteen Gothas took off from Ghent and headed towards England. As they crossed the Channel alarm bells started ringing in England and at 1pm the bombers reached London. Anti-aircraft fire commenced but, due to the poor siting of the guns and lack of training for the crews, this was ineffective, and the Gothas bombed docks, railway stations and warehouses. Of the thirty British fighters sent up to intercept them, not one was effective. A few of the Gothas were hit but not badly enough to bring them down, and two hours after dropping their bombs the whole squadron landed in Ghent.

The next day, 14 June 1917, Brandenburg was summoned to Supreme Headquarters and in front of the Kaiser described the whole raid in detail; he was immediately promoted to Hauptmann and the Kaiser personally awarded the *Pour le Mérite* and invited him to stay for the weekend. He was one of only two *Bombengeschwader* commanders to be given this honour. On his return to the front his Albatros, piloted by Oberleutnant Freiherr von Trotha, took off, but as the aircraft lifted from the airfield the engine spluttered and the Albatros crashed back to the ground. Brandenburg was pulled from the wreckage severely injured, his shattered leg having to be amputated.

After recovering, he returned to his squadron and organised many more raids, but he was soon taken off the active service duty list. At the end of the war the squadron was disbanded and Brandenburg returned to Germany. In 1924 he was appointed Director of Civil Aviation and helped to form the Luftwaffe. Former senior army officers were enrolled in commercial pilot schools and some 27 million marks were channelled to the *Reichswehr* through the ministry for military aviation. However, with the rise of the Nazis, he was pushed aside in favour of Ernst Udet. Not much is known about the rest of his life.

He died in Berlin in 1952.

Leutnant Franz BÜCHNER (40 victories)

The son of a wealthy businessman, Franz Büchner was born in Leipzig on 2 January 1898. At the start of the war he was only 16 years old but volunteered for Saxon Infantry Regiment Nr 106. His unit saw action at Ypres, and even at his young age Büchner was already showing leadership qualities, but he contracted typhoid fever in November 1914 and it was not until February 1915 that he rejoined his unit. In March the regiment was sent to the Eastern Front and Büchner went with it, being commissioned Leutnant in August. In September he and his regiment were back on the Western Front, where, after several actions, he was awarded the Iron Cross 2nd Class. On 3 April 1916 he was wounded; while in hospital he applied for a transfer to the German Army Air Service, and was sent to FFA270 for pilot training. In July 1916 he was posted to *Jasta* 9, but between July 1916 and August 1917 he shot down only one aircraft, a Nieuport, which he brought down on 17 August over Chappy.

In October Büchner was posted to *Jasta* 13, but was still having difficulties in shooting down any aircraft, managing only one that month, but his leadership qualities were flourishing. In the summer of 1918 he shot down two Spads, one each on 10 and 11 June, and on 28 June an SE5a flown by Major J.C. Callaghan MC, a five victory ace. Despite his low scoring, Büchner was appointed Staffelführer on 15 June, such was the high regard in which he was held. His tally started to improve during July and by the end of the month his total stood at twelve, including another ace, Lieutenant M.S. Taylor (seven victories), brought down on the 7th. The Iron Cross 1st Class came in August, followed by the Knight's Cross of the Royal Hohenzollern House Order and the Saxon Merit Order 2nd Class with Swords. In celebration he shot down another eight aircraft by the end of August, including two doubles on the 11th and 20th, bringing his tally to twenty.

On 12 September he shot down three aircraft, two DH4s, one from the 8th Aero Squadron USAS, and a Breguet XIV bomber over Hattonville. By the end of the month Büchner had become the scourge of the USAS by shooting down seventeen of their aircraft, including four Spad XIIIs on the 26th, bringing his tally to thirty-seven. He was now awarded the Saxon Albert Order 2nd Class with Swords and the Military St Heinrich's Order (Saxony's highest award).

On 1 October he shot down a Salmson 2A2 bomber, but then on the 10th he collided with another member of his *Jasta* while they were attacking a bomber; both pilots were able to parachute to safety, a rare occurrence in those days. He then added two more to his tally and on 25 October 1918 was awarded the *Pour le Mérite*, ending the war with forty victories.

During the postwar revolution he fought on with the *Reichswehr*, but on 18 March 1920 he was shot down and killed while on reconnaissance near Leipzig – another air ace killed by his own countrymen, something the Allies could not do in four years of fighting. He is buried in Leipzig, but the site of his grave is unknown.

Leutnant der Reserve Julius BUCKLER (36 victories)

Julius Buckler was born on 28 March 1894 in Mainz. He wanted to be an architect and when he left school at 15 worked in the design office of Anthony Fokker for a short time. As the war clouds were gathering in 1913 he joined Infantry Life Regiment Nr 117. Within days of the war starting he was in action on the Western Front and within a few weeks was awarded the Iron Cross 2nd Class. But in August 1914 he was badly wounded and on his release from hospital in October was deemed unfit for army duty.

In November he volunteered for flying duties and was trained as an observer. He joined FEA6 at Leipzig-Lindenthal and after just four weeks' instruction passed his flight exams. He remained at FEA6 as an instructor until being posted to FA(A)209 as an observer six months later. Buckler spent a year with this unit, in which time he was awarded the Iron Cross 1st Class, but in the spring of 1916 he applied for pilot training. He was posted to *Jasta* 17 in November with the rank of Vizefeldwebel. On the 17th he shot down his first enemy aircraft, a twin-engine Caudron, over Bras.

Two more Caudrons followed on 14 and 15 February 1917 and by the end of April his tally stood at six. He continued to shoot down enemy aircraft until 17 July, when his squadron ran into a flight of Sopwith Pups and Camels while on patrol over Keyem. Buckler shot down one Pup but was badly wounded by another. However, he managed to break away and return to his airfield. Then on 12 August, with thirteen victories to his name, he was again wounded in a dog-fight with a Sopwith Camel, but again he was able to return to his airfield. Buckler shot down nine in October, including doubles on the 11th, 29th (one of which was a balloon) and the 31st. He shot down an RE8 (nicknamed the 'Harry Tate' by the British) on 15 November, and was commissioned Leutnant and awarded the Golden Military Service Cross on the 18th, on which day he shot down an RE8 and two balloons. Another balloon followed on 29 November but the next day, with his tally at thirty, he was shot down after being attacked by two enemy fighters. His aircraft crashed to the ground from 2500ft, breaking both his arms. On 4 December 1917, while still in hospital, he was awarded the *Pour le Mérite*, making him one of only five pilots to be awarded both the *Pour le Mérite* and the Golden Military Service Cross.

He returned to *Jasta* 17 at the beginning of April 1918 and had two aircraft made available to him, which he named 'Lilly' and 'Mops'. On 16 April he shot down a Breguet XIV over Vaux and on the 21st brought down another over Mareuil. He shot down his last balloon on 3 May and was then wounded in the left ankle on 6 May; this wound would keep him out of the war for eight months, during which he was awarded the Golden Wound Badge; he is believed to be the only German ace to receive it. He returned to his *Jasta* at the beginning of July and settled down to a period of inactivity. On 22 September he was made Staffelführer, a post he held until the end of the war. During October he brought down three enemy aircraft, bringing his total to thirty-six, but the last of these may never have been officially confirmed.

During the Second World War Buckler served with Luftwaffe training units. He died in Berlin on 23 May 1960. His memoir is called *Malaula: The Battle Cry of my Jasta*.

Hauptmann Hans-Joachim BUDDECKE 'The Hunting Falcon' (13 victories)

The son of an army general, Hans-Joachim Buddecke was born on 22 August 1890 in Berlin. He left school at 14 in 1904 and joined the army as a cadet, and was commissioned Leutnant in 1910. In 1913 he resigned his commission and went to work for his uncle in the USA as an engineer. After a year he had earned enough money to buy a second-hand French Nieuport and learned to fly. Buddecke could see that aviation was going to have a great future, so with the help of his uncle he set up his own company to build aircraft to his own design. However, as the war in Europe started he made his way back to Germany.

In June 1915 Buddecke joined the German Army Air Service with the rank of Leutnant due to his experience in the army. After a short period at *Jastaschule* he was posted to FA23 as a scout and reconnaissance pilot. While flying with Rudolf Berthold over St Quentin on either 15 or 19 September, they sighted a British patrol from 8 Squadron. Berthold came under attack from a BE2c, but Buddecke closed in on the British aircraft and shot it down. Buddecke scored his second victory on 23 October, another BE2c (its observer was Second Lieutenant W. Lawrence – brother of T.E. Lawrence – who became a POW) and his third on 11 November. By the end of the year he had been awarded the Iron Cross 2nd Class, was posted to Gallipoli with Ottoman FA6 flying Halberstadt DIIs, DVs and Fokker EIIIs, and was promoted to Oberleutnant.

FA6 was based at Smyrna. On 6 January 1916, over Cape Narors, Buddecke shot down a Maurice Farman from 2 Squadron RNAS. By the end of the month he had brought down another three, bringing his tally to seven, plus five unconfirmed, and was awarded the Silver Liaket Medal and the Iron Cross 1st Class. On 14 April 1916 he was awarded the Golden Liaket Medal, the Saxon Military St Heinrich Henry Order 4th Class, the Knight's Cross with Swords of the Royal Hohenzollern Order and the *Pour le Mérite*, only the third airman to be awarded it. The Turks called him 'The Hunting Falcon', but he was also known as 'The Shooting Hawk'.

At the beginning of August 1916 Buddecke was posted back to the Western

Front, where he was appointed commander of *Jasta* 4 on 28 August and promoted to Hauptmann. During September he raised his score to ten, but in December he was posted back to Turkey and joined Ottoman FA5; the rest of the year was very quiet, flying mostly reconnaissance missions. On 30 March 1917 he encountered a patrol of British aircraft over Smyrna and in a brief dog-fight he shot down a Farman F27 and a Nieuport XII from 2 Squadron RNAS. The rest of 1917 was also very quiet.

At the beginning of 1918 he was asked by Rudolph Berthold to join him as his deputy. He immediately accepted the offer and returned to France at the beginning of February, first going to *Jasta* 30 and then to *Jasta* 18. On 19 February Buddecke shot down a Sopwith Camel from 80 Squadron over Neuve Chapelle. On 10 March, while on patrol over Harmes with Berthold, they encountered a patrol of Sopwith Camels from 3 Squadron RNAS. Berthold was attacked; Buddecke again went to his friend's aid but the long periods of inactivity on the Turkish Front were taking their toll: he was shot down and killed. As well as his thirteen confirmed victories, he also had seven unconfirmed.

Hans-Joachim Buddecke was buried with full military honours on 22 March 1918 in the Invaliden Friedhof, Scharnhorst Strasse, Berlin.

Leutnant Walter von BÜLOW-BOTHKAMP 'Jonny Bülow' (28 victories)

The son of a wealthy landowner, Walter von Bülow-Bothkamp was born on 24 April 1894 in Borby, Holstein. Walter was very bright and broke away from the family tradition of joining the army to study law at Heidelberg University, but at the outbreak of war he joined Saxon Hussar Regiment Nr 17, the Death's Head Hussars. His regiment was soon in action, and in early 1915 was fighting in the Alsace region. Bülow-Bothkamp took well to soldiering and after several skirmishes was given a field commission as Leutnant and awarded the Iron Cross 2nd Class.

In the spring of 1915 he applied for a transfer to the German Army Air Service and was posted to Valenciennes in June for pilot training. On passing out, he was sent to FA22 flying twin-engined AEG GIIs. Walter opened his tally on 10 October 1915 when he shot down a Voisin over Metz. The next day he brought down a Maurice Farman in the Champagne region; for these successes he was awarded the Iron Cross 1st Class.

January 1916 saw him posted to FA300 in Palestine. With little action in prospect, he did not score again until 8 August, over El Arish. His next victory came on 17 September, when he shot down a Sopwith Baby from the seaplane carrier *Ben-my-Chree*, again over El Arish. After numerous requests he was posted back to the Western Front in December 1916 to join *Jasta* 18.

His fifth and sixth victories came on 23 January 1917, when he shot down a

1½ Strutter from 45 Squadron and an FE8 from 41 Squadron over Gheluvelt. By the end of April his tally had reached twelve and he had been awarded the Knight's Cross with Swords of the Royal Hohenzollern House Order and the Saxon Military St Heinrich Henry Order. On 7 May he shot down an FE2d over his own airfield and on 10 May was appointed commander of *Jasta* 36. By the beginning of October his score stood at twenty-one, and on 8 October 1917 he was awarded the *Pour le Mérite*. By the time he was appointed commander of *Jasta* 2 on 13 December he had shot down twenty-eight aircraft.

His command did not last long, however. On patrol over Ypres his *Jasta* engaged enemy aircraft from 23 and 70 Squadrons and after a brief dog-fight his Albatros DV was seen to spin down out of control and crash into the front-line trenches.

Bülow-Bothkamp is buried in the family Chateau Cemetery, Borby, Germany.

Kapitänleutnant Horst Freiherr Treusch von BUTTLAR-BRANDENFELS

Horst Treusch von Buttlar-Brandenfels was born in Hannau, Darmstadt, on 14 June 1888. In 1903 he followed the family tradition and joined the Imperial German Navy as a sea cadet. On completing his training, he was commissioned Leutnant zur See and then sent for radio-telephony training. On passing out, he was posted as RT Officer to the staff of the Commander of Reconnaissance Ships. In 1910 Zeppelin trials began, with the intention of using them as aerial scouts for the navy. The first air-to-ship radio test flight involved the airship *L2*, but, due to the extra equipment onboard, some of the crew, including Buttlar-Brandenfels, were left behind. During the trial the *L2* crashed, killing all on board. Later trials were more successful and in 1916 Zeppelins were used to radio back the positions of the British fleet during the Battle of Jutland.

Buttlar-Brandenfels went on to train as an airship pilot and soon after the start of the war was given command of the *L6*. His first action took place on 25 December 1914: during a patrol off Heligoland he sighted three minelayers accompanied by two cruisers and eight destroyers. Unable to send a radio message as his radio equipment was faulty, he decided to attack and dropped three 100lb bombs from 4000ft. The attack did no damage and only succeeded in drawing very heavy and accurate fire from the cruisers, so he withdrew into the clouds and then, using them as cover, came in low and strafed the ships with machine-gun fire. The British ships returned fire, puncturing the airship and forcing Buttlar-Brandenfels to abandon the attack; his airship was losing height but he managed to limp home. He was awarded the Iron Cross 2nd Class and promoted to Kommander for this action.

On 19 January 1915 *L6* set off on a mission to bomb England but had to turn back due to engine trouble. Buttlar-Brandenfels had to wait until 17 August to carry out his first raid, with *L11*. In all, he carried out more than nineteen missions against England, receiving the Iron Cross 1st Class and being promoted to Kapitänleutnant. He was awarded the *Pour le Mérite* on 9 April 1918 after his fifteenth raid and his crew were awarded the Iron Cross 1st Class.

At the end of the war, and in defiance of the Treaty of Versailles, he was one of those responsible for destroying the entire airship fleet at Nordholz.

Buttlar-Brandenfels served with the Luftwaffe during the Second World War and was killed in action in 1943.

Kapitänleutnant zur See Friedrich CHRISTIANSEN (13 victories)

The son of a sea captain, Friedrich Christiansen was born on 12 December 1879 in Wyk on Fohr. The naval tradition in his family ensured that on leaving school in 1895 he joined the merchant navy, with which he served until 1901, when he volunteered for military service, serving on MTBs. After a year with the MTBs, Christiansen went back to the merchant navy and was appointed as second officer on *Preussen*, then the biggest sailing ship in the world. In 1913 he decided to learn to fly and after graduating became an instructor at a civilian flying school in 1914.

At the outbreak of war Christiansen was called up and posted to Zeebrugge as a naval aviator, flying Brandenburg W12 seaplanes over the North Sea and England. He even bombed Dover, for which he was awarded the Iron Cross 2nd Class. For the next year he carried out raids and reconnaissance patrols, making *C-Staffel* one of the most successful units in the German Naval Air Service. Leutnant der Matrosen Artillerie Christiansen was awarded the Iron Cross 1st Class and the Knight's Cross with Swords of the Royal Hohenzollern House Order on 27 April 1916.

Christiansen shot down his first opponent on 15 May 1917, when he brought down a Sopwith Pup while on patrol near Dover. On 1 September he was promoted to Oberleutnant and given command of the Naval Air Station at Zeebrugge, and celebrated by shooting down a Porte FB2 Baby flying-boat near Felixstowe. On 11 December 1917 he shot down the airship *C27*, and was awarded the *Pour le Mérite* on the same day, having completed 440 missions.

On 15 February 1918 he shot down a Curtiss H12b flying-boat, followed by two more on 24 and 25 April. In June and July he brought down three more F2a flying-boats from Felixstowe. On 6 July he attacked the submarine *C–25* while it was on the surface, killing the captain and five of her crew; Christiansen believed the submarine had sunk but in fact she limped back to harbour. Christiansen was credited with shooting down thirteen enemy aircraft by the end of the war, but he may also have 'sunk' some vessels and shot down into the sea some aircraft that are often credited to him but cannot be confirmed. His total may have been as high as twenty-one or twenty-seven according to some records.

After the war he returned to the merchant navy and for a while worked for the

Dornier Company. In 1930 he flew the largest seaplane in the world, the Dornier Do X, on its maiden Atlantic flight to New York. In 1933 he joined the German Aviation Ministry to help rebuild the air force and was appointed Korpsfuhrer of the NSFK in 1937. After the fall of Holland in 1940, Christiansen was appointed commanding officer of occupied Holland, a post he held until the end of the war, when he was arrested and imprisoned by the Allies. On his release he returned to West Germany. He died at the age of 93 at Innien on 5 December 1972, fifty-four years after the award of his *Pour le Mérite* – thus entitling him to the fifty-year Crown had it still been awarded.

Leutnant Carl DEGELOW 'Charly' (30 victories)

Carl Degelow was born in Munsterdorf on 5 January 1891. At the age of 21 he went to the USA, where he worked his way from Chicago to El Paso. Returning to Germany just prior to the start of the war, he joined Nassauische Infantrie-Regiment Nr 88 and was sent to the Western Front. Within three months he had been promoted to Unteroffizier and was awarded the Iron Cross 2nd Class. At the beginning of 1915 his regiment was transferred to the Eastern Front; after several patrols, for which he was promoted to Vizefeldwebel and awarded the Iron Cross 1st Class, he was wounded in the arm. While still in hospital he was commissioned Leutnant on 31 July. But by now he had had enough of the mud and cold, so he applied for a transfer to the German Army Air Service. On his release from hospital, however, Degelow was posted back to the front. Not until April 1916 was he finally sent for flying training, and after graduating he was posted to FA(A)216 at the beginning of 1917, on the Western Front. He started flying reconnaissance missions with Leutnant Kurten as his observer in an Albatros CV. On 22 May 1917 they were attacked by a Caudron GIV, which they shot down, but this was unconfirmed so did not count towards Degelow's tally. Three days later they were attacked by another Caudron GIV and again shot it down; this time it was confirmed.

Degelow applied to fly single-seat fighters and was posted to *Jasta* 36 for training, but was sent away within three days for accidentally shooting an airman during gunnery practice. On 17 August he was posted to *Jasta* 7, where he brought down two more enemy aircraft, but again they were unconfirmed. After another unconfirmed claim on 23 January 1918 things started to improve: on 25 January he shot down a Bf2b from 20 Squadron, followed by a Sopwith Camel from 54 Squadron on 21 April; then on 16 May he shot down an RE8, and on the same day was posted to *Jasta* 40, shooting down three more in June. On 11 July he took command of the *Jasta*, and to celebrate he shot down six more enemy aircraft in July. His aircraft was painted with a white stag on the fuselage sides.

Degelow was awarded the Knight's Cross with Swords of the Royal Hohenzollern House Order on 9 August and during September shot down another six aircraft, brining his total to nineteen. In the first eight days of October Degelow shot down seven enemy aircraft, ending the month with twenty-nine victories to his credit; he rounded it up to thirty on 4 November when he shot down a DH9. On 9 November 1918 he was awarded the *Pour le Mérite* – the last man ever to receive it.

After the war Carl Degelow formed the Hamburg *Zeitfriwillingen Korps* and fought during the revolution against the communists. He wrote *With the White Stag Through Thick and Thin* in 1920. When the Second World War started he joined the Luftwaffe, reaching the rank of Major. He survived this war too and went into business.

Degelow died in Hamburg on 9 November 1970, fifty-two years to the day since he was awarded his *Pour le Mérite*, entitling him to the fifty-year Crown had it still been awarded.

Leutnant der Reserve Albert DOSSENBACH (15 victories)

Albert Dossenbach was born on 5 June 1891 in St Blasien in the Black Forest. He had intended to follow in his father's footsteps by studying medicine and had started his medical training when war broke out. Dossenbach enlisted into the army and was promoted to Unteroffizier within weeks. He was awarded the Iron Cross 2nd Class for carrying his wounded CO to safety after only four weeks at the front, and within four months had been awarded the Iron Cross 1st Class, the Golden Military Merit Cross (considered to be the enlisted man's *Pour le Mérite*) and been promoted to Feldwebel. On 27 January 1915 he was commissioned Leutnant, but he was already thinking of flying and applied for a transfer to the German Army Air Service toward the end 1915. In the spring of 1916 he was sent to *Jastaschule* and was posted to FA22 in June. Dossenbach and his observer Oberleutnant Hans Schilling were straight into the thick of the action and within three months had shot down eight enemy aircraft. They were shot down themselves by their eighth victim on 27 September, both pilot and observer suffering minor burns, but they were soon back in action. Dossenbach was awarded the Knight's Cross 2nd Class with Swords to the Order of the Zahringer Lion, and on 21 October the Knight's Cross of the Royal Hohenzollern House Order. To celebrate he went out on 3 November and shot down an FE2b from 25 Squadron, but his observer was badly wounded in the dog-fight. On 11 November 1916 Dossenbach was awarded the *Pour le Mérite*, the first two-seater pilot to receive it. On 9 December he was awarded the Knight's Cross of the Karl Friedrich Military Merit Order, but his success was marred by the death of his friend and observer Hans Schilling, who was killed while on a bombing mission. Soon afterwards Dossenbach applied for single-seat fighter training, and after passing out was sent to command *Jasta* 36 on 22 February 1917. On 5 April he scored the unit's first victory, downing a Caudron from *Escadrille* 12. By the end of April he had raised his personal score to fourteen, including Sous-Lieutenant M.J.M. Nogues on the 13th. Nogues was taken prisoner but escaped and returned to his unit, shooting down thirteen enemy aircraft by the end of the war. Dossenbach was badly wounded by shell splinters when his airfield was attacked on 2 May, leaving him in hospital for a month. On his return he was posted to *Jasta* 10, taking command on 21 June. While on patrol on 27 June he shot down an observation balloon over Ypres, bringing his score to fifteen. Then, on 3 July 1917, his luck ran out. On patrol over Frenzenberg his unit was attacked by fighters from 57 Squadron; during the ensuing dog-fight he was attacked by four enemy fighters and his airplane caught fire. It remains unclear whether he jumped or fell from the blazing wreck, but he was killed. His body was returned to the Germans and was buried with full military honours in Frieberg.

Oberleutnant Eduard Ritter von DOSTLER (26 victories)

The son of a surveyor, Eduard Dostler was born in Pottenstein, Bavaria, on 3 February 1892. He joined the 2nd Pioneer Battalion as a cadet on leaving school and was commissioned Leutnant on 28 October 1912, being posted to the 4th Pioneer Battalion. During an exercise that involved crossing the flooded Danube River in 1913 he saved the life of a fellow officer, for which act of bravery he was awarded the Bavarian Lifesaving Medal.

At the outbreak of war Dostler's battalion was in the thick of the fighting and in November he was awarded the Iron Cross 2nd Class. In March 1915 he was awarded the Iron Cross 1st Class and the Bavarian Military Service Order 4th Class with Swords. In November he heard that his brother, a pilot, had been killed in action, so he applied for a transfer to the German Army Air Service; in February 1916 he was posted to *Schutzstaffel* 27 and on 15 June to *Kampfstaffel* 36 flying Roland CIIs. During most of 1916 he carried out reconnaissance missions with his observer Leutnant Boes and then on 17 December shot down his first enemy aircraft, a Nieuport Scout, over Verdun.

Dostler and Boes were posted to *Jasta* 13 on 27 December 1916 and on 22 January 1917 they shot down a Caudron while on patrol over Nixeville. Early in February they were posted to *Jasta* 34 and by 3 June Dostler had raised his score to eight. Then on 10 June he was given command of *Jasta* 6, shooting down just one more that month. During July he shot down thirteen enemy aircraft, including doubles on the 12th, 13th and 28th, bringing his total to twenty-one; he was awarded the Knight's Cross with Swords of the Royal Hohenzollern House Order, and on 6 August 1917 the *Pour le Mérite*. He continued to shoot down enemy aircraft, bringing his total to twenty-six by 18 August 1917. On 21 August, while on patrol over the East Roulers area, his luck ran out. His patrol was attacked by RE8s from 7 Squadron, and Dostler's aircraft was hit and set on fire by Lieutenant Norman Sharples and Second Lieutenant M.A. O'Callaghan, the latter firing only fifty rounds before his gun jammed. Dostler did not survive the crash.

He was a well liked and respected officer, and his loss was greatly felt by his men. He was posthumously awarded the Bavarian Military Max Joseph Order, making him a Knight, the award being backdated to 18 August 1917.

Leutnant der Reserve Wilhelm FRANKL (20 victories)

The son of a salesman, Wilhelm Frankl was born in Hamburg on 20 December 1893. After leaving school he joined his father as a salesman, but he was already thinking about aeroplanes. At the age of 20 he learnt to fly at his local flying school, taking part in many competitions. One in Berlin-Johannisthal resulted in him being awarded his international licence.

At the start of the war he applied to join the German Army Air Service and was accepted as an observer, even though he was qualified as a pilot. He carried out a number of reconnaissance missions with FA40 in Flanders, earning himself the Iron Cross 2nd Class. On 10 May 1915 he shot down his first enemy aircraft, a Voisin, using a rifle, for which action he was awarded the Iron Cross 1st Class and later promoted to Vizefeldwebel.

In late 1915 Frankl applied for training as a fighter pilot and was sent to *Jastaschule* in November. On passing out he was posted to *Kek* Vaux in January 1916, flying Fokker EIII Eindeckers. Within just a few days he shot down another Voisin while on patrol over Woumen. Nine days later he added yet another Voisin to his score. By the end of May he had shot down three more and been commissioned Leutnant. Within a few days he was awarded the Knight's Cross of the Royal Hohenzollern House Order and the Hanseatic Cross. On 10 July he took his tally to eight and on 12 July 1916 was awarded the *Pour le Mérite*.

Frankl was posted to *Jasta* 4 on 1 September 1916 and by the end of the month his tally had risen to thirteen. Then things went quiet for him, and by the end of the year he had brought down just two more. In April 1917 things started to change: on 6 April he shot down four aircraft in one day, the first before dawn and the remaining three within one hour of each other. On 7 April he shot down number twenty.

In the afternoon of 8 April Frankl took off and flew straight into a patrol of British fighters from 48 Squadron. His Albatros was heavily shot up and was seen to break up in mid-air; his body fell to the ground near Vitry-Sailly. He was buried with full military honours in Berlin-Charlottenburg.

In the 1930s the Nazis removed his name from the list of air heroes of the First World War because he was Jewish. In 1973 his name was restored and Luftwaffe Squadron Nr 74 was renamed in his honour.

Oberleutnant Hermann FRICKE

Hermann Fricke was born in Munster, Westphalia, on 16 June 1890. He had a keen interest in photography and at the age of 22 he took to the air as an aircraft passenger; realising this was for him, he applied for the German Army Air Service, and on being accepted was sent to *Feldflieger Abteilung* II. On 1 July 1914 he was posted to the German Flying School at Johannisthal for pilot training and on graduating returned to his unit in September as a reconnaissance pilot.

The war had by now started, and his unit was soon posted to the Western Front and immediately began reconnaissance and artillery spotting. With his knowledge of photography, Fricke also began taking photographs of Allied positions. His efforts were recognised by the High Command with the award of the Iron Cross 2nd Class and Knight's Cross of the Royal Hohenzollern House Order. He made the most unusual request to command an infantry unit, in order to experience what the infantry were going through; this was granted and for several weeks he commanded an infantry company. On rejoining his unit he believed he was now better able to understand the problems of the infantrymen.

During the Somme, Arras and Flanders battles he flew mission after mission taking photographs of the struggle on the ground and then, during the winter of 1916/17, the High Command instructed the newly promoted Oberleutnant Fricke to establish a War Photography Office. He was appointed to command the Group 2 Series Photography Unit and he equipped his aircraft with Reihenbilder built-in cameras capable of photographing a mile-long strip; put together, these gave an invaluable picture of Allied positions.

Fricke had by now flown well over 160 combat missions and his unit had photographed some 3,700 square miles of enemy positions. On 23 December 1917 he was awarded the *Pour le Mérite* for his outstanding work in photography. He continued to fly until the end of the war.

Fricke also flew in the Luftwaffe during the Second World War; he died in hospital while still in captivity on 14 May 1946.

Leutnant der Reserve Heinrich GONTERMANN (39 victories)

The son of a cavalry officer, Heinrich Gontermann was born in Siegen, Westphalia, on 25 February 1896. In 1914 he joined the 6th Uhlan Cavalry Regiment and after training was sent to the front line, where within days his regiment was in action and Gontermann's leadership skills started to show through. He was lightly wounded in September and was promoted to Feldwebel. Early in the spring of 1915 he was given a field commission as Leutnant and was awarded the Iron Cross 2nd Class. He continued with his regiment until October, when he was transferred to Fusilier Regiment Nr 80.

This was not what he wanted, and he applied for the German Army Air Service instead. He was accepted and sent for pilot and observer training. On graduation early in 1916, he was posted to *Kampfstaffel* Tergnier as a reconnaissance pilot flying Roland CIIs. Then he was posted again, this time to FA25, flying AGO CIs. After almost a year on reconnaissance missions he applied for transfer to a fighter unit, and was accepted. On 11 November 1916 he was posted to *Jasta* 5 and within three days shot down his first enemy aircraft, an FE2b, over Morval.

For the next four months he failed to score again, although he was in combat regularly, then on 5 March 1917 he was awarded the Iron Cross 1st Class. On the 6th he shot down an FE2b from 57 Squadron, and by the end of March had brought down another three, bringing his total to six. By the end of April he had raised his score to seventeen, including five balloons, and had been appointed Staffelführer of *Jasta* 15. In celebration of this he shot down a Spad over Caronne on 4 May, and on 6 May was awarded the Knight's Cross with Swords of the Royal Hohenzollern House Order. On 10 May he shot down two aircraft in one day, a Spad and a Caudron R4, and the following day shot down another Spad and received the Bavarian Order of Max Josef. The *Pour le Mérite* came next, on 14 May 1917.

From June 1917 until the end of September Gontermann added six more enemy aircraft and eleven balloons. Four balloons and a Spad fell to his guns on 19 August, the balloons within three minutes of each other, and this brought his score to thirty-five. During September and October he shot down four more to bring his total to thirty-nine, of which seventeen were balloons. On 30 October 1917 he took one of the latest Fokker Triplanes up for a test flight; within minutes the top wing suffered structural failure, and the aircraft spun out of control into the ground. Gontermann was pulled from the wreckage alive but died from his injuries several hours later. He was buried outside the airfield but the grave site is no longer known.

Oberleutnant Hermann GÖRING 'The Iron Man' (22 victories)

The son of Dr Heinrich Göring, Governor of German South West Africa, Hermann Göring was born in Rosenheim, Upper Bavaria, on 12 January 1893. A rebellious and undisciplined child, he was sent to the military academy at Karlsruhe, and from there to Lichterfelde, an army cadet college for future officers. He graduated with the highest honours a cadet could achieve, and received praise from the Kaiser himself. Göring was commissioned into Prinz Wilhelm Regiment Nr 112. He had a passion for mountain climbing and did not shrink from the danger, believing nothing bad could happen to him.

At the outbreak of war his regiment went straight into action as it was stationed at Muhlhausen in Alsace-Lorraine, on the wrong side of the Rhine. When the regiment moved to the Vosges region, Göring contracted rheumatic fever. While in hospital he was visited by his friend Bruno Loerzer, who had served in the same regiment but was now a pilot with the German Army Air Service. His visit gave Göring much to think about, not least the dismal prospect of returning to the cold and the mud. He therefore wrote to his CO requesting a transfer to the Freiburg flying school. After having had no response for two weeks, he 'obtained' the papers and signed them himself. He spent the next two weeks flying with Loerzer and getting all the training he could. However, his transfer was refused and he was ordered to rejoin his unit; the situation was serious, as he had left himself open to charges of desertion and forging papers. He immediately telegraphed his godfather, Ritter von Epstein, who moved in high circles, and suddenly Crown Prince Friedrich Wilhelm intervened, asking that Göring be posted to the German Fifth Army field air detachment. The charges were reduced to one of 'lateness', and Göring was given a medical certificate saying he was unfit for front-line duty. It should be remembered here that he was not trying to get out of the fighting – he just wanted to fight in the air.

In the autumn of 1914 he completed his training and then joined Bruno Loerzer at FFA25. They flew together as often as possible, soon winning a reputation for carrying out the most dangerous missions, and in March 1915 were awarded the Iron Cross 2nd Class. In May they were sent to carry out a reconnaissance of the French fortresses of Verdun, a task that many others had tried – and failed. For three days they flew over the Verdun area and took pictures so detailed that General Erich von Falkenhayn asked to see them personally. The High Command were so impressed with the results that Crown Prince Wilhelm exercised his royal prerogative and awarded them both the Iron Cross 1st Class in the field. In June 1915 Göring was posted to Freiburg for pilot training, passing out in October and being sent to FA25. On 16 November, while flying an Albatros, he shot down his first enemy aircraft, a Maurice Farman, over Tahure.

In 1916 Göring was posted to *Kek* Stennay flying Fokker EIIIs, and then in March to *Kek* Metz, where he shot down a Caudron on the 14th; on 30 July he shot down another Caudron over Memang. On 9 July he went back to FA25, and again to *Kek* Metz on 7 September. He was posted to *Jasta* 7 in early October and then on 20 October to *Jasta* 5. While on patrol on 2 November he came across a Handley-Page bomber; as he closed in on it, he came under fire, which he returned, killing one of the gunners. Then he came under attack from an escorting Sopwith, being hit in the thigh; losing consciousness momentarily, he came to as his aircraft was plummeting to the ground. He was able to regain control and landed next to an emergency hospital just inside the German lines, and within a very short time he was in the operating theatre.

At the beginning of February 1917 Göring was posted to *Jasta* 26, now under the command of his friend Bruno Loerzer, and by the end of the month had brought his score to six. On 10 May he shot down a DH4 of 55 Squadron over Le Pave and one week later was given command of *Jasta* 27. Although it had been in existence for three months, this unit had yet to score its first kill. On 16 July Göring shot down an SE5a for his ninth victory but was himself brought down in the process, both pilots claiming a kill. On 21 September Göring shot down the Bristol Fighter flown by Lieutenant R.L. Curtis (fifteen victories) and Lieutenant D.P.F. Uniacke (thirteen victories). His scoring was much slower at this time due to the responsibility of command, and it took until the end of October to bring his tally to fifteen. On 27 October Göring was awarded the Military Karl Friedrich Merit Order, the Knight's Cross with Swords of the Royal Hohenzollern House Order and the Knight's Cross 2nd Class with Swords of the Baden Order of the Zahringer Lion. On 7 November he achieved his final score for that year, a DH4 north-west of Poelcapelle, although much confusion surrounds this claim as the only British aircraft reported lost on this date was an AWFK VIII two-seater.

It was not until 21 February 1918 that Göring scored again, bringing down an SE5a from 60 Squadron, followed by an RE8 from 48 Squadron on 7 April. On 2 June 1918 he was awarded the *Pour le Mérite* by the Kaiser, and by the end of that month he had brought down three more aircraft to bring his tally to twenty-one. On 9 July he was given command of JGI, the Richthofen Wing, with promotion to Oberleutnant. His only victory while leading this unit came on 18 July, bringing his total to twenty-two. From then on he did very little flying, having either decided or been ordered to take a more administrative role due to the lack of experienced officers.

On 9 August 1918 the order to cease all further air operations came and he was ordered to transfer his unit's aircraft to an Allied airfield; Göring obeyed the order but, knowing full well the Allies wanted the latest Fokkers, he ordered his pilots to set fire to their planes on landing. After fighting in the post-war revolution with the rank of Hauptmann, he went to Denmark in a flight advisory capacity, but returned to Germany in the early 1920s.

Göring joined the Nazi Party in 1922 and was appointed commander of the SA in 1923. In November 1923 he was involved in the 'Beer Hall Putsch': Ludendorff, Hitler and Göring marched in front of a large column with Ulrich Graf carrying a swastika flag before them; shots were fired and Göring was hit in the hip and thighs. As a result of his wounds he was given two shots of morphine a day for a month.

In 1925 he went into a sanatorium three times to be cured of his morphine addiction, which he did by will-power alone. In 1928 he was elected to the Reichstag, and in 1932 became its President. When Hitler was appointed Chancellor in January 1933, Göring became Reich Minister, Reich Commissioner for Aviation and Acting Prussian Minister of the Interior; later the same year he was appointed Minister President of Prussia. He was promoted to General in May 1933, but from April his old wounds started to give him problems and he was back on painkillers. In March 1934 he was named as Hitler's successor. March 1935 saw him appointed General of the Luftwaffe with the rank of Generalleutnant and he was soon promoted Oberstgeneral.

In April 1935 he was appointed Dictator of Raw Material, a post that allowed him to channel resources into the Luftwaffe. In October 1936 he was appointed the person responsible for the 'Four Year Plan' intended to make the Reich independent from imports. Göring also appointed himself Commander-in-Chief of the Luftwaffe in June 1937. Throughout that year he tried many weight cures, which only weakened him, and he was still being treated for his addiction to pills. Yet another promotion came in February 1938, this time to Airmarschall. On 30 September 1939 he was awarded the Knight's Cross of the Iron Cross.

Published in 1940, his authorised biography is called *Hermann Göring; The Man and his Work*. On 19 July 1940, after the fall of France, he was promoted to Reichsmarschall and, uniquely, was awarded the Grand Cross of the Iron Cross. He was now at the height of his power.

From the Battle of Britain onwards his influence started to decline, not least because the Luftwaffe proved unable to dominate the skies as he had promised the Fuhrer it would. In 1941 his paratroopers suffered heavy losses in the battle of Crete. He became known throughout Germany as 'Meier', due to his boast that no enemy plane would ever fly over the Reich – by now a common occurrence. The Fuhrer lost even more faith in him after the fall of Stalingrad in 1943, as Göring had promised he could re-supply the city from the air, though by now he was completely unable to prevent the bombing of German cities. Reproached by Hitler, he feared being relieved from command of the Luftwaffe, and mood swings now became part of his persona.

In April 1945 Göring sent Hitler his famous telegram stating that he would assume overall leadership of the Reich if he [Hitler] was unable to act freely. Two days later Göring was relieved of all offices and Hitler ordered his arrest. He was supposed to be shot after Hitler's death but the SS guard was unsure of this and telephoned Feldmarschall Kesselring, who forbade it and told the guard to leave Göring to himself. On 8 May he fell into the hands of the Americans. He was sent to trial at Nuremberg in 1946 and found guilty of war crimes, and killed himself with poison on 15 October 1946. His ashes were scattered in an unknown German river.

Oberleutnant Robert Ritter von GREIM (28 victories)

The son of a police captain, Robert Greim was born in Bayreuth, Bavaria, on 22 June 1892. At 14 he became a cadet, joining the regular army on 14 July 1911 at the age of 19. He was immediately put forward for officer training and on 29 October 1912 joined Bavarian Field Artillery Regiment Nr 8 and was commissioned Leutnant on 25 October 1913. When the war broke out his regiment was one of the first into action; he commanded a battery at the Battle of Lorraine at Nancy-Epinal, and at the assaults on St Mihiel and Camp des Romains. For these actions he was awarded the Iron Cross 2nd Class, and on 15 March 1915 was appointed the 1st Battalion's Adjutant. At the end of April Greim was awarded the Bavarian Military Merit Order 4th Class with Swords.

Like so many other young men, he began to look at the newly formed German Army Air Service and applied for a transfer. He started his training as an observer on 10 August 1915 and was posted to FFA3b. Greim opened his tally by shooting down a Maurice Farman on 10 October. He was then sent to FA(A)204 as an observer during the Battle of the Somme in 1916, but applied for pilot training towards the end of the year. After graduating he was sent to FA46b as a reconnaissance pilot on 22 February 1917 and then to *Jastaschule* in March for single-seater training. On completing this he was posted to *Jasta* 34b on 3 April 1917; he now had his aircraft painted with his own markings of a red nose, two red fuselage bands and a white/silvery tail. On 18 May 1917 he was awarded the Bavarian Military Merit Order 4th Class with Crown and Swords.

On 24 May he shot down a Spad over Mamey but this was unconfirmed. The next day he shot down a Caudron R4 over Ramaucourt, and was awarded the Iron Cross 1st Class. By the end of 1917 he had brought down seven enemy aircraft. On 29 April 1918, with his tally at nine, he was awarded the Knight's Cross with Swords of the Royal Hohenzollern House Order and on 21 March he was given command of *Jagdgruppe* Nr 10 and later *Jagdgruppe* Nr 9. In April, May and June he brought down only four enemy aircraft, but in August he shot down six, including two on the 8th. On 8 October 1918 he was awarded the *Pour le Mérite* and by the end of the month had brought his score to twenty-eight, and subsequently was awarded the Bavarian Max Joseph Medal, entitling him to use the term 'Ritter von' (thus making him a knight); he was also promoted to Oberleutnant. After the war he served with the Bavarian Air Service and later became an adviser to the Chinese Nationalist Air Force.

In the early 1930s he became Director of the Bavarian Sport Flyers Association, then in 1934 he joined the newly formed Luftwaffe with the rank of Major, taking command of the Richthofen *Geschwader*. In 1938 he was promoted to General and during the Second World War commanded Fliegerkorps V, and was awarded the Knight's Cross of the Iron Cross on 24 June 1940. The Oak Leaves to this medal followed on 2 April 1943 and the Swords on 7 August 1944. By 1944 he was commanding the air fleets in Russia with the rank of Generaloberst. By the time he was captured by the Americans in 1945 he was head of the Luftwaffe, a post given to him by Hitler, who also promoted him to Generalfeldmarschall. He committed suicide on 24 May 1945, his last words being 'I am head of the Luftwaffe with no Luftwaffe.' He is buried in the Communal Cemetery, Salzburg, Austria.

Leutnant der Reserve Wilhelm GRIEBSCH

Born on 30 June 1887 in Posen, Wilhelm Griebsch developed an interest in flying during his school days, and it soon became his passion. In 1908, at the age of 21, he entered the technical college in Danzig and four years later went to flying school at Berlin-Johannisthal, training on an Etrich Taube. He earned his flying certificate on 29 December 1913 and looked forward to joining the newly formed German Army Air Service. On the outbreak of war he volunteered for the Army Air Service and left the training school with the rank of Leutnant der Reserve, joining *Flieger Abteilung* 250 as a reconnaissance pilot. He began to fly as an observer and was immediately in the thick of the fighting on the Western Front. Soon he was transferred to *Flieger Abteilung* 213, where his technical knowledge proved its worth. His speciality was long-range reconnaissance patrols, and he completed no fewer than 345 such missions. The information and technical detail he provided proved of great value to the German High Command in planning their ground battles. Even when under enemy attack he would continue to observe and record Allied positions below him, fighting back at the same time with his machine-gun.

On 30 September 1918 his outstanding work was rewarded with the *Pour le Mérite* – one of only a few observers to receive it. Having spent almost four years in the thick of things, he was taken off operational flying and sent to Berlin to use his hard-won battle expertise at the Albatros Aircraft Company, where he spent the last few months of the war.

Still passionate about flying, after the war Griebsch took a position with the Junkers Aircraft Company as a test pilot. On 20 July 1920 he took off to flight test a new aircraft but, with an injured arm, he was apparently unable to control the aircraft and it plummeted down from 1900ft, killing him instantly.

Hauptmann Jürgen von GRONE

The youngest son of an army officer, Jürgen von Grone was born in Schwerin on 14 November 1887. After leaving school, he went to college to study law and political sciences. Towards the end of his studies Jurgen volunteered for a one-year enlistment with the 1st Guard Field Artillery Regiment.

When the war broke out he was serving with the 11th Field Artillery Regiment with the rank of Leutnant, and was sent to the Western Front. His regiment was heavily engaged in the Namur sector and the experience gained was to be put to good use later. In 1915 he was posted to the Eastern Front, where, during heavy fighting, he was wounded. On his return to duty he became commander of the new mobile anti-aircraft trains the Germans were using. He was awarded the Iron Cross 2nd Class, which was shortly followed by the Iron Cross 1st Class.

In December 1915 he applied to become an observer in the Air Service and was accepted. After his training, he was posted to *Flieger Abteilung* 222, where his specialist role as a reconnaissance observer was to take photographs of Allied positions and their troop movements. By the summer of 1917 he had flown some 130 missions and was appointed to command the Photography Troop of the German 7th Army with the rank of Oberleutnant. By the end of May he had flown fifty long-range reconnaissance missions over enemy territory, contributing considerably to the knowledge of the area. He was the first observer to photograph Paris on 10 September 1917 from a height of just over 2000ft. For his outstanding contribution to the war effort he was awarded the *Pour le Mérite* on 13 October 1918.

Grone survived the war and was discharged from the army in 1920 with the rank of Hauptmann. Not much is known about the rest of his life, but he died in 1978, making him entitled to the fifty-year Crown had it still been awarded. His nephew Volkmar von Grone, inspired by stories from his uncle, flew with the Luftwaffe during the Second World War.

Leutnant Walter HÖHNDORF (12 victories)

The son of a schoolteacher, Walter Höhndorf was born in Prutzke on 10 November 1892. He had a passion for all things mechanical, and on leaving school went to Paris to study motor and engineering mechanics. While in Paris he learnt to fly in 1913.

Höhndorf returned to Germany and took part in many air displays, becoming one of the best aerobatic pilots in the country, often carrying out manoeuvres never seen before. He also helped with the designs of production aircraft with the Union *Flugzeugwerke* at Teltow. At the start of the war he immediately volunteered for the German Army Air Service, being commissioned Leutnant on 15 March 1915. Due to his experience he was assigned to Siemens-Schuckert as a test pilot. After almost a year he applied for fighter training and was sent to *Jastaschule*. On passing out, he was posted to FA12 and later to FA67 as a reconnaissance pilot, where he was soon awarded the Iron Cross 2nd Class. At the beginning of January 1916 he was posted back to FA12, where he shot down his first enemy aircraft, a French Voisin from *Escadrille* VB105, on 17 January in the Alsace region. Two days later he shot down another Voisin from *Escadrille* VB101 over Medevich.

Höhndorf was then sent to *Kek* Vaux at the beginning of April 1916, flying Fokker SVIIIs, and brought down number three, a Nieuport, on 10 April. The award of the Iron Cross 1st Class and the Knight's Cross with Swords of the Royal Hohenzollern House Order came in June, followed by the *Pour le Mérite* on 20 July 1916, with nine enemy aircraft to his credit. He shot down three more in July on the 19th, 22nd and 31st. At the beginning of August he was posted to *Jasta* 1 and from there to *Jasta* 4. His last victory came on 17 September 1916 when he shot down a Caudron G.IV over Morval. His experience in testing aircraft meant a return to test pilot duties at Valenciennes, but on 15 August 1917 he was given command of *Jasta* 14. His command was to be short-lived. He returned to Valenciennes in early September to test fly an AEG DI, an aircraft he had helped to design. During the flight on 5 September 1917 he experienced problems and crashed while landing at Ire-le-Sec, near Marville, later dying from his injuries.

General der Kavallerie Ernst von HOEPPNER

Ernst Hoeppner was born on 14 January 1860 in Tonnin on the Pomeranian island of Wollin. At just 12 years of age he entered the cadet school at Potsdam, being commissioned Leutnant in Dragoon Regiment Nr 6 in 1879. In 1890 Hoeppner was posted to the Prussian Military Academy, graduating in 1893 and being sent to Dragoon Regiment Nr 14 with the rank of Oberleutnant. An appointment to the General Staff in 1902 heralded the beginning of a distinguished staff career. In 1904 he was promoted to Major and appointed as a staff officer to IX Army Corps in Altona.

In 1906 Hoeppner was again promoted, this time to Oberstleutnant, and was given command of Hussars Regiment Nr 13. Two years later he was appointed Chief of Staff of the VII Army Corps and in 1912 he was sent to command the 4th Cavalry Brigade in Bromberg, one of the most prestigious commands in the German Army. In 1913 he was granted the title of 'von', making him a knight.

At the start of the First World War von Hoeppner was at III Army Corps HQ, where he remained until the spring of 1915, when he took up command of the 14th Reserve Division. Within a few months he was appointed Chief of Staff of II Army Corps and in June 1916 became commander of the 75th Reserve Division. Then in October 1916 Ludendorff decided that the German Army Air Service needed unity of command and von Hoeppner was promoted to the rank of Generalleutnant and appointed Chief of the Air Service. He immediately set about reorganising the fragmented air services, greatly increasing the number of *Jastas* and forming them into *Jagdgeschwaders*. On 8 April 1917 his efforts were rewarded with the *Pour le Mérite*, though it seems the award did not go down well with some of his junior officers.

After the surrender in 1918 the German Army Air Service was disbanded and the German War Ministry issued orders for von Hoeppner's post to be dissolved on 16 January 1919, although it appears to have taken some time as his last order was issued on 21 January. He took up command of XVIII Army Corps on 10 April 1919 but resigned from active service at his own request in November 1919. Von Hoeppner retired as General der Kavallerie with permission to wear the uniform of Hussars Regiment Nr 13. His book *Germany's War in the Air* was published in 1921.

Von Hoeppner died on 26 September 1922 and is buried at Tonnin.

Oberleutnant Erich HOMBURG

The son of a forester, Erich Homburg was born in Rosenthal, Bavaria, on 2 October 1886. On leaving school he joined the army as a cadet with Reserve Field Regiment Nr 12. By the time the war started Homburg had already been given a commission and was the regiment's ordnance officer as well as its adjutant. The regiment was moved to the Western Front and saw some very heavy fighting, for his part in which Homburg was awarded the Iron Cross 2nd Class.

During a lull in the fighting early in 1915 Homburg was offered a flight in an aircraft. He was so taken with the relative freedom it afforded him that he applied for a transfer to the German Army Air Service and in the spring was accepted, being posted for flying training. In the autumn of 1915 he graduated and was sent to Field Flying Unit 34 as a reconnaissance pilot. He quickly developed an interest in communications and was assigned the position of communications officer. On 25 September he was awarded the Iron Cross 1st Class for his work in reconnaissance. Over the next two years he created a reporting system that used ground-to-air radio, and became the first airman to use it. He also spent time on aerial photography and carried out strip photographic flying missions over the Somme battlefield, Verdun, Champagne and Romania. During the German offensive in Italy Homburg was sent to carry out aerial photographic missions which greatly helped in the campaign. He returned to the Western Front at the beginning of August 1918 and was given command of Army Flight Unit 260. On 13 October he was awarded the *Pour le Mérite*, one of only a few non-fighter pilots to receive it. He was also promoted to Oberleutnant in recognition of the 239 reconnaissance and photographic missions he had flown over enemy territory. When the armistice came, Homburg managed to get all of his aircraft, every piece of equipment and all the personnel back to Germany.

Homburg continued with his interest in aerial photography after the war, using it for the planning of new airfields for commercial use. He was appointed Director of Air Transport-AG for Lower Saxony in 1926, and in the early 1930s was appointed President of the Reich's Association of Regional Air Traffic Companies. He was also president of a number of sporting flying organisations, including Director of the Aviation Office in Hamburg.

At the start of the Second World War he joined the Luftwaffe, reaching the rank of Generalmajor on 1 November 1940. He survived the war but died in Wiesbaden in 1954.

Leutnant Hans-Georg HORN

The son of a Lutheran pastor, Hans-Georg Horn was born in Berbisdorf, Silesia, on 28 April 1892. After finishing school, he attended military school at Danzig as a cadet. At the start of the war Horn was an Unteroffizier at college; sent to an

144

infantry regiment on the Western Front, he was in action within days. He took part in the storming of Maas Heights during the Battle of Longwy, and a month later the Battle of Combres, where his leadership earned him promotion to Leutnant and the Iron Cross 2nd Class.

On 17 July 1915 Horn was wounded while leading an attack on enemy positions. He returned to the front after a week in hospital, but was wounded again at the end of July. While in hospital he was awarded the Iron Cross 1st Class, and had a chance meeting with a pilot that led him to apply for a transfer to the Air Service on his release. He was accepted and sent to Flying Reserve Unit 10 and on 5 December went for training as an observer. Graduating in February 1916, he was sent to a defence *Jasta* flying reconnaissance missions for the infantry for the rest of the year. Then in January 1917 he was posted to defence *Jasta* 11 for two months and then to *Kagohl* 221 in April.

This move was to bring him into some of the most intense fighting of the war, including the battle for Verdun. Horn and his pilot Otto Jahnke flew almost daily missions, which were recognised by the High Command with the award of the Knight's Cross with Swords of the Royal Hohenzollern House Order on 15 July 1917. It was known that Horn was one of the best observers in the Air Service and this was borne out in November when he and Jahnke flew six missions in horrendous weather conditions during the fighting near Gheluveld. The information they brought back enabled the infantry to make important advances and doubtless saved the lives of many men.

On 23 December 1917 Horn was awarded the *Pour le Mérite*, while Otto Jahnke received the Golden Military Merit Cross (considered to be the enlisted man's *Pour le Mérite*). Horn was one of only five observers to receive it. In May 1918 he was posted for two months to the 7th Infantry Division as a flying liaison officer with the rank of Oberleutnant. On his return to his unit in August Horn was wounded, which ended his flying during the war. He had over 300 sorties over enemy territory to his credit. When the armistice was signed he was sent to *Kagohl* 401 flying reconnaissance missions for the border police.

In November 1919 Horn resigned from the army. Not much is known about his later life apart from the facts that he joined the Nazi Party and died in March 1946. He is buried in Berlin Central Cemetery, Plot Group 71B, Vault 70.

Oberleutnant Max IMMELMANN 'The Eagle of Lille' (17 victories)

The son of a factory owner, Max Immelmann was born in Dresden on 21 September 1890. His father (also called Max) died from tuberculosis when he was only 7 years old. At 15 he was sent to the Dresden Cadet School and by 1912 was an ensign serving in the prosaically named Railway Regiment Nr 2. He spent the next two years studying at the War Academy at Anklam, only returning to his regiment on the outbreak of war.

By this time he had become interested in aviation and applied for a transfer to the German Army Air Service; when this was approved, he was sent to *Jastaschule* at Johannisthal, Berlin, in November 1914. From there he was posted to Aldershof for advanced training before being awarded his pilot's badge. In February 1915 Immelmann was posted to FFA62 (later *Kek* Douai) flying two-seaters on observation and escort missions. It was during this time that he met Oswald Boelcke; both men would soon be known as top scouting pilots.

In May he was moved to the unit's single-seater, the Fokker EIII Eindecker. He was awarded the Iron Cross 2nd Class and in July was commissioned Leutnant. On 1 August he shot down his first enemy aircraft, a BE2c of 2 Squadron RFC, and by the end of September his score had reached three, the last of these brought down on his 25th birthday. By the end of the year he had raised his tally to seven and promotion to Oberleutnant followed, along with the Iron Cross 1st Class and the Knight's Cross with Swords of the Royal Hohenzollern House Order. On 12 January 1916 Immelmann, or 'The Eagle of Lille' as he had become known, shot down number eight and was awarded the *Pour le Mérite* on the same day. His score had risen to thirteen by the end of March and more awards followed: the Saxon Commander's Cross to the Military St Heinrich's Order 2nd Class, the Knight's Cross to the Military St Heinrich Order, the Saxon Albert Order 2nd Class with Swords, the Saxon Freidrich August Medal in Silver and the Bavarian Military Merit Order 4th Class with Swords. He shot down one enemy aircraft in both April and May, bringing his tally to fifteen.

On 18 June 1916 he engaged with FE2s from 25 Squadron and shot down one at 17.00 hours. By 21.45 he was again in the air and taking on 25 Squadron; he shot down another FE2, but then came under fire from another FE2 flown by Captain G.R. McCubbin and his gunner Corporal J.H. Waller. According to the British, Immelmann's propeller was shot away and he plunged to his death. The German High Command announced that Immelmann had died due to a defective synchronised gun which shot off his own propeller. This seems unlikely as a pilot of Immelmann's experience would have just switched off his engine and glided down.

His last two victories do not seem to have been officially confirmed, but there is little doubt that they were his. Immelmann was greatly respected by the British and on the day of his funeral they flew over the spot where he was killed and dropped a wreath. On it was a notice: 'In memory of Oberleutnant Immelmann, our brave and knightly opponent, from the British Royal Flying Corps.' Despite the fact that he was buried with full military honours by the British, Immelmann has no known grave.

Leutnant Josef JACOBS (48 victories)

The son of a middle-class businessman, Josef Jacobs was born in Kreuzkapelle in the Rhineland on 15 May 1894. He had an interest in all things mechanical and in 1912 he learned to fly. At the outbreak of war he enlisted in the German Army Air Service and was posted to FEA9 for training; on graduating, he was posted to FAI1 as a reconnaissance pilot. For over a year Jacobs was engaged in reconnaissance missions. Then in early 1916 he was sent to Fokker *Staffel* West to fly Fokker EIIIs. His first claimed kill came on 1 February, a Caudron, but this was unconfirmed. His first confirmed victory came on 22 March, when he shot down a balloon, for which he was awarded the Iron Cross 2nd Class. Jacobs, however, wanted his *Ehrenbecher* inscribed 12 May, perhaps because he had wanted his first official victory to be the shooting down of another flyer.

On 25 October Jacobs was posted to join his long-time friend Erich Honemanns's *Jasta* 22. After two weeks he was temporarily posted to *Jastaschule* I as an instructor, returning to *Jasta* 22 at the end of January 1917, when he was awarded the Iron Cross 1st Class. On 23 January he shot down a Caudron R4 while on patrol over Terny Sorny. Between 7 May and 28 July he had a run of seven unconfirmed claims, but by the end of August, with his score at six, he was appointed commander of *Jasta* 7, and was awarded the Knight's Cross with Swords of the Royal Hohenzollern House Order. On 10 September 1917 he shot down Captain G. Matton, a nine-victory ace, and by the end of the year had brought down another five, bringing his total to twelve. When his unit was re-equipped with the new Fokker DrI Triplane, Jacobs painted his all black and it soon became well known to the Allies.

With a lull at the start of 1918 Jacobs used the time to mould his men into a fighting unit. It was not until April that he scored again, an RE 8 from 7 Squadron, over Ostend. The fighting soon became intense and by the end of July, after surviving a mid-air collision with another Fokker, his tally had risen to twenty-four, bringing the award of the *Pour le Mérite* on 18 July 1918. During September he shot down nine, including doubles on the 16th and 28th. October was even more successful for him, as he shot down fifteen enemy aircraft, again including doubles on the 2nd, 3rd, 9th and 19th. Jacobs became Germany's greatest pilot in the Fokker Triplane and by the end of the war had brought down forty-eight Allied aircraft, plus another eleven unconfirmed.

After the Armistice Jacobs, along with Theodor Osterkamp and Gotthard Sachsenberg, fought the communists in the Baltic. In the early 1920s he became a flight instructor with the Turkish Army, helping them to develop a formidable air force. In 1931 he was appointed director of the Adler works, still maintaining his interest in aviation. In 1933 he started his own aircraft plant at Erfurt, although this was not a great success. Speed was still his passion and he became involved in the world of car and powerboat racing and bobsledding. He did not get involved with the newly formed Luftwaffe until the onset of the Second

World War, when he was commissioned as a major in the reserves. His views on the National Socialist Party were well known and at some point he moved his company from Germany to Holland to prevent Göring becoming a major shareholder.

After the war Jacobs became President of the German Bobsleigh Society and started a crane operating company, and he later became one of the greatest sources of historical information on German aviation and its personnel in the First World War. He died in Munich on 29 July 1978, fifty years and eleven days after the award of his *Pour le Mérite*, making him entitled to the fifty-year Crown had it still been awarded.

Hauptmann Alfred KELLER

The son of a tax collector, Alfred Keller was born in Bochum, Westphalia, on 19 September 1882. On leaving school in 1897 he went into the army as a cadet, graduating in 1902, and was posted to Pioneer Battalion Nr 7 at Thorn. Keller was commissioned Leutnant in 1903; it would be nine more years before he was promoted to Oberleutnant. In the autumn of 1912 Keller applied for a transfer to the German Army Air Service, and was posted to Metz for training as an observer. As soon as he completed this course he reapplied for pilot training. He was then sent to the flying school at Niederneuendorf in the spring of 1913, and upon graduating was posted to the flying station at Darmstadt.

On the outbreak of war in 1914 Keller was sent to the Western Front in command of *Kagohl* 27 and was promoted to Hauptmann. He carried out a number of reconnaissance missions during the following year, including a flight over Paris in October, causing a great deal of concern to Parisians, who had thought that the distant fighting offered no direct threat to the city. For this mission Keller was awarded the Iron Cross 2nd Class. In 1915 Keller was given command of AFP5 and saw extensive action in reconnaissance in the area of the Somme and Verdun. In September 1915 he was given command of *Kagohl* 40, a position he held until the autumn of 1916, when he was asked to command Night Flying Unit 1. Keller spent the next few months developing this unit and then, on 1 April 1917, he was given command of *Bogohl* 1 and was awarded the Iron Cross 1st Class for his work in this field.

Bogohl 1 was the first official bombing *Jasta* to carry out night-bombing. Keller and his bomber crews carried out numerous missions, including one on Dunkirk in September 1917. Over 100,000kg of bombs were dropped, causing a large number of casualties and considerable damage which forced the British to move to the safety of Calais. For this attack Keller was awarded the Knight's Cross with Swords of the Royal Hohenzollern House Order, and then, on 4 December, he was awarded the *Pour le Mérite*.

Keller and his crews continued night-bombing, and on the night of 30/31

January 1918 made a surprise attack on Paris, causing great panic. Although anti-aircraft guns put up a great deal of fire, all the bombers returned safely. Keller's men continued to bomb the city, with the result that vital artillery had to be moved from the front to defend the capital. At the war's end Keller left the Air Service and became the head of the German *Luftreederei*, which was involved in airship transports.

In the early 1930s Keller was asked by Göring to help build new the Luftwaffe. He joined the Luftwaffe in 1935 with the rank of Oberst and was given command of *Bogohl* 154. He was promoted to Generalmajor in April 1936, then to Generalleutnant on I February 1938, and given the post of Commanding General of the East Prussian Luftwaffe. Keller held this post for one year, after which he was given command of the 4th Air Division HQ Brunswick. On 24 June 1940 he was awarded the Knight's Cross of the Iron Cross and promoted to Generaloberst. His next appointment was to Commander-in-Chief of *Luftflotte* I in Berlin and the Russian Front. At the end of the war he was Commanding Officer of the Luftwaffe Anti-Tank Service.

Keller died in Berlin on II February 1974 at the age of 92.

Leutnant Hans KIRSCHSTEIN (27 victories)

The son of the head of the Provincial Government, Hans Kirschstein was born in Koblenz on 5 August 1896. At the outbreak of war he volunteered for the 3rd Pioneer Battalion, and soon saw action on both the Eastern and Western Fronts. In the spring of 1915 his battalion was shipped to Macedonia, where he contracted malaria. He was sent back to Germany for treatment, and while in hospital he started to make enquiries about the German Army Air Service. He returned to Macedonia in December but in February 1916 he applied for a transfer to the Air Service and was accepted. He was sent to the flying school at Schliessheim at the beginning of May and after graduating was posted to FA19, a bomber squadron. He was one of the first pilots to carry out a bombing raid on Dover, for which he was awarded the Iron Cross 2nd Class. During the battles in Flanders he became notorious for his low-level strafing of tanks.

During 1917 Kirschstein flew with FA256 and FA3, and at the beginning of February 1918 he applied for a fighter posting and was sent to *Jastaschule* for training. On 13 March he was posted to *Jasta* 6, part of the Richthofen Circus. He opened his score on 18 March by shooting down a Sopwith Camel from 54 Squadron, and on 27 March he shot down two more. During April he brought down another three and in May he shot down ten, including three on the 15th and a double on the 16th, bringing his tally to sixteen. One of the aircraft he shot down on the 16th was flown by Captain T. Durrant, an eleven-victory ace. Also in May he was awarded the Iron Cross 1st Class, followed by the Knight's Cross with Swords of the Royal Hohenzollern House Order.

Kirschstein shot down eleven in June, including two on the 2nd and 3rd, three on the 5th and another two on the 14th. He was given command of *Jasta* 6 on 10 June, and by the end of that month had brought his score to twenty-seven. He was awarded the *Pour le Mérite* on 24 June 1918. Just one month later, on 11 July, Kirschstein took his personal Fokker to the aircraft park at Fismes for its annual overhaul, followed by Leutnant Johannes Markgraf flying a Hanover CLII. Just after take-off on the return flight the Hanover crashed, killing both men instantly. It was revealed at the board of inquiry that Markgraf had never flown a Hanover before and, as nothing else seemed to have contributed to the crash, it was considered to be pilot error.

Oberleutnant Otto KISSENBERTH (20 victories)

The son of a local businessman, Otto Kissenberth was born in Landshut, Bavaria, on 26 February 1893. After leaving school he was sent to study engineering at Grenoble University in France, then he went on to technical college in Munich. Upon graduating, he started work at the Gustav Otto Aircraft Works, where he took a diploma in aircraft engineering.

At the outbreak of war Kissenberth volunteered for the newly formed German Army Air Service as a pilot, being sent for training at FEA1 at Schliessheim, where he was awarded his pilot's certificate and badge. He was sent to FA8b in October as a reconnaissance pilot and early in March 1915 he was promoted to Vizefeldwebel. On 21 March, while on a reconnaissance mission, his aircraft was attacked by Allied fighters; he was seriously wounde but managed to get his aircraft back to his base. His injuries put him in hospital for over three months. On 8 July, once fully recovered, he was posted to FA9b, based at Toblach in Italy.

Kissenberth's first mission with his new unit was a long-range bombing raid on Cortina on 31 July. The raid was a complete success, raising his status dramatically among his fellow pilots. Shortly after this his *Jasta* moved to the Vosges Mountains area, where the lack of action soon prompted him to apply for fighter pilot training and in early 1916 he was accepted, being posted to *Jastaschule*. A number of his comrades had also requested fighter training, and on completion they were all posted to *Kek* Einsisheim. There followed several uneventful months. On 12 October 1916, while on a bombing raid on Oberdorf, Kissenberth shot down three enemy aircraft: two Maurice Farmans from *Escadrille* F123 and a Breguet V from 3 Naval Wing, RNAS. For his part in this raid Kissenberth was awarded the Iron Cross 2nd Class and commissioned Leutnant.

The Air Service was expanding and *Kek* Einsisheim formed part of *Jasta* 16. By the middle of July 1917 Kissenberth's score had reached six, including a balloon, and on 4 August he was given command of *Jasta* 23. He was awarded the Iron Cross 1st Class later the same month and continued to increase his score steadily, flying his Albatros DV with his personal insignia: a white and yellow edelweiss on the fuselage. He shot down six enemy aircraft in August, including a double on the 20th, and five in September. On 2 October he shot down his eighteenth enemy aircraft and on 5 December 1917 was awarded the Bavarian Military Merit Order 4th Class with Crown and Swords.

His twentieth victory was scored using a captured Sopwith Camel. But on 29 May 1918, still flying the Camel, he crashed on landing and was so severely injured he was told he would never fly again. In hospital Kissenberth was awarded the Knight's Cross of the Royal Hohenzollern House Order and on 24 July the *Pour le Mérite*. Two days after being discharged from hospital on 19 August he was promoted to Oberleutnant and made commandant of the Flying School at Schliessheim, where he ended the war. He was one of only a handful of pilots who wore glasses.

Kissenberth was killed while mountaineering in the Bavarian Alps on 2 August 1919.

Leutnant Hans KLEIN (22 victories)

Hans Klein was born in Stettin, Bavaria, on 17 January 1891. He had an uneventful childhood, but all that changed on the outbreak of war. Klein volunteered for the army and after training served with the 34th Infantry Regiment and then with the 210th Reserve Infantry Regiment, seeing action on the Western Front. He was in action almost immediately and his leadership qualities were rewarded with promotion to Unteroffizier and then to Feldwebel; he was also awarded the Iron Cross 2nd Class. In March 1915 Klein was given a field commission as Leutnant, just six months after volunteering. He continued to fight and by the end of the year had been awarded the Iron Cross 1st Class. He then applied for the German Army Air Service at the end of 1915 and was accepted.

In the spring of 1916 Klein began training, graduating in July. He was sent to a *Kek* where he was immediately in action. On 20 August he claimed a BE2c, but this was unconfirmed. Next he was posted to *Jasta* 4 in November, where he underwent intensive fighter training. In April 1917 he shot down six enemy aircraft, including a balloon on the 7th, one of the very first night victories of the war on the 8th and two each on the 11th and 13th; the second of these was flown by Captain L.L. Richardson MC, a seven-victory ace, and Second Lieutenant D.C. Wollon, both of whom became POWs. This brought Klein's tally to eight. May brought him only one victory but there were three in June, including two balloons, and in July he shot down another four, including two more balloons. On 13 July, with his score standing at sixteen, Klein was wounded in action in a dog-fight with 29 Squadron. He managed to get his aircraft back to base but was hospitalised. On his return to *Jasta* 4 at the end of August he was awarded the Knight's Cross with Swords of the Royal Hohenzollern House Order and given command of *Jasta* 10, which he took over on 27 September. By the end of November he had shot down twenty-two enemy aircraft and was awarded the *Pour le Mérite* on 2 December 1917.

At the beginning of 1918 Klein was promoted to Oberleutnant, but on 19 February 1918 he was brought down while flying a Pfalz DIII by Lieutenant N. Clark and Second Lieutenant A.T.W. Lindsay of 54 Squadron. Injuries to his right hand meant the loss of his thumb, thus ending his flying days.

After the Armistice Klein went back to school and gained an engineering degree, but he was enticed back into the newly formed Luftwaffe in 1935 with the rank of Major. From October 1939 to January 1940 he commanded JG53, and then he was promoted to Oberst and given command of a fighter area. In 1942 Klein was again promoted, this time to Generalmajor. He also became Duty Commander of all Luftwaffe fighters.

Klein died on 18 November 1944 as a result of a car accident, but his family suspected he had been murdered, as there appeared to be a bullet wound to his head.

Kapitänleutnant Rudolf KLEINE

The son of an infantry colonel, Rudolf Kleine was born in Minden on 28 August 1886. In 1901, after leaving school, it came as no surprise when he joined the army as a cadet; graduating as a Leutnant on 14 June 1905, he was posted to Infantry Regiment Nr 65, where he made rapid progress, becoming the battalion adjutant in 1910. But the infantry was losing its appeal and in the spring of 1913 he applied for and was accepted into the German Army Air Service.

In September Kleine was sent to the Herzog-Karl-Eduard Flying School at Gotha for pilot training and on passing out in June 1914 was assigned to Air Battalion Nr 3 at Cologne. In August he took part in one of the first battles of the war when he flew reconnaissance missions for the forces tasked with the capture of the fortress city of Liege. For his part in this Kleine was awarded the Iron Cross 2nd Class and promoted to Oberleutnant. For the next year he carried out numerous reconnaissance missions over enemy lines, including one in July 1915 when he was wounded. On recovering, he was promoted to Hauptmann and in December was posted to Ostend to take command of *Kagohl* I. His Silver Pilot's Badge must have been unusual as most *Kagohl* commanders were observers.

For the next year his unit made numerous scouting and reconnaissance missions over enemy lines, including one he made himself when he reported the massing of French troops for the battle of Champagne. His precise reports helped the German infantry prepare for the coming assault, thus reducing their casualties. For this Kleine was awarded the Iron Cross 1st Class and the Knight's Cross with Swords of the Royal Hohenzollern House Order. On 23 August 1916 Kleine was given command of Field Flying Unit 53, a post he held until June 1917, when he took command of *Kagohl* 3.

His primary assignment was the bombing of London, but he believed this served no real purpose and he made himself unpopular with the German High Command on this issue. He duly set about planning his first raid, deciding to bomb the port of Harwich and the Royal Naval Air Station at Felixstowe. On 4 July 1917 twenty-five Gotha bombers took off but, by the time they reached the coast, seven had turned back due to engine problems; the rest headed north towards their targets. On reaching Harwich one flight dropped its bombs, but only two fell on the town, the remainder dropping into the sea. The other flight attacked Felixstowe, with more success: a number of bombs fell on the naval base, destroying one aircraft and damaging several others, as well as killing seventeen and wounding twenty-nine personnel. All the Gothas returned safely, despite eighty-three Allied aircraft being sent to intercept them.

During the next few months Kleine planned and carried out six more raids, all on London, and on 4 October 1917 he was awarded the *Pour le Mérite*. On 12 December, during an attack on Ypres, his flight came under attack from Allied fighters. Kleine's bomber was raked from nose to tail, killing him and his crew. The aircraft came down in no-man's-land, the bodies being recovered by the Germans.

Hauptmann Hermann KÖHL

The son of a general, Hermann Köhl was born in Neu-Ulm, Bavaria, on 15 April 1888. Following in his father's footsteps, he joined the army as a cadet on leaving school, being commissioned Leutnant in Bavarian Infantry Regiment Nr 20. On the outbreak of war his regiment was posted to the Western Front and in October he was severely wounded. He did not return to the front until January 1915 when he was also awarded the Iron Cross 2nd Class. Having had enough of fighting on the ground, he applied for the newly formed German Army Air Service, much to the annoyance to his father. In the spring of 1915 Köhl was awarded his pilot's badge.

For the next few months he worked as a reconnaissance pilot and flew a number of sorties in support of the artillery. In October 1915 he was transferred to a new *Bombengeschwader* unit, which spent the next few months training in bombing techniques. In February 1916 they started their raids, which were not a great success at first. Then, on the night of 6/7 November, Köhl and his crew attacked the ammunition depot at Ceresy. The explosions could be seen and heard for miles and caused the French serious munition problems, albeit only for a short period. This raid earned Köhl the command of *Bogohl 7*.

Bogohl 7 was equipped with the Gotha C-type bomber and Köhl concentrated his attacks on railway stations and similar targets. He next attacked two of the French Army's largest ammunition dumps with devastating effect. Köhl was awarded the *Pour le Mérite* on 20 May 1918 for flying over 200 missions. He was one of only two *Bombengeschwader* commanders to be given this honour. On 20/21 May his squadron of Gothas flew at less than 200ft to attack the French ammunition depot near Blargies; the raid was a complete success. On another raid in July his Gothas came up against strong opposition in the air and Köhl's bomber was brought down behind enemy lines. Together with his crew, he set fire to the aircraft and they set off towards their own lines, but all three men were captured and sent to a POW camp. In September Köhl managed to escape and made his way back to Germany, but by this time the war was nearly over and he left the army.

Joining the Junkers Company, he helped create new civil air routes in Europe and within Germany. On 13 April 1928 he flew 36½ hours across the Atlantic and landed his Junkers W.33 *Bremen* on Greenly Island, Labrador. He was fêted in New York and Washington, putting German aviation back on the map.

Herman Köhl died on 7 October 1938, and is buried in Pfaffenhofen an der Roth, Germany.

Leutnant Otto KÖNNECKE (35 victories)

The son of a carpenter, Otto Könnecke was born in Strasbourg on 20 September 1892. After qualifying from the Building Trade School at Frankfurt-am-Main in 1909, he worked as a carpenter's assistant for two years, then in 1911 he volunteered for the military, joining Railroad Regiment Nr 3 at Hanau, in which he served for two years. Then in 1913 he was transferred to FEA4 at Metz and promoted to Unteroffizier. By the time war broke out in 1914 Könnecke was a qualified NCO flying instructor. He stayed at Metz training until December 1916, when he was posted to *Jasta* 25 in Macedonia.

Könnecke claimed his first victory on 9 January 1917, but this was unconfirmed. He opened his score officially on 5 February when he shot down a Henri Farman over north-west Moglia. The next day he shot down another Farman. In March he was posted to the Western Front as a reconnaissance pilot in AFP2, then in April 1917 he was sent to *Jasta* 5. It was here that he met two other NCO pilots, Fitz Rumey and Joseph Mai; later they were to become known as 'The Golden Triumvirate' and together they shot down a total of 109 enemy aircraft. By the end of 1917 Könnecke had raised his score to eleven. His Albatros DV was painted green with the *Jasta* 5 red-edged tail, and a black and white chequerboard marker with red edge just in front of the fuselage cross.

Könnecke continued to score and on 12 May 1918 was awarded the Golden Military Merit Cross (considered to be the enlisted man's *Pour le Mérite*). The following month he was commissioned Leutnant and on 20 July, with his score at twenty-three, he was awarded the Knight's Cross with Swords of the Royal Hohenzollern House Order. He shot down nine in August, including three each on the 8th and 9th. The *Pour le Mérite* came in September with his tally at thirty-two, making him one of only five airmen to have been awarded both the *Pour le Mérite* and the Golden Military Merit Cross. He ended the war with thirty-five victories.

In 1926 he joined the newly formed Lufthansa as a pilot, then in 1935 he enlisted into the Luftwaffe and became Commandant of the Fying Schools with the rank of Major.

He died in Germany on 25 January 1956.

Oberleutnant Heinrich KROLL (33 victories)

The son of a schoolteacher, Heinrich Kroll was born in Flatsby, Flensburg, on 3 November 1894. He was studying to be a teacher when the war broke out in 1914; he immediately volunteered to join the army and was sent to 'Queen Augusta Victoria' Fusilier Regiment Nr 86. However, he was sent to the front with Fusilier Regiment Nr 92 and with only basic training was soon in the thick of the fighting. Proving an able soldier, within a year he had been awarded the Iron Cross 2nd Class, and commissioned Leutnant in May 1915.

Late in 1915 he applied for a transfer to the German Army Air Service; he had to make a number of such requests before being accepted, and in January 1916 was sent to flying training school. After graduating in April he was posted to FA17 as a reconnaissance pilot, flying Rumpler two-seaters. At his own request he was sent to *Jastaschule* for pilot training, on completion of which he was posted to *Jasta* 9 at the beginning of November 1916.

On 24 November, during his first combat mission, Kroll's aircraft was shot up and he was forced to land, unharmed apart from his pride. He was awarded the Iron Cross 1st Class on 12 February 1917. At around this time he wrote about the difficulty of confirming victories, saying, 'It is difficult to get confirmation of a victory – especially the first one! It must be confirmed by our own ground troops.' On 1 May he opened his score by shooting down a Spad in his Albatros over Moronvillers. By the end of May he had shot down five confirmed and one unconfirmed, including on 25 May the French ace René Pere Dorme, who had shot down twenty-three Germans.

Kroll was given command of *Jasta* 24 on 1 July and shot down an SE5 of 56 Squadron on 20 July, then on 27 July he himself was shot down over Menin. He said of it later:

> I was shot down in flames – machine destroyed. I attacked 10 Spads and brought one out of the formation and circled with him from 4,000 to 2,500 metres. Then he suddenly turned tail and went on the defensive. He shot my inlet pipes and induction valve, resulting in a fire in the carburettor. I immediately turned off the petrol, switched off the ignition and dived steeply, the machine smoked and burned, my face full of fuel and oil, and I could not see through my goggles; tore them off at

800 metres and looked for a place to land. With the prop stationary I pulled over a row of trees, under a high-tension cable, took some telephones wires with me, and landed in an open field where the machine came to rest on its nose; it was completely broken.

The victor was probably Captain Clive Warman of 23 Squadron. Kroll escaped uninjured. He continued to shoot down enemy aircraft, ending 1917 with fifteen confirmed victories. The new year started well as he shot down another four aircraft in January and on 22 February, with his tally now at twenty, he was awarded the Knight's Cross of the Royal Hohenzollern House Order. On 17 March he shot down a Sopwith Camel flown by Captain C. Taylor, a ten-victory ace from 80 Squadron. On 29 March he was awarded the *Pour le Mérite* and promoted to Oberleutnant. During June he shot down five more, including two each on the 9th and 29th. On 18 June he was awarded the Knight's Cross 2nd Class with Swords of the Order of Albert. On 27 July Kroll was shot down in flames for a second time, but again he managed to walk away unharmed. On 25 May the first Fokker DVIIs arrived at his *Jasta*, and soon afterwards Kroll was given command of JG12. His last victory came on 9 August 1918 when he shot down an SE5a. His luck changed on 14 August when he was badly wounded in the left shoulder during a dog-fight. The injury was so severe it effectively ended his combat career, with thirty-three enemy aircraft to his credit.

Kroll joined the Hamburg police with the rank of Hauptmann after the war. After running his own business he joined the Hamburg Flying Club in 1928 and one year later closed down his business to become a commercial pilot.

Kroll died from pneumonia on 21 February 1930. He is buried in Ohlsdorf Cemetery, Hamburg.

Leutnant der Reserve Arthur LAUMANN (28 victories)

Arthur Laumann was born in Essen on 4 July 1894. He had an uneventful child-hood and on the outbreak of war he joined Field Artillery Regiment Nr 83. During the next two years he fought on both the Western and Eastern Fronts, was awarded the Iron Cross 2nd Class and was commissioned Leutnant. During 1916 and 1917 he made a number of requests to join the German Army Air Service, finally being accepted in August 1917.

On graduating in March 1918 he was posted to FA(A)265 (which his brother commanded) as a reconnaissance pilot. In May 1918 Laumann was posted to *Jasta* 66 as a fighter pilot, albeit with no training. He opened his score on 27 May by shooting down a Spad II while on patrol over Couvrelles, the same day as his CO Rudolph Windisch was shot down, never to be seen again. By the end of June his tally was four, all Spads. In July 1918 he shot down eleven, including three on the 18th, and was given command of *Jasta* 66. During August he shot down another twelve, including his only balloon on the 7th, three on the 9th, and two each on the 10th and 22nd.

On 14 August Laumann was posted as CO to *Jasta* 10, part of JGI, to replace Erich Löwenhardt, who had been killed. His Fokker DVII had a monogrammed interlocking 'AL' on the fuselage. Laumann was awarded the Iron Cross 1st Class and the Knight's Cross of the Royal Hohenzollern House Order on 29 September. On 25 October 1918, with his score at twenty-eight, he was awarded the *Pour le Mérite*. He was to stay in command of *Jasta* 10 until the end of the war. It is worth noting that he shot down all of his twenty-eight victories in just three months.

After the war Laumann worked as an instructor but he joined the newly formed Luftwaffe in 1935 and was given command of the new JG Richthofen Squadron. He survived the war and became the German air attaché to Yugoslavia and Greece.

Laumann died from a stroke in Munster on 18 November 1970.

Leutnant der Reserve Gustav LEFFERS (9 victories)

The son of a naval officer, Gustav Leffers was born in Wilhelmshaven on 2 January 1892. He was studying naval engineering before the war, being interested in all things mechanical. On its outbreak he immediately volunteered for the German Army Air Service, and was sent for pilot training to FEA2 at Aldershof during the autumn and winter of 1914. After graduating, he was posted to FFA32 on 14 February 1915 as a reconnaissance pilot flying LVG Bs.

On 21 March Leffers was promoted to Unteroffizier, to Vizefeldwebel in April and to Offiziersstellvertreter on 29 May, finally being commissioned Leutnant on 25 July. Then he was sent for fighter pilot training, graduating on 15 September, and was posted to FA32's fighter unit *Kek* Bertincourt. A new Fokker EIII Eindecker arrived on 5 November and Leffers was asked to fly it; unfortunately he crash-landed it, but walked away unhurt.

Leffers opened his score on 5 December when he shot down a BE2c of 13 Squadron over Achiet-le-Grand, and then on 29 December he brought down another BE2c, this time from 8 Squadron. By the end of March 1916 he had shot down four and been awarded the Iron Cross 1st and 2nd Class. His unit became officially known as *Jasta* 1 at the end of July, by which time he had been awarded the Knight's Cross of the Royal Hohenzollern House Order and two classes of the Oldenburg Friedrich August Cross.

Leffers shot down an FE2b on 9 July, followed by a Martinsyde G100 on 31 August. Three more Allied aircraft were brought down by the end of November, bringing his total to nine. On 5 November 1916 he was awarded the *Pour le Mérite*. His good luck came to an end on 27 December 1916 when he was flying a captured Nieuport and got involved in a dog-fight with FE2bs from 11 Squadron over Cherisy south-east of Wancourt; after a long fight he was shot down and killed. He was buried with full military honours in his home town of Wilhelmshaven.

Oberst Hermann von der LEITH-THOMSEN
(born Hermann THOMSEN)

Hermann Thomsen was born on 10 March 1867 in Flensburg, the son of a wealthy farmer. His early years were spent on the family farm until he joined the army in 1887 as a cadet, graduating two years later as a Leutnant in Pioneer Battalion Nr 9. The next few years were spent working on his organisational skills to such an extent that he was sent to the Prussian War Academy, after which he was appointed head of the newly formed Technical Section of the German Greater General Staff, a position he held until the outbreak of war.

In February 1914 he was transferred to the staff of Railway Regiment Nr 2. In May he was promoted to Oberleutnant and took part in the Battles of Tannenberg, Ypres and the winter campaigns in the Carpathian Mountains, being awarded the Iron Cross 2nd Class. At the beginning of 1915 he was appointed Chief of Field Air Forces within the German Army Air Service while still only a Major. The following year, and now with the rank of Generalleutnant, he was named Chief of Staff of the Air Service, a position he would hold until the end of the war. On 8 April 1917 Leith-Thomsen was awarded the *Pour le Mérite* and promoted to Oberst for his outstanding work within the Service, but as with von Hoeppner, it seems that the award did not go down well with some of his junior officers.

At the end of the war Leith-Thomsen took part in the deactivation of the German Army Air Service and was for a short time Head of the War Ministry Aviation department, resigning his position in August 1919. In the 1920s he actively participated in efforts to secretly build an air force in the Soviet Union, but he started to have sight problems which eventually led to him going blind.

In 1935, despite his blindness, he offered his services again and was given the rank of Generalmajor by Hitler personally, being assigned to the Luftwaffe section of the War Department. Two years later he was promoted to Generalleutnant and in 1939 to General der Flieger.

Leith-Thomsen died from a heart attack on 5 August 1942 and was buried in the Invaliden Friedhof, Scharnhorst Strasse, Berlin.

Hauptmann Leo LEONHARDY 'The Iron Commander'

Leo Leonhardy was born in Rastenburg on 13 November 1880. He joined the army as a cadet on leaving school in 1895. Five years later he graduated as a Leutnant and was sent to the East Prussian Infantry. In late 1913 he applied for and was accepted by the German Army Air Service, being posted to flying school at Johannisthal for pilot training.

Just ten days after starting his training he was involved in a mid-air collision. He managed to land his aircraft, but had suffered a fractured skull, a broken breastbone, a broken nose, two broken vertebrae, and broken legs. He was rushed to hospital, where they somehow managed to rebuild him. After more than a year in hospital Leonhardy was declared fit and was posted to the Inspectorate of Flying in Berlin. He managed to convince the High Command that he was fit for active duty and in the summer of 1915 was posted to the army airfield of the Southern Army in Muncacz. Within a very short time he started to fly again, albeit secretly. Then, after three months he applied for flying duties as an observer and was posted to Field Flying Unit 59.

With his pilot, Leonhardy carried out numerous artillery and infantry reconnaissance missions during 1916, for which he was promoted to Oberleutnant and awarded the Iron Cross 2nd Class. In September he was posted back to flying school for pilot training and on graduating in January 1917 he was sent to FA25. After flying a few missions Leonhardy took command of *Bombengeschwader* VI in the summer of 1917. He was soon promoted to Hauptmann and awarded the Knight's Cross of the Royal Hohenzollern House Order. He was to lead a number of raids against the Allies but his most notable one took place on 18 February 1918, when his unit attacked the airfield at Malzieuville, dropping over 300 bombs, destroying ten hangers, thirteen Nieuport fighters, and the fuel and ammunition dumps.

During the next three months he bombed a number of airfields. In May his squadron raided the French bomb and fuel dump at Etaples, causing much damage, and for this Leonhardy was awarded the Iron Cross 1st Class. On 2 October 1918, after completing eighty-three missions, he was awarded the *Pour le Mérite*.

After the war he returned to being an observer again, but this time it was to witness the destruction of German aircraft in accordance with the Versailles Treaty. He retired from military service in 1919 suffering from ill-health.

He died in Berlin on 12 July 1928.

Hauptmann Bruno LOERZER (44 victories)

Bruno Loerzer was born in Berlin on 22 January 1891. At 17 he joined the army as a cadet in Infantry Regiment Nr 112 (Prinz Wilhelm). He was later accepted to military school and after graduating in 1913 rejoined his regiment with the rank of Leutnant. It was while serving with this regiment that he met Hermann Göring, and they were to become inseparable. Loerzer soon became tired of the infantry and applied for the German Army Air Service, starting his flying training in August 1914. Graduating in October, he was posted to FA25 as a reconnaissance pilot, and was soon joined by Göring as his observer. They flew many missions together and were both awarded the Iron Cross 2nd Class on 7 March 1915. But by the end of June Loerzer was bored of observation missions and asked to be transferred to a fighter unit; he was sent initially to FA60, and from there to FA(A)203.

On completion of his training, Loerzer was posted to *Kek* Jametz, where on 21 March 1916 he shot down his first enemy aircraft, a Farman. On 31 March he shot down his second, and in late 1916 was posted to *Jasta* 5 and from there to *Jasta* 17. On 18 January 1917 he was given command of *Jasta* 26 and his score began to increase slowly, shooting down two in March, one in April and another two in August. Things started to pick up in September when he shot down five, followed by eight in October. By the end of 1917 he had been awarded the Iron Cross 1st Class and the Knight's Cross with Swords of the Royal Hohenzollern House Order. With his tally at twenty-three, Loerzer was awarded the *Pour le Mérite* on 12 March 1918 and nine days later was given command of *Jagdgeschwader* Nr III. He was now flying the new Fokker DVII, usually with *Jasta* 26, and his younger brother Fritz (who would end the war with eleven victories). Loerzer shot down eleven enemy aircraft between 23 March and 29 August, bringing his tally to thirty-four. He shot down five enemy aircraft in the first five days of September, plus two on the 16th, one on the 22nd and two more on the 26th. He flew a distinctive black-and-white striped aircraft throughout his career. On 10 October 1918 he was promoted to Hauptmann and by the war's end had shot down forty-four enemy aircraft.

During the Second World War he was promoted to Generalleutnant of the Luftwaffe and on 29 May 1940 was awarded the Knight's Cross of the Iron Cross. He was promoted to Generaloberst, and it seems clear that his friendship with Göring had some influence on the decision.

Loerzer died on 23 September 1960. He is buried in Ohisdorfer Cemetery (now called Haupt Cemetery), Hamburg.

Oberleutnant Erich LÖWENHARDT (54 victories)

The son of a doctor, Erich Löwenhardt was born in Breslau on 7 April 1897. He was educated at the military cadet school in Lichterfelde and at the start of the war he was posted to Infantry Regiment Nr 141. His regiment was sent to the Eastern Front and on 2 October 1914 he was commissioned Leutnant, aged just 17. At the end of October he was severely wounded, and awarded the Iron Cross 2nd Class. On release from hospital at the beginning of January 1915 he was sent to the Carpathian Mountains, and while in action there he saved the lives of five wounded soldiers, for which he was awarded the Iron Cross 1st Class, and transferred to the Alpine Corps. In October he applied for the German Army Air Service as an observer and this was granted. After nearly a year as observer he requested pilot training and was posted to FA(A)265 in early 1916. After another year in reconnaissance Löwenhardt undertook fighter pilot training early in 1917 and on graduating in March was posted to *Jasta* 10.

A week later he scored his first victory, shooting down an observation balloon over Recicourt on 24 March. By September he had raised his score to five but nearly got himself killed on the 20th when he was wounded in a dog-fight with a British fighter, managing a forced-landing near Roulers. Then, on 6 November, with his score at seven, his lower wing broke while in combat and again he had to make a forced-landing, this time near Winkel St Eloi.

The year 1918 started well for Löwenhardt. On 5 January he shot down another balloon, bringing the number of balloons he had brought down to five. Another two balloons followed on 12 and 15 January, together with a BF2b on 18 January. By the end of March he had raised his score to fifteen. One week short of his 21st birthday Löwenhardt was given command of *Jasta* 10, making him one of the youngest commanders in the Air Service. On 11 May, with his tally at twenty, he was awarded the Knight's Cross of the Royal Hohenzollern House Order, followed on 31 May 1918 by the *Pour le Mérite*. He was also awarded the Austrian Verdienstkreuz 2nd Class. During June he shot down eight, including two on the 28th. In July he shot down sixteen enemy aircraft, including doubles on the 2nd, 18th, 19th and 30th, and was also made acting commander of *Jagdgeschwader* I between 19 June and 6 July.

While leading a patrol on 8 August 1918 Löwenhardt encountered a patrol of Sopwith Camels, shooting three down himself, bringing his tally to fifty-one. He was now the second of only three Germans to shoot down fifty or more enemy aircraft. On the 9th he shot down two more Sopwith Camels. Then on 10 August 1918, just after shooting down an SE5a from 56 Squadron for his fifty-fourth victory, Löwenhardt collided with Leutnant Alfred Wentz from *Jasta* 11. Both pilots jumped but Löwenhardt was killed when his parachute failed to open properly. He is buried in Douai Cemetery, Rue de Sin-le-Noble, Douai, Nord, France.

Oberleutnant Carl MENCKHOFF (39 victories)

Carl Menckhoff was born in Herford, Westphalia, on 4 April 1883. He enlisted into the army in 1903 at the age of 20, but was invalided out within six weeks due to acute appendicitis. When war broke out he immediately volunteered, joining Infantry Regiment Nr 106 at Leipzig. Such was the demand for men that his training was a matter of collecting his uniform, cleaning his rifle and heading for the front line at Alsace-Lorraine and the battle of the Marne. He was an aggressive soldier and soon made his mark. Towards the end of 1914 he was selected for a mission behind enemy lines, dressed in a French uniform, for which he was awarded the Iron Cross 1st Class. Within months of this he was wounded and returned to Herford.

Menckhoff's recovery was very slow and after his convalescence he was deemed unfit for infantry duties. He immediately applied for flying duties. He took to flying naturally, being a good pilot, but on the ground his cavalier attitude towards army discipline and etiquette caused some problems. It was only the fact that his instructors maintained that his flying ability outweighed his indifference towards the rules that kept him in the Air Service. His first posting was to the Eastern Front, where he gained a great deal of flying experience but saw very little combat. Early in 1916 he was recalled for duty as an instructor, but it was soon clear that his aggressive nature meant he was better employed with a fighting *Jasta*, so he was posted to Flamers for a special course in air combat. On its completion in early 1917 he was sent to *Jasta* 3 in Flanders with the rank of Vizefeldwebel. Within days he shot down his first opponent, a Nieuport XXIII from 29 Squadron. Two more followed within a month, and by September he had shot down twelve. On 28 September he was himself shot down and wounded by a 56 Squadron pilot. After recovering, he threw himself back into the war and by the end of 1917 had raised his score to eighteen. In February 1918 he was commissioned Leutnant and given command of *Jasta* 72. He was also awarded the Knight's Cross with Swords of the Royal Hohenzollern House Order, followed by the *Pour le Mérite* on 23 April.

The next four months saw him raise his tally steadily and by 19 July 1918 it stood at thirty-nine. Then, just six days after his thirty-ninth victory, he met his equal when was shot down by Lieutenant William Avery from the US 95th Aero Squadron and taken prisoner. His impatience at being a POW was fuelled by his aggression and on 23 August he escaped and headed for Switzerland. One week later he crossed the border, remaining there until the end of the war. Seeing the state of Germany after the war Menckhoff decided to stay in Switzerland and set himself up in business.

He died in Switzerland in 1948.

Leutnant Max Ritter von MÜLLER (36 victories)

Max Müller was born in Rottenburg, Lower Bavaria, on 1 January 1887. After serving his apprenticeship as a locksmith, he joined the army in 1912 as a driver and soon discovered that he had a natural mechanical aptitude. Becoming noticed by his superiors, he was assigned as chauffeur to the Bavarian War Minister. Müller had by now acquired an interest in aviation and it is said that every time he opened the door for the minister he asked for a transfer to the German Army Air Service. His persistence paid off, probably more out of a desire to get rid of him than to help. Müller was posted to the army flying school at Schliessheim on 1 December 1913 and after four months' training he qualified as a pilot on 4 April 1914. He was posted to FAIb as a reconnaissance pilot and carried out observation work once the war started. On 18 August he was just taking off when his engine failed and his aircraft plunged to the ground, breaking both his legs. When he recovered he was soon back in the air, now with the rank of Offiziersstellvertreter. For an extremely dangerous photographic mission on 13 December 1915 he was awarded the Bavarian Bravery Medal in silver. By May 1916 he had flown over 160 missions and been awarded the Iron Cross 1st and 2nd Class and the Bavarian Military Merit Cross 3rd Class with Crown and Swords. By now one of the most experienced reconnaissance pilots in the air service, he applied for a transfer to a fighter *Jasta*. This was reluctantly granted and Müller was posted to single-seater training at Mannheim, where on 18 May 1916 he graduated and was sent to *Kek* B attached to FA32.

Müller was to remain with *Kek* B until 1 September, when he was posted to *Jasta* 2. On 10 October he shot down his first enemy aircraft, a DH2 from 24 Squadron, and by the end of 1916 he had brought down a total of five. A new unit, *Jasta* 28, was being formed and Müller and Leutnant Ray were sent to it to form its backbone. By the end of May, during which he shot down six enemy aircraft, his score had reached thirteen, making him the top scorer in the unit. On 26 August he was commissioned Leutnant in the Regular Army (usually these promotions were in the Reserve and this was the first time this had ever happened).

Müller went from strength to strength and by the end of September 1917 he had shot down twenty-seven enemy aircraft and been awarded the *Pour le Mérite*. After a well-earned leave he requested to return to his old unit to assist his friend Erwin Böhme in bringing the *Jasta* into shape. This was granted and he rejoined *Jasta* 2 on 3 November. Following the death of Walter von Bulow, and with his tally now at thirty-six, Müller took over command of *Jasta* 2 on 6 January 1918. Three days later his patrol was attacking an RE8 from 21 Squadron when two SE5s flown by Captain F. Soden and Captain R. Childlaw-Roberts jumped him from behind; his aircraft, reeling from the attack, spiralled down to earth in flames. When the flames reached the cockpit, Müller, who was not wearing a parachute, jumped to his death rather than burn alive.

The most highly decorated man in the German Army Air Service after von Richthofen, he was posthumously awarded the Knight's Cross of the Military Max Joseph Order, making him a knight; this was backdated to 11 November 1917. Some lists say he had shot down thirty-eight enemy: the war diary of *Jasta* 2 states that his last confirmed victory on 16 December 1917 was his thirty-eighth, but this figure seems to include two unconfirmed victories.

Oberleutnant Albert MÜLLER-KAHLE

The son of a Lutheran pastor, Albert Müller-Kahle was born on 29 June 1894. When the war began he enlisted as a cadet in Foot Artillery Regiment Nr 20, but after a year he requested a transfer to the German Army Air Service. In January

1916 he underwent training as an artillery spotter and observer, graduating in the spring of 1916. He was posted to *Flieger Abteilung* 202 and later served with FA215, FA47 and FA6, seeing active service on the Western Front in the Douai and Somme sectors, as well as along the North Sea coast.

Müller-Kahle became very proficient at calling in artillery fire on specific targets. The Germans had begun to use very heavy artillery mounted on railway tracks, and Müller-Kahle was able to direct their fire on to important strategic targets such as the coal mines at Bethune. He was so proficient at artillery spotting that he was selected in early 1918 to become an observer for the new long-range guns, named the *Kaiser Wilhelm Geschutz* intended to bombard Paris. These giant guns had originally been designed at the request of the navy and were manned by naval personnel, much to the disappointment of the army. They weighed nearly 300 tons and the barrels were over 100ft long.

At 7.15 am on 23 March one of the *Geschutz* guns, the *Pariskanone*, opened fire on Paris from 110 kilometres behind the German lines, with Müller-Kahle, it is said, acting as artillery fire controller. He climbed to 5,000 metres, then flew to within 40 kilometres of Paris to direct the fire. Despite coming under heavy anti-aircraft fire and machine-gun fire from British fighters, he managed to complete his task and return to base. During the five months the gun was used, its shells killed over a thousand Parisians, including one incident on Good Friday, 29 March, when a shell crashed through the roof of St Gervais L'Eglise, killing ninety-one worshippers and injuring over a hundred more. This act only made the Germans more hated, and before the bombardment of Paris was over a large number of Germans were against it. For his role as observer Müller-Kahle was awarded the *Pour le Mérite* on 13 October 1918.

Müller-Kahle survived the war and served in the Luftwaffe during the Second World War with the rank of Generalmajor. He committed suicide on 17 October 1941 at Brieg Military Airfield.

Leutnant Max Ritter von MULZER (10 victories)

The son of a doctor, Max Mulzer was born in Kimratshofen, Bavaria, on 9 July 1893. He enlisted into the army as a cadet in 1910 and graduated as an officer cadet in the 8th Cavalry Regiment on 10 July 1914. He was commissioned Leutnant on 13 December 1914 after taking part in some of the earliest battles of the war at Peronne, Lille and Epinal. He applied for the Army Air Service and was sent to the army's flying school at Schliessheim on 20 August 1915, where after just four months' training he graduated.

Mulzer was posted to FFA4b on 13 December and after two months was posted, with Oswald Boelcke and Max Immelmann, to FFA62. He scored his first, albeit unconfirmed, victory on 13 March 1916 when he claimed a Morane Saulnier and was awarded the Iron Cross 2nd Class. On 30 March he shot down a VFB5 from 11 Squadron over Wancourt. At the beginning of June he was posted to *Kek* Nord on the Eastern Front, where he made his presence felt by shooting down three enemy aircraft in nine days, bringing his score to six, for which he was awarded the Iron Cross 1st Class. In June Mulzer was posted to Douai on the Western Front and joined FFA32, then temporarily to *Kek* B, where he increased his score to eight, bringing with it the *Pour le Mérite*. He was the first Bavarian to be awarded it. On 26 September 1916 he was awarded the Knight's Cross of the Military Max Joseph Order, making him a knight. By 3 August he had ten enemy aircraft to his credit.

On hearing of the death of a close comrade he said: 'Immelmann died, Parschau died, Wintgens died. Now I am next.' Shortly afterwards, at the beginning of September 1916, he was assigned to AFP6 at Valenciennes to test a number of new aircraft. On 26 September he took off to test an Albatros DI but during the flight the aircraft suffered structural failure and crashed. Mulzer was killed. He was just 23 years old.

Leutnant Ulrich NECKEL (30 victories)

Ulrich Neckel was born in Gustrow on 23 January 1898. His early life was uneventful and he joined the army at 16 on the outbreak of war in 1914. He was sent for training as an artilleryman with the Holstein Field Artillery Regiment Nr 24. In January 1915, after completing his training, he was sent to the Eastern Front and was in action immediately. Within six months he had been awarded the Iron Cross 2nd Class. The conditions on the Eastern Front were having an effect on him and in September 1916 he applied for a transfer to the German Army Air Service; he was sent to flying school at Gotha in November and graduated as a pilot in February 1917.

Ironically, having joined the Air Service to get away from the Eastern Front, he was posted back to it as part of FA25. After flying a number of reconnaissance missions, he applied for fighter pilot training and in August was sent to the *Jastaschule* at Valenciennes. On 8 September he was posted to *Jasta* 12 on the Western Front and promoted to Gefreiter. He opened his score on 21 September by shooting down a Sopwith Pup from 46 Squadron, while on patrol over Monchy-le-Preux. By the end of the month he had also shot down a DH5 from 41 Squadron. His third victory came on 18 October 1917.

Such was his success in the first part of 1918 that he was commissioned Leutnant in April and awarded the Iron Cross 1st Class, and by the end of the month had shot down ten enemy aircraft. In July he shot down eight more, including two each on the 14th, 25th and 27th. He only shot down two in July, but four in August, including Major Charles D. Booker DSC, CO of 201 Naval Squadron, an ace with twenty-nine victories. Neckel was awarded the Knight's Cross of the Royal Hohenzollern House Order on 24 August. At the beginning of August he was transferred to *Jasta* 19 and in that month he raised his score to twenty-four; he was given command of *Jasta* 6 on 1 September 1918. Neckel continued to shoot down enemy aircraft and by 8 November had increased his tally to thirty; he was awarded the *Pour le Mérite* on 8 November 1918.

Neckel died from tuberculosis in Italy on 11 May 1928. He is buried in the Invaliden Friedhof, Scharnhorst Strasse, Berlin. In the 1930s Lufthansa named one of its Junkers 52 airliners after him.

Leutnant der Landwehr Friedrich NIELEBOCK

The son of a retired army officer, Friedrich Nielebock was born in Weissenwarthe on 4 July 1882. He was an outstanding all-round athlete at school, and later became an expert shot. He started his military service on 1 October 1899 as a volunteer reserve with a Foot Artillery Regiment at Lauenburg, being promoted to Leutnant in the spring of 1915. He soon realised that his training could best be used in the air as an artillery spotter. So he applied for observer training, and after a month's training he joined *Flieger Abteilung* 250 in October 1916.

For the rest of the war Nielebock was continuously at the front, and he flew 280 sorties. As an artillery spotter, he made 196 artillery fire missions, of which 134 were effective. Of 728 newly discovered battery positions, 331 could be attacked at once due to his work. He achieved superior results with directed low trajectory fire during day and night. During two days of strictly relying on Nielebock's reports, the commanding general of 18 Reserve Corps was able to take measures that were decisive for the success of subsequent battles. His work deserved recognition not only in the field of artillery observation, but also in the area of continued progress in artillery flying activity and in the cooperation between airmen and the artillery. He was badly wounded on 24 January 1918 during a reconnaissance mission. His *Pour le Mérite* was awarded on 2 June 1918 for his outstanding work.

After the war he returned to civilian life to earn professional qualifications in the building trade and became a director of a large company in Venezuela. He died there on 2 June 1962.

Oberleutnant zur See Theodor OSTERKAMP 'Uncle Theo' (32 victories)

The son of a forestry worker, Theodor Osterkamp was born in Duren in the Rhineland on 15 April 1892. He was studying forestry himself when the war started, and he volunteered for the Naval Flying Corps in August 1914, requesting to be trained as a pilot. However, the need for observers was greater at that time. On completion of his training he was posted to the Marine Flying

166

Detachment, where for the next two years he flew reconnaissance missions along the Belgian coast. Osterkamp's success was rewarded with the Iron Cross 2nd Class and a commission to Leutnant zur See in June 1916.

The routine nature of these missions soon started to get to him and in February 1917 Osterkamp applied for pilot training and was accepted in March. On graduating on 14 April, he was posted to MFJ I and the same week shot down his first enemy aircraft, a Sopwith, while on patrol over Oostkerke. By the end of July his tally was five and on 29 August he was awarded the Iron Cross 1st Class and the Knight's Cross of the Royal Hohenzollern House Order. His sixth victory came on 24 September when he shot down a Spad from *Escadrille* 31. Then on 15 October 1917 he was given command of MFJ I and promoted to Oberleutnant zur See.

While on a solo familiarisation flight in a new Fokker EV monoplane he was jumped by three Spads and had to bale out of his aircraft, landing behind his own lines. At the beginning of 1918 he spent some time reorganising his unit to make it more efficient and the results started to show. By the end of July his personal tally had risen to nineteen and by the end of August stood at twenty-three. On 2 September 1918 he was awarded the *Pour le Mérite*. His total stood at thirty-two by the war's end. After the Armistice he, along with Peter Jacobs and Gotthard Sachsenberg, fought the communists in the Baltic.

Osterkamp took part in the FAI International Tourist Plane Contest Challenge three times, finishing eleventh in 1930, twelfth in 1932 and fifth in 1934. In 1935 he joined the Luftwaffe, and was given command of *Jagdfliegerschule* Nr I in 1939. He held this post until taking over command of JG51 the following year. During the invasion of France Osterkamp was almost immediately in action, shooting down four enemy aircraft in May and two more during the Battle of Britain, including three Hurricanes and a Spitfire (so perhaps his final score should be thirty-eight). For this he was awarded the Knight's Cross of the Iron Cross on 22 August 1940. He was appointed commander of fighters in northern France and later Sicily, with the rank of Generalleutnant. He was very critical of the High Command and the way they were directing the air war, and because of this he was retired in 1944. It was probably only the respect that Luftwaffe pilots and ground crew held for him that prevented a worse fate.

He died in Baden-Baden on 2 January 1975.

Leutnant Otto PARSCHAU (8 victories)

The son of a land-leaser, Otto Parschau was born in Kluznitz, East Prussia, on 11 November 1890. On his 20th birthday he joined as a cadet Infantry Regiment Nr 151, and was commissioned Leutnant in 1911. However, he was already watching with great interest the new German Army Air Service. He started flying training in February 1913 at Darmstadt, then moved to Johannisthal and

Hanover, finally graduating on 4 July. Within a year he had won a number of awards, mostly for long-distance flights. At the Ostmark Flight Competition in 1914 he won the Honour Prize of Prince Friedrich Sigismund of Prussia.

At the start of the war Parschau applied for the Air Service and was immediately accepted. Due to his experience, he was posted to FA42, then to FA261. He was awarded the Iron Cross 2nd Class early in 1915 for his reconnaissance work. He was soon posted to KGI flying single-seat fighters. He opened his tally on 11 October 1915 while on patrol over Argonne, shooting down a Maurice Farman. Before the year was out he shot down a BE2c from 12 Squadron over Oostkampe. The observer, who was killed, was the brother of future ace Captain A. Cunningham-Reid DFC.

Two more aircraft fell to Parschau in early 1916, then in May he was appointed commander of KGI and was awarded the Iron Cross 1st Class and the Knight's Cross with Swords of the Royal Hohenzollern House Order on 3 July. On 9 July he was transferred to FA32 and shot down number eight the same day, and on the 10th he was awarded the *Pour le Mérite*. His last two victories were balloons. On patrol over Grevillers on 21 July 1916 his unit was attacked, and after a long fight Parschau was badly wounded in the head and chest. He managed to crash-land his aircraft but died later from his wounds.

Oberleutnant Paul Freiherr von PECHMANN

Paul Pechmann was born in Gaudismuhl on 28 December 1889. His military career started in Foot Artillery Regiment Nr 7. In 1911 he was promoted to Leutnant and when the war started he was posted to the *Flieger Abteilung Artillerie* at Wahn. It was with this unit he went to the front but he was soon transferred to FA6. Pechmann saw service on the Western Front as an artillery observer with FA215, and with FA217 on the Flanders front. During his three years with these units he flew 700 operational missions, was awarded the Iron Cross 1st and 2nd Class, and the Knight's Cross with Swords of the Royal Hohenzollern House Order.

In the summer of 1917 Pechmann was promoted to Oberleutnant and was appointed Commander of FA(A)215. On 31 July 1917 the Kaiser personally presented him with his *Pour le Mérite*, making him the first observer to be awarded it. In January 1918 he was given command of FA(A)217 and played an important role in the March offensive. One mission was carried out in fog and Pechmann flew so low that he was under constant ground fire. On his return his aircraft had over 150 bullet holes in it. He flew a number of missions without fighter escort and on one of these he and his pilot were so engrossed with directing the artillery fire that they failed to notice two Sopwith Camels closing in on them, and their aircraft was raked with fire. With their engine and radiator riddled with bullet holes, and the light fading, they managed to glide across the front line to safety.

Pechmann remained with his unit and was flying during the battle of Cambrai when the British made use of tanks. He was also responsible for resupplying the attacking German forces with food and ammunition from the air. After the war he started in the Air Service, retiring in 1920 with the rank of Hauptmann.

He died in Cologne on 11 May 1955.

Leutnant Fritz PÜTTER (25 victories)

Fritz Pütter was born in Dulmen, Westphalia, on 14 January 1895. He had an uneventful childhood and when the war started he joined a Westphalian infantry regiment, which was sent to the Eastern Front and was almost immediately involved in heavy fighting. In early 1915 Pütter was awarded the Iron Cross 2nd Class and commissioned Leutnant, and in October 1915 he transferred to Infantry Regiment Nr 370. February 1916 saw him apply for the German Army Air Service, and he was sent to FEA8 at Graudenz on 20 May.

On graduating from flying training he was posted to FA251 as a reconnaissance pilot on 9 December 1916. After just two months of this he requested fighter-pilot duties, and was sent to *Jastaschule*; on graduating, he was posted to *Jasta* 9 on 17 March 1917. His first victory came on 14 April when he shot down a French observation balloon over Suippes. By the end of the year he had shot down four more French balloons.

On 12 January 1918 he shot down his first aircraft, a Spad, but ended the day with another balloon. By the end of January Pütter had shot down two more aircraft and two more balloons, bringing his tally to ten. Pütter was awarded the Iron Cross 1st Class in February, although it was one of the quietest months his *Jasta* had had. Next he was given command of *Jasta* 68 on 3 February and spent the month familiarising himself with the pilots and aircraft. In March 1918 he shot down five more aircraft to bring his score to fifteen, including another balloon. He was awarded the Knight's Cross with Swords of the Royal Hohenzollern House Order at about this time. During April he shot down six more, including on the 6th the Frenchman P.A. Petit, himself an ace, and a double on the 7th.

Pütter continued to shoot down Allied aircraft, bringing his total to twenty-five by the end of May, including two on the 30th. On 31 May 1918 he was awarded the *Pour le Mérite*. His luck finally ran out on 16 July when, during a dog-fight, his tracer ammunition ignited in his aircraft, badly burning him. He managed to land and was rushed to hospital but died from his injuries on 10 August 1918. He is buried in Munster Central Cemetery.

Leutnant Lothar Freiherr von RICHTHOFEN 'The Butcher' (40 victories)

Younger brother of the famous Red Baron, Lothar von Richthofen was born on the family estate in Breslau on 27 September 1894. Before the war he joined a cavalry regiment and by the time hostilities began he was serving in 'Von Bredow's Own' Dragoon Regiment Nr 4. Inspired by his brother, he transferred into the German Army Air Service in late 1915. He served in KG4 on the Verdun and Somme fronts as an observer and gained his pilot's certificate in 1916.

On 6 March 1917 he was posted to *Jasta* 11, his brother's command, at Manfred's request. Lothar scored his first victory on 28 March 1917, a FE2b from 25 Squadron. His victory tally began to increase almost daily, and in April he shot down fifteen enemy aircraft (no wonder the British called it 'Bloody April'), including two each on the 11th, 13th, 14th, 29th and 30th, bringing his total to sixteen. For this he was awarded the Iron Cross 1st Class to go with his Iron Cross 2nd Class.

On 1 May Lothar continued his relentless, even reckless (he was dubbed 'The Butcher' by his brother) pursuit of the enemy, bringing down an FE2b from 25 Squadron. On 7 May 1917 he took off, having already shot down one aircraft earlier in the day and encountered fighters from 56 Squadron. A running battle followed in deteriorating visibility. Lothar took on a Sopwith Triplane before engaging two SE5s, one of which may well have been piloted by Albert Ball. Both men came down behind the German lines; Ball was killed, but Lothar survived. There is, however, some doubt as to exactly what happened. Richthofen's claim was for a Sopwith Triplane but Ball was flying an SE5, and the two are very unlikely to be confused – however, no British Triplanes were lost this day. German propaganda of the time made great play of their aces, and Richthofen may well have been ordered to take the credit for shooting down Ball.

With his total at twenty-two, on 10 May Richthofen was awarded the Knight's Cross with Swords of the Royal Hohenzollern House Order. Then on 13 May, after shooting down a BE2 for his twenty-fourth victory, he was wounded in the left hip by ground fire. He managed to land in a field on the German side of the line, and woke up in hospital the next day, when he was awarded the *Pour le Mérite*, five months after his brother. Lothar returned to flying on 24 September 1917 but did not score again until 9 November, when he shot down a BF2b from 8 Squadron over Zonnebeke, his first victory in the new Fokker Dr.I Triplane. His last victory of 1917 came on 23 November, a BF2b shot down west of Seranvillers.

The year 1918 started slowly and he did not score again until 11 March, shooting down a BF2b from 62 Squadron, followed the next day by two more. On 13 March he attacked a BF2, whose rear gunner took careful aim and put a burst of fire into the Fokker; the top wing began to shed fabric and then the whole centre section peeled away, causing Lothar to lose control. In the subsequent crash-landing Lothar's jaw was broken and to his discomfort was 'wired up' for months. However, he was promoted to Oberleutnant while in hospital and awarded the Bavarian Military Merit Order. He was still in hospital when he heard the news of his brother's death.

Returning to *Jasta* 11 on 19 July, he shot down his thirtieth opponent on the 25th, a Sopwith Camel from 73 Squadron. Ten more enemy aircraft were credited to him during August, including two on the 1st, three on the 8th, and two more on the 9th; his last two, both on the 12th, were Sopwith Camels from 209 Squadron and 73 Squadron, the latter flown by Captain John Summers MC MID, an eight-victory ace. Summers was captured.

The next day was 13 August 1918; he was, of course, acutely aware of the date, and could have no doubt justified a day on the ground but instead led his *Jasta* into action. He was just about to attack a two-seater when he was fired on from behind, being wounded in the leg. His Fokker DVII crash-landed on the old Somme battlefield. This time he did not return to combat before the war's end.

Lothar von Richthofen resumed flying after the armistice, and was killed in a flying accident on 4 July 1922. He is buried with his brother in the family grave at Garrison Cemetery, Schweidnitz (Westhain Section, Plot 77).

Rittmeister Manfred Freiherr von RICHTHOFEN 'The Red Baron' or 'Der Rote Kampfflieger' (80 victories)

The legendary 'Red Baron' was born on the family estate in Breslau on 2 May 1892. At 11 years old he entered the military school at Wahlstatt, before moving on to the Royal Prussian Military Academy. In 1911 he joined Uhlan Regiment Nr 1 'Kaiser Alexander III', and in the autumn of 1912 was commissioned Leutnant. At the outbreak of war he went with his unit to the Eastern Front, but within two weeks was transferred to the Western Front, being awarded the Iron Cross 2nd Class.

With trench warfare being established, the role of the cavalry was undermined so Richthofen applied for a transfer to the German Army Air Service in May 1915; after four weeks' training as an observer with FEA7 at Cologne and FEA6 at Grossenheim, he was posted to FA69 on the Eastern Front.

In August 1915 he was posted to *Brieftauben Abteilung Ostende* (Carrier Pigeon Unit, Ostend), the code-name for a long-range bomber unit. Richthofen's first aerial combat came on 1 September 1915; flying as an observer with Leutnant Zeumer, he spotted a Farman and ordered his pilot to close with it. Armed only with a rifle, he opened fire but scored no hits. A week later, flying again as observer with Leutnant Osteroth as pilot, they sighted a Farman and attacked. Richthofen fired 100 rounds from his machine-gun and the Farman crashed to earth behind the Allied lines; however, it was not confirmed.

On 1 October Richthofen was posted to Metz to join another bomber unit.

On the train he met Oswald Boelcke, who was already a legend. Inspired by this meeting, Richthofen asked Zeumer to teach him to fly. On his first flight he crashed on landing. But he persisted and on Christmas Day 1915 qualified as a pilot. He was again posted to the Eastern Front, and it was not until March 1916 that he would return to France, and even then he was flying a two-seater and not the fighter he so badly wanted. Richthofen adapted the Albatros with a machine-gun on the top wing so that he could fire from the pilot's seat.

On 26 April 1916 he shot down a French Nieuport over Douaumont, but again this was unconfirmed. On 1 September 1916 Richthofen was posted to *Jasta* 2 flying the new Albatros DIII. His first confirmed victory came on 17 September when he shot down an FE2b which landed behind the German lines; Richthofen himself was able to land nearby, and found the pilot mortally wounded and the observer dead. By the end of October his score was at six, and he had started to collect relics from each of them which he sent home for display. His tally continued to increase and by 22 November stood at ten. The next day he encountered his most famous opponent, Major Lanoe Hawker, a seven-victory ace and Victoria Cross holder. After an epic fight Hawker was hit in the head and crashed just behind the German lines. On 20 December Richthofen scored his first double in one day, bringing his tally to fourteen. His fifteenth confirmed victory on 27 December may have been over James McCudden (a future VC holder), who was believed at the time to have crashed, though in fact he got away. The British would have counted this as an 'out of control victory', but not in the German Air Service; Richthofen thought he saw it crash but this was not the case. Richthofen was by now flying an aircraft with an all-red fuselage and was well known to the Allies. After his sixteenth victory on 4 January 1917 Richthofen was awarded the *Pour le Mérite*, promoted Rittmeister and given command of *Jasta* 11. By 5 March his tally was twenty-three, including two doubles on 14 February and 4 March. On 6 March Richthofen was in action again. As he was lining up to attack an aircraft he was fired on from behind; his engine and petrol tank were hit and he was forced to break off the attack and land. He was unhurt and was back in the air later the same day, shooting down a BE2e from 16 Squadron. He had another double victory on 17 March. During April he shot down twenty-one enemy aircraft, including two each on the 2nd, 5th and 8th, three on the 13th and four on the 29th, bringing his total to fifty-two confirmed victories. No wonder the British called it 'Bloody April'. Then on 30 April he encountered Billy Bishop (another future VC holder) but neither man could get the better of the other.

On 26 June 1917 the German High Command grouped their *Jastas* into *Jagdgeschwaders* and Richthofen was given command of JGI, consisting of *Jastas* 4, 6, 10 and 11. Richthofen increased his score to fifty-seven by 2 July, but then on 6 July he was hit a glancing blow to the head when in combat with 20 Squadron; for a moment he was paralysed and blinded. However, he somehow managed to crash-land his Albatros near Wervicq. He returned to duty at the end of the month still suffering with headaches and dizziness, and was never really the same man again. His next flight and victory came on 16 August, when, despite feeling nauseous and dizzy, he shot down a Nieuport XXIII from 29 Squadron. By the end of November he had brought his total to sixty-three, by now flying his famous Fokker Dr.I. He would not score again until March 1918.

Regaining some of his old self, Richthofen brought down eleven aircraft in March 1918, including two on the 26th and three on the 27th, bringing his total to seventy-four. On 2 April, the day of his seventy-fifth victory, the Kaiser awarded him the last of his twenty-six decorations, the Order of the Red Eagle with Crowns and Swords. Shooting down another one on the 6th, two on the 7th and two on the 20th brought his final score to eighty.

On Sunday, 21 April 1918 Richthofen took off with his *Jasta* and headed toward the Allied lines. When they encountered fighters from 209 Squadron, a large dog-fight ensued. Lieutenant May, on his first combat mission, was told not to get drawn into the fight, but he was tempted and had a go at a Fokker triplane probably flown by Wolfram von Richthofen. May was soon in the thick of it, but, outclassed and with his guns jammed, he fell away and headed for the Somme valley.

Richthofen saw him and was soon on his tail, driving May down until they were only a few hundred yards above the Somme river, heading west. Brown, who was meant to be looking out for May, dived down from 3,000ft to help him. Richthofen was sure of his victory but May was so inexperienced it was difficult to predict what he would do next.

Closing in, Richthofen loosened his shoulder straps and crouched forward, focusing along the sights.

Brown, now diving down at a much faster speed than the triplane, got in a burst before overshooting it, later saying that he saw the pilot slump forward. Richthofen, alerted by the fire, looked up at Brown's Camel as he flew past, then, seeing him climb away, he returned his attention to May, still crouched at his guns. Richthofen was now only 150 yards behind May's Camel, and about 2 miles inside the British lines. Flying parallel to the Somme river, the two aircraft came upon rising ground along the north bank. A number of machine-gun positions spread across the whole area and the two aircraft were now well within their range.

Situated on the rise were Sergeant Cedric Popkin and Private R. Weston manning a Vickers gun, and they could see May and Richthofen coming straight at them from the direction of Vaux. The planes turned to the left of the machine-gun's position and were so close that Popkin had to wait for May to pass before he fired a seven-second burst at the triplane. Weston thought the aircraft faltered and wobbled. But still it clung to May's tail.

Next the two aircraft passed the positions of Gunner Robert Buie and Gunner William Evans, going almost directly over Buie. He and Sapper Tom Lovell saw Richthofen looking around, his triplane hard on May's tail. They could not fire for fear of hitting May; they did, however, see Richthofen firing short bursts at the Camel. Then Evans opened fire with his Lewis gun, followed by Buie. As Buie fired, splinters flew off the triplane, which jerked and banked hard, seemingly to avoid the fire. Evans fired again. At the first shots Richthofen tore off his goggles and threw them out. He had done this before when he was shot down in July. For a second or two the engine throttled up, then it died down, finally cutting out.

Richthofen then came under rifle fire from a group of men manning a reserve trench and Popkin got in another burst as the triplane seemed to turn to attack the gunners and believed he hit it. The triplane wobbled, side-slipped and slowed to near stalling speed as it slid to the ground. About half a mile to the west Brown reappeared; getting a clear view of the stricken triplane, and thinking its end was due to his fire, he later claimed Richthofen as his victory.

Within seconds the triplane crashed into a beet field alongside the Bray–Corbie road, the undercarriage breaking after the aircraft bounced 10ft into the air and fell back to the ground. Richthofen was found mortally wounded with a broken nose, cut lip and a single bullet wound to the body. But who had fired it? Was it Evans, Buie or Popkin with their machine-guns, or an unknown rifleman in the reserve trench? Clearly Brown could not have fired the fatal round, as apart from anything else the triplane was still under control some time after his attack. We will almost certainly never know for sure.

Manfred von Richthofen was buried with full military honours at Bertangles but in 1920 his remains were moved to the German Cemetery at Fricourt, Plot 4, Row 7, Grave 12. Then in 1925 he was re-interred in the Berlin Invaliden Friedhof. Now he rests with his brother in the family grave at Garrison Cemetery, Schweidnitz (Westhain Section, Plot 77).

Leutnant der Reserve Peter RIEPER

Peter Rieper was born near Hanover on 13 April 1887. He studied chemistry and qualified as a doctor in 1912. The following year he enlisted into the Army Reserve for one year's service, but in August 1914 transferred to Field Artillery Regiment Nr 74 in the Regular Army with the rank of Vizewachtmeister. His regiment was soon in the thick of the fighting and Rieper was wounded. On his return to duty he applied for training as a balloon observer, and due to his training as an artillery spotter he was accepted.

On qualifying, Rieper was posted to *Ballonzug* 19 as a spotter and intelligence gatherer, and soon found out how dangerous it was to be in balloons. On 17 October 1915 he was in a balloon at a height of 1,300 metres when he was told that two enemy aircraft were approaching. The ground crew opened fire on them to little or no effect and as an incendiary rocket punctured the balloon Rieper decided it was time to jump. Swinging his legs over the side he lowered himself out of the basket and was about to jump when he noticed one of the parachute lines had snagged. So he climbed back into the basket, freed the line and then plunged head first over the side. Seconds later the blazing balloon swept past him, the heat searing him as it went.

By 1916 Rieper had been promoted to Leutnant der Reserve Balloon Observer, but had another close call in the spring when his balloon was attacked by four enemy fighters. Busy directing artillery fire on an enemy rail marshalling yard, he failed to notice the enemy aircraft approach; armed only with his rifle, he returned fire but was no match for the machine-guns. Luckily Max Immelmann came to his rescue and saw off the fighters, which allowed Rieper's artillery spotting to result in the destruction of the marshalling yards.

His luck ran out on 3 June 1918 when Allied gunfire opened up and his balloon began to burn. In the barrage of fire Rieper was badly wounded in the shoulder. He decided to jump, which he did with only seconds to spare; landing in front of the German lines, he was dragged along by strong winds with such force that he broke his leg and suffered severe injuries to his arm. In hospital his arm was amputated and after two months he was declared unfit for active service, being then posted to the *Luftschifferschule* in Namur as an instructor. In July 1918 he was awarded the *Pour le Mérite* for his dedication to duty, the only balloon observer to be awarded it.

Rieper survived the war and went into business. He died on 21 March 1942.

Oberleutnant Friedrich 'Fritz' Ritter von RÖTH (28 victories)

Friedrich Röth was born into a military family in Nuremberg on 29 September 1893. Commonly known as Fritz, he started his military career at the outbreak of war in 1914, volunteering for Bavarian Field Artillery Regiment Nr 8. Due to his family background he was immediately promoted to Unteroffizier. He was seriously wounded almost immediately and spent nearly a year in hospital. On 29 May 1915 he was commissioned Leutnant while still in hospital. It was also at this time that he started to think about the German Army Air Service. After recovering, he applied for pilot training, but after just a few weeks he was injured in a flying accident which put him back in hospital for almost another year. Finally in February 1917 he qualified as a pilot and was posted to FA(A)296b on 1 April.

Röth carried out a number of reconnaissance missions and on 11 June was awarded the Bavarian Merit Order 4th Class with Swords. On 10 September he was posted to *Jastaschule* I and trained as a fighter pilot. He was sent to *Jasta* 23 on 4 October, and was awarded the Iron Cross 1st Class on 1 November for his reconnaissance work. Then on 25 January 1918 he shot down three observation balloons within ten minutes. On 25 February he was awarded the Knight's Cross with Swords of the Royal Hohenzollern House Order.

With his score now at ten, nine of which were balloons, Röth took command of *Jasta* 16 on 24 April. On 29 May 1918 he shot down an unheard of five balloons in fifteen minutes. Unusually for him, in July he shot down three airplanes, then in August he shot down an SE5a on the 12th, followed by three balloons the next day, and was promoted to Oberleutnant on 19 August. Having reached twenty-three victories, he was awarded the *Pour le Mérite* on 9 September 1918. By the end of the war his total stood at twenty-eight, of which twenty were balloons, all of them scored in multiple numbers within minutes of one another. At the war's end, Röth could not come to terms with Germany's defeat, believing that his country was invincible. On New Year's Eve 1918 he committed suicide. He is buried in an unmarked grave in St Joannis Cemetery, Nuremberg. He was posthumously awarded the Knight's Cross of the Military Max-Joseph Order in 1919, backdated to 25 January 1918, for shooting down three balloons in ten minutes, thus making him a knight.

Leutnant der Reserve Fritz RUMEY (45 victories)

Fitz Rumey was born in Konigsberg, Bavaria, on 3 March 1891. On leaving school at 16 he became an apprentice roof slater, and in 1911 volunteered for Infantry Regiment Nr 45. At the outbreak of war Rumey was sent with the 3rd Grenadier Regiment to the Eastern Front and was immediately in action. During the next year he distinguished himself and was awarded the Iron Cross 2nd Class.

At the beginning of 1915 Rumey applied for a transfer to the German Army Air Service and on 5 August was posted to the flying school at Hundsfeld, near Breslau. On graduating, he was sent to FA(A)219 as an observer. With a year of reconnaissance missions completed, Rumey applied for pilot training, and was posted to *Jastaschule* on the Western Front in early 1917. On completing his training, he was sent to *Jasta* 2 in May and then to *Jasta* 5 on 10 June 1917 with the rank of Vizefeldwebel. At *Jasta* 5 he met two other NCO pilots, Otto Könnecke and Joseph Mai; later they became known as 'The Golden Triumvirate' and together they shot down a total of 109 enemy aircraft. Rumey's first victory came on 6 July, a balloon shot down over Boursies. On 25 August 1917 he was involved in a dog-fight with some British aircraft; he was wounded and only just managed to get back to his airfield. But within two weeks he was back in the air. By the end of 1917 he had shot down five enemy aircraft. On 22 November he shot down Captain G.B. Crole MC, a five-victory ace.

In January 1918 Rumey shot down three, with another one in February and four in March. By the end of May 1918 his score stood at twenty-one and he had been awarded the Golden Military Merit Cross (considered to be the enlisted man's *Pour le Mérite*). On 7 June he shot down Lieutenant J.J. Davies, an eight-victory ace, and then on 26 June 1918 he shot down five-victory ace Lieutenant E.C. Eaton of 65 Squadron. For this he received the Bavarian Military Merit Order 2nd Class with Swords. At the end of June he was commissioned Leutnant. He continued to score and with his tally at twenty-nine was awarded the *Pour le*

Mérite on 10 July 1918, making him one of only five airmen to have been awarded both the *Pour le Mérite* and the Golden Military Merit Cross.

Rumey continued to score against the British, shooting down sixteen during September, including three each on the 16th and 26th. The next day he shot down his last enemy aircraft, a Sopwith Camel, at 12.05 east of Marquion. The same day Rumey is said to have been in a collision with Lieutenant G.E.B. Lawson, but Lawson's action was timed at 09.30, and Rumey's last victory was claimed at 12.05. Rumey did, however, parachute from his damaged aircraft on this day - and this must have happened on a later patrol as he had already put in the claim for victory number forty-five — but he was killed when his parachute failed to open. It is not known where he is buried.

Oberleutnant zur See Gotthard SACHSENBERG (31 victories)

The son of a wharf owner, Gotthard Sachsenberg was born in Dessau on 6 December 1891. His early years were uneventful until he joined the Imperial German Navy in 1913 as a cadet, spending most of his first year aboard the battle-ship *Pommern*. Almost immediately the war started he volunteered for flying duties in the newly formed German Naval Air Service. He wanted to be a pilot but the need for observers was greater, and after training he was posted to Marine FA2. After only ten missions as an observer Sachsenberg was awarded the Iron Cross 2nd Class in 1915, still with the rank of Fähnrich. In January 1916 he was commissioned Leutnant, and with it came a posting to training school as an instructor. In the meantime his application for pilot training had been approved and he was sent to the *Jastaschule* at Mannheim in February. With his training complete, Sachsenberg was posted back to his old unit flying Fokker EIIIs from Mariakerke.

Due to the lack of activity in this area he was not able to shoot any aircraft down for the remainder of the year, but he did continue to carry out reconnais-sance missions. From 1 February 1917 he commanded MFJ I, then on 1 May he shot down his first two enemy aircraft, a Belgian Henri Farman over Dixmude and a Sopwith 1½ Strutter over Oudercapelle. On 20 August, with his tally at six, Sachsenberg was awarded the Knight's Cross with Swords of the Royal Hohenzollern House Order. By the end of the year his tally was eight and he had also been awarded the Iron Cross 1st Class, the House Order of Albert the Bear, Knight's 1st Class with Swords. The year 1918 was a good one for Sachsenberg. He scored steadily, including three on 16 July, and by August his tally stood at twenty-four, including two each on the 12th and 16th. His *Pour le Mérite* was awarded on 5 August. More honours came his way with the Friedrich Cross of Anhalt 1st and 2nd Class, the Friedrich-August Cross 1st and 2nd Class of Oldenburg and the Hanseatic Cross of Hamburg. He shot down six more in

October, including three on the 23rd. By the end of the war he had shot down thirty-one enemy aircraft.

In 1919 Sachsenberg was given the task of forming a Marine *Freikorps*, MJGr I, for operations in the Baltic, with Theodor Osterkamp and Peter Jacobs. Fighter Squadron 'Sachsenberg', as it became known, was very successful, but political pressure saw it returned and disbanded within seven months.

After the war Sachsenberg continued in aviation and helped the development of air traffic control in Germany. He also became an anti-Nazi member of parliament.

Sachsenberg died from a heart attack in Bremen on 23 August 1961.

Leutnant Karl SCHÄFER (30 victories)

The son of a silk cloth manufacturer, Karl Schäfer was born in Krefeld, Bavaria, on 17 December 1891. In 1909 he served his compulsory year in *Jäger* Regiment Nr 10. After this he went to Paris and was still there when the war broke out; with difficulty he returned to Germany and was immediately assigned to *Jäger* Regiment Nr 7. His regiment went into action within weeks of him joining, and in September he was awarded the Iron Cross 2nd Class and promoted to Vizefeldwebel. Just days after receiving the award he was badly wounded, spending the next six months in hospital. It was while there that he first had the idea of joining the Air Service. On his release from hospital Schäfer returned to his unit, and in May 1916 was commissioned Leutnant, awarded the Iron Cross 1st Class and the Military Merit Order 4th Class with Swords from Bavaria. Then he asked to be transferred to the German Army Air Service and was accepted. After only two months' training, he passed out of the flying school at Koslin.

On 30 July 1916 Schäfer was sent to KG2 on the Eastern Front. Over the next six months he flew more than fifty reconnaissance and bombing raids. He dropped over 5,000lb of bombs in the area of Wolhynien, inflicting heavy casualties. Then in January 1917 his unit was transferred to the Western Front and he joined *Kasta* 2, part of KG3. He shot down his first enemy aircraft on 22 January, a French Caudron over Pont-a-Mousson. Next he was posted to Richthofen's *Jasta* 11 on 21 February and made his presence felt by shooting down five aircraft in five days during March. During 'Bloody April' he shot down fifteen enemy aircraft, including two each on the 6th, 11th, 14th and 25th, bringing his tally to twenty-three. He was awarded the Knight's Cross with Swords of the Royal Hohenzollern House Order and the *Pour le Mérite* on the 26th, and to cap it off was given command of *Jasta* 28. His victory on 13 April was over Captain L.L. Richardson, a seven-victory ace, and his observer Second Lieutenant D.C. Woollen, both of whom became POWs. During May Schäfer raised his tally to twenty-nine and on 4 June shot down a DH4 from 55 Squadron to bring his score to thirty. On 5 June 1917 he took off with his *Jasta* and engaged fighters from 20 Squadron, but just after 4pm he was shot down and killed by Lieutenant H.L. Satchell and his observer T.A. Lewis. He had no bullet wounds, but it is said that every bone in his body was broken.

Schäfer is buried in Krefeld.

Oberleutnant Eduard Ritter von SCHLEICH 'The Black Knight' (35 victories)

Eduard Schleich was born in Munich on 9 August 1888. Very little is known about his early life, but his military career started in 1908 when he joined Bavarian Infantry Regiment Nr 11 as a Fahnrich. Two years later he was commissioned Leutnant and put on the reserve list. On the outbreak of war in 1914 he was called up to rejoin his old regiment and was in the thick of the action within months. He was severely wounded on 25 August and sent to Munich. While recovering, he decided to apply for transfer to the German Army Air Service; being accepted, he was posted to FEAI at Schliessheim in May 1915, completing his training on 11 September.

His first posting was to FA2b on 24 October. In February 1916, after a number of reconnaissance flights, Schleich was wounded in combat with Allied fighters. On his return in September he was suddenly put in command of *Fliegerschule* I, where he became a flying instructor. He was then transferred to *Schutzstaffel* 28 as its commanding officer on 12 February 1917. But a shortage of aircraft meant he was unable to lead his unit in the air. Within weeks he had written furious letters to Fifth Army HQ requesting a transfer to a fighter unit. Although he had himself been an instructor, Schleich was sent to the fighter training school at Famars. After just two weeks his instructor announced that he could teach him no more and suggested he be sent to a fighter unit.

Posted to *Jasta* 21 on 21 May 1917 with the rank of Oberleutnant, Schleich was given temporary command of the unit. He scored his first victory on 25 May 1917 when he shot down a Spad VII flown by the French 43-victory ace Sous-Lieutenant Rene Pierre Marie Dorme over Moronvillers. Dorme's gold watch was later dropped over a French airfield with a note saying he had died bravely. Schleich's second victory came on 17 June when he shot down a 1½ Strutter and then he was given command of the unit permanently – which is when his problems started. *Jasta* 21 was a Prussian unit that had just been redesignated a Saxon unit, and was now commanded by a Bavarian. This became a source of embarrassment to the senior Prussian members of the old military guard who still held high positions in Germany. *Jasta* 21 was closely watched and any infringement, no matter how small, was leapt upon by Schleich's superiors.

Over the next four months Schleich shot down twenty-three enemy aircraft, bringing his score to twenty-five. However, his unit was not doing so well. After one incident involving three of his pilots, which earned him a severe reprimand,

179

Schleich assembled his men and threatened that they would be removed from the unit in disgrace if their performance did not improve – and within days the pilots starting scoring victories. This helped ease the pressure from above. In July 1917 his friend Leutnant Limpert was shot down and killed. In his honour Schleich had his Albatros painted black with a white band around the fuselage, and he soon became known to the Allies as 'The Black Knight'. During September Schleich shot down seventeen enemy aircraft, including two each on the 3rd, 16th and 21st, bringing his tally to twenty-five.

Although a unit commander, Schleich was also prone to acts of foolishness. Once, when a Spad fighter had been forced down intact, Schleich had it painted in German markings and took it up, joining a French squadron on patrol. It was some minutes before the French pilots realised what was happening, but before they could react he headed back for his own lines, only to be fired on by the German anti-aircraft gunners. He made it back safely and was again severely reprimanded by Fifth Army HQ. Just after his twenty-fifth victory Schleich was taken ill with dysentery and rushed to hospital in a serious condition. Some months later, while recovering, he was informed that he had been removed from *Jasta* 21 as it had been decreed that no Bavarian should serve in a Prussian unit, let alone command one.

On 23 October 1917 Schleich was given command of the all-Bavarian *Jasta* 32, his tally by now having risen to thirty-five. He was awarded the *Pour le Mérite* on 4 December but did not receive the Royal Hohenzollern House Order that usually accompanies it. The following month he was given command of *Jastaschule* I and on 15 March 1918 *Jagdgruppe* 8, consisting of *Jastas* 23, 34 and 35. It was not until the end of 1918 that he learned he had also been awarded the Knight's Cross of the Military Max-Joseph Order, the Saxon Knight's Cross, the Albrecht Order 2nd Class and the Bavarian Military Merit Order 4th Class with Crown and Swords. With these awards came promotion to Hauptmann and the nobility title of 'Ritter'. Schleich given command of *Jasta* 21 in October, with which he shot down his last enemy aircraft on the 1st. The year 1919 saw Schleich with an aviation unit of the Bavarian State Police fighting against Communist revolutionaries, and the following year he served as a member of the Armistice Committee.

In the 1920s Schleich joined Lufthansa, staying with them until 1933, when he joined the Luftwaffe; he even visited Britain. He then took part in the Spanish Civil War as part of the Condor Legion. During the Second World War Schleich rose to the rank of Generaloberst, commanding combat units. He held a post in occupied Denmark, before being appointed General der Fliegers in Norway. He was taken prisoner by the Allies at the end of the war and interned in a POW camp for high-ranking officers. While there, he died from a heart condition on 15 November 1947. He is buried in Dissen am Ammersee in Germany.

Leutnant Wilhelm Paul SCHREIBER

The son of a pharmacist, Wilhelm Schreiber was born on 21 December 1893 in Bramsche. He studied law before joining Field Artillery Regiment Nr 62 at the outbreak of the First World War. Then he transferred to Field Artillery Regiment Nr 20, serving with it on all the major fronts for the next two years, being awarded the Iron Cross 2nd Class. Then in October 1916 he applied for a transfer to the German Army Air Service and was sent to *Armee Flugpark* I for evaluation as an observer. At the beginning of November he was posted to the observers' school at Konigsberg, East Prussia, where he completed the six-month course in three months.

On 14 February 1917 he was posted to FA(A)221 for operational duties over the Somme. The next day he met his pilot, Unteroffizier Heinrich-Ernst Schäfer, and almost immediately they were sent out on low-level reconnaissance missions. Their first mission nearly ended in disaster when they were jumped by ten British fighters and their Albatros was raked with machine-gun fire, forcing them to make an emergency landing. Over the next few months Schreiber and Schäfer completed numerous reconnaissance and support missions, including one bombing raid on a British airfield near Bailleul, where they dropped twenty-five bombs. For this daring raid Schreiber was awarded the Iron Cross 1st Class and Schäfer was promoted to Vizefeldwebel.

For the remainder of 1917 they carried out many reconnaissance and support missions, seemingly flying lower and lower every time. On 7 March 1918 Schreiber was awarded the Knight's Cross with Swords of the Royal Hohenzollern House Order. Two weeks later their armour-plated Albatros was hit by armour-piercing bullets and the fuel tank was punctured, forcing Schäfer to make an emergency landing. This time the aircraft was a write-off; it was replaced with an armour-plated Junkers JI, an all-metal aircraft.

When the 1918 German offensive started in March, Schreiber and Schäfer continued to fly longer and lower missions over enemy territory, bringing back information about enemy troop movements and spotting for the artillery. So good was their information that Schreiber was recommended for the *Pour le Mérite* and Schäfer for the Golden Military Merit Cross (the NCO's *Pour le Mérite*). Then, on 29 May 1918, while flying at treetop height, their Junkers came under heavy ground fire. Schäfer was hit in the head and the aircraft went crashing into the ground. (It was found later to have over 200 bullet holes in it.) Both men were killed.

Both men's awards were approved by the Kaiser on 8 June 1918, and Schäfer's family duly received his Golden Military Merit Cross. However, Schreiber's *Pour le Mérite* was never presented as, although it had been approved by the Kaiser, it could not actually be awarded posthumously. His family received the following letter from the commander of 17th Army:

> The exceptionally vigorous spirit, the constantly driving forward characteristics of the fallen fighter which he displayed time and time again on numerous missions

over the lines and which led to his great accomplishments, were the determining factors in the Supreme Commander's recommending your son for the highest of all awards, the *Orden Pour le Mérite*. It is an honour-laden duty for me to tell you that it has pleased his Majesty, the Emperor and King, on June 8 to award your son the *Pour le Mérite*.

Under the regulations, unfortunately, there can be no transmittal of the high award if the bestowal of the award has been made posthumously. May it, however, be of some consolation to you in your great sorrow that your son, who fell as a brave hero for his Fatherland, was considered deserving of the highest of all recognition by the Supreme War Lord because of his outstanding service.

Schreiber is buried in the Military Cemetery at Menen, Belgium, Block M, Grave 953.

Fregattenkapitän Peter STRASSER

Peter Strasser was born on 1 April 1876 in Hanover. Following the family tradition, after leaving school he joined the Navy as a cadet at the age of 15. His initial training was aboard the training ships *Stein* and *Moltke*, and on graduating he was sent to the Navy School in Kiel. He received further training in gunnery on the ships *Mars* and *Blucher*. When his training was completed, he was commissioned Leutnant zur See.

In 1897 Strasser was posted to the cruiser *Hertha* and spent the next two years touring East Asia. He returned to a shore base before being posted to the gunboat *Panther* as gunnery officer from 1902 to 1904. After a short period on another shore base, he was sent to the battleship *Westfalen*, where he won the *Kaiserpreis* for the best gunnery officer in the service. He was a dedicated professional seaman, and a strict but fair disciplinarian. In 1910 he was posted to the battleship *Mecklenburg*, where his reputation preceded him. He won the *Kaiserpreis* for the next three years, during which time he applied for a transfer to the navy's aviation wing. This was refused as he was considered too valuable as a gunnery officer. Then on 1 September 1913 Strasser was ordered to report to naval headquarters in Berlin, where he was shown into the office of a senior naval officer and told of the demise of Leutnantkommander Matzing in the crash of Zeppelin L1. He was then told that he would be put in command of the naval Zeppelins. Strasser said he had no knowledge of airships, but was told that all the most experienced airship men had been killed on the L1, and that new crews would have to be trained. The High Command needed a dedicated disciplinarian and an officer of strength of character to see it through.

Less than a month after taking over his new command, Strasser's mettle was tested when the airship L2 exploded in mid-air, killing all those aboard. By careful interrogation of all the witnesses, Strasser found the cause and arranged for modifications to all future airships. At the start of the war the Naval Air Division had only one airship, the L3. Strasser immediately requested new airships to be built, making sure the High Command was aware of their ability to fly over any blockade the British could impose and to bomb London.

On 19 January 1915 the first raid on Britain took place. The L3, L4 and L6, with Strasser aboard, took off but the L6 had to return due to engine problems. The remaining airships bombed Great Yarmouth. Although little damage was done, the British suddenly found they were vulnerable to attack at home. Strasser was promoted to Korvettenkapitän for his part in planning the raid and was soon to build a fleet of airships that would carry out over 200 raids and over 1,000 reconnaissance missions. Strasser was promoted to Fregattenkapitän on 20 August 1917 and awarded the *Pour le Mérite*. He continued to lead raids against Britain and then on 5 August 1918 he led the whole squadron of airships on a raid to London. As they approached the coast, Strasser's airship, the L70, the biggest and newest type, was attacked by a DH4 flown by Lieutenant Peter Cadbury. Cadbury opened fire and his tracer bullets ripped into the gas bags and fuel tanks of the L70. Seconds later it exploded in a mass of burning fuel and gas and plunged into the North Sea; all the crew were killed. The remaining airships turned back.

In just four years Strasser had taken an idea – to disrupt the British at home – and turned it into reality, and in so doing made them keep hundreds of artillery pieces and soldiers at home to deal with this new threat.

Leutnant Karl THOM (27 victories)

The son of a field-hand, Karl Thom was born on 19 May 1893 in Freystadt, West Prussia. After leaving school he had a succession of jobs, and in 1911 he volunteered for three years' service in the army, being posted to Hussar Regiment Nr 5. When the war broke out in 1914 Thom, now an experienced soldier, was posted to *Jäger* Regiment Nr 10 and promoted to Unteroffizier in September. His regiment was soon in action. Thom was seriously wounded in November and awarded the Iron Cross 2nd Class. After his release from hospital in June 1915 he applied for a transfer to the German Army Air Service and was accepted.

Thom was sent for pilot training in September 1915 and graduated in January 1916. He was then posted to FA216 and operated in the area of Vosges on recon- naissance missions. On 16 May 1916 he crashed on landing and was badly injured. On his recovery, he was promoted to Vizefeldwebel on 24 July and sent to FA48 in Romania in October. Later that month he was shot down and captured, but he managed to escape and make his way back to his unit, and for this he was awarded the Iron Cross 1st Class. Bored with reconnaissance work, Thom made numerous requests for pilot training and on 24 April 1917 he was sent to *Jastaschule*; gradu- ating on 15 May, he was posted to *Jasta* 21 on the Western Front.

Flying his personalised Albatros with a large capital T on the fuselage sides, Thom opened his account on 22 August 1917 when he shot down a French AR2 over Avocourt. September was good for Thom; he shot down eleven enemy aircraft, including three on the 18th, two on the 19th and another two on the 22nd, and he was awarded the Golden Military Merit Cross on 11 October. A quiet period followed. He shot down only one in October and one in December, bringing his tally to fourteen. (He did also have an unconfirmed victory in December, the same day he brought down number fourteen.) Thom was wounded in the leg while attacking an observation balloon on 23 December. He returned to duty on 24 January 1918 and was promoted to Offiziersstellvertreter. Another quiet period followed but, as before, when it ended his score would leap forward. In June 1918 he shot down five enemy aircraft and in July another six, including three on the 24th, bringing his score to twenty-five. He capped his career with one each on 1 and 4 August 1918, and was awarded the Members' Cross with Swords of the Royal Hohenzollern House Order.

On 11 August he was wounded yet again, this time in the hip, but by the end of the month he had been commissioned Leutnant. Then, while still in hospital, he was awarded the *Pour le Mérite* on 1 November, making him one of only five men to have been awarded it and the Golden Military Merit Cross. Thom returned to his unit on 6 November 1918 and on the 9th he crashed, suffering multiple fractures.

During the Second World War he joined the Luftwaffe and held posts in Eastern Germany. He died in obscure circumstances on 3 March 1945 in Pillau, East Prussia, while visiting the Russian Front. It is believed he was taken prisoner. He was never seen again and has no known grave.

Leutnant Emil THUY (35 victories)

The son of a schoolteacher, Emil Thuy was born on 11 March 1894 in Hagen, Westphalia. His childhood was uneventful, but Thuy was one of the first in his town to enlist at the outbreak of war in 1914. He was sent almost immediately to the Western Front with Rhineland Pioneer Regiment Nr 3, with the most basic of training. In October he was badly wounded and returned to Germany. While in hospital he was declared unfit for further front-line duties and discharged from the army.

Thuy applied instead for the German Army Air Service and was accepted. On completion of his training on 10 July 1915, he was posted to FFA53 as a reconnaissance pilot with the rank of Gefreiter. He was awarded the Iron Cross 2nd Class on 7 August, possibly for his previous war service as there seems to be no other reason for it to be awarded. Thuy opened his score on 8 September and later the same month was promoted to Unteroffizier. Then on 10 November he was awarded the Iron Cross 1st Class and promotion to Vizefeldwebel followed in December 1915. On 26 March he was commissioned Leutnant, and for most of 1916 he carried out reconnaissance missions. He applied for fighter pilot training in November and was sent to *Jastaschule*, from which he graduated on 28 January 1917, being sent to *Jasta* 21. His second victory came on 16 April 1917, when he shot down a Caudron while on patrol over Berry-au-Bac. He would score only one in each of June and July, but shot down four in August, including a balloon on the 10th. September was a good month for Thuy: he brought down seven, including two on the 18th, thus bringing his tally to fifteen. He would only get two more by the end of the year, but he was given command of *Jasta* 28 on 6 November and was awarded the Knight's Cross with Swords of the Royal Hohenzollern House Order.

The next year, 1918, started well as he shot down a Sopwith Camel on 29 January over Poelkapelle, but then on 2 February he was wounded in a dog-fight; he managed to get his aircraft back to his airfield, but was once again hospitalised. He was back in command on 21 February and by the end of May 1918 had raised his score to twenty-one, and was awarded the Knight's Cross of the Military Merit Order of Wurttemberg. On 6 June he was appointed commander of JG7, consisting of *Jastas* 28, 33, 57 and 58. The *Pour le Mérite* came on 30 June 1918 with his score now at twenty-three. For the rest of the war he was to keep scoring steadily, with two in July, three in August, four in September and three in October, bringing his final score to thirty-five.

After the war Thuy stayed in aviation, training pilots, but as the Luftwaffe took shape he became a flying instructor at the Luftwaffe school near Smolensk. He was killed there on 11 June 1930 in a flying accident.

Oberleutnant Adolf Ritter von TUTSCHEK (27 victories)

The son of a soldier, Adolf Tutschek was born on 26 April 1896 in Ingolstadt, Bavaria. Both his father and grandfather were military men, so it was only natural that he joined the army in 1911 as a cadet in Bavarian Infantry Regiment Nr 3. He was commissioned Leutnant the following year. When war broke out Tutschek was assigned to Bavarian Infantry Regiment Nr 40 and was immediately thrown into action on the Western Front. He was wounded on 2 May 1915 and for this and other actions he was awarded the Iron Cross 1st and 2nd Class and the Bavarian Military Merit Order 4th Class with Swords. He was back in action within days of his discharge from hospital in June. On 15 August he was awarded the Military Max Joseph Order, making him a knight. Promoted to Oberleutnant on 17 January 1916, he then went back to the Western Front at Verdun. While there he was gassed on 26 March and spent several months recovering in hospital. It was at this time his application was accepted for the German Army Air Service, although his regiment was not too happy about losing such an experienced officer.

Tutschek was sent to Schliessheim for pilot training on 25 July 1916 and in October, after qualifying as a pilot, he was posted to FA6b to train on single-seaters. The Bavarian Military Merit Order 4th Class with Crown and Swords was awarded to him on 17 January 1917. On 25 January he was posted to *Jasta* 2 and opened his score on 6 March by shooting down a DH2 over Beugny. On 28 April, with his tally at three, he was given command of *Jasta* 12, not only for his flying but for his experience as an infantry officer. He got one more in April, on the 30th, but May was good to Tutschek as he brought down seven. However, June was a complete blank. He made up for it in July, bringing down ten, including two on the 28th. Also in July, on the 15th, he was awarded the Knight's Cross with Swords of the Royal Hohenzollern House Order. With his total now at twenty-one, he was awarded the *Pour le Mérite* on 3 August 1917. He scored a double victory on 23 August but was shot down and wounded in the right shoulder on the same day by Flight Commander C.D. Booker; he survived the crash and after recovering was promoted to Hauptmann on 6 December. He was then given command of JG2, made up of *Jastas* 12, 13, 15 and 19, on 1 February 1918. His twenty-seventh victory came on 10 March, then on 15 March 1918 he was shot down while flying his all-green Fokker Dr.I, this time by Lieutenant H.B. Redler from 24 Squadron. Tutschek was seen to be waving, having got out of his aircraft, but was found dead by German soldiers having suffered a blow to the head.

Oberleutnant Ernst UDET 'The Flying Clown' (62 victories)

The son of a wealthy landowner, Ernst Udet was born on 26 April 1896 in Frankfurt-am-Main. He had a flair for anything mechanical, and owned a motor-cycle. He tried to join the army first at the age of 17 but was rejected several times before being accepted on 21 August 1914 as a motorcycle messenger for the 26th Wurttemberg Reserve Division. For the next few months he delivered messages up and down the lines. Then one night he swerved to miss a shell hole and crashed; after ten days in hospital, he was sent to find his division but could not. While in Liege he met a pilot, Leutnant von Waxheim, who convinced him to join the German Army Air Service.

Udet made several applications but all were refused and he was ordered back home. He trained as a pilot at his own expense while putting forward more requests to fly. In early 1915 he was ordered to Darmstadt for pilot training, on completion of which he was sent to FA(A)206 with the rank of Gefreiter. Leutnant Bruno Justinus was appointed as his observer. After three long weeks, during which time they never even saw an Allied aircraft, they spotted a French monoplane attacking a railway station. As they approached and got in behind it, it became obvious that the Frenchman was having difficulties. Noticing that the monoplane had a machine-gun mounted *behind* the propeller, Udet 'encouraged' the French pilot to make a forced-landing on the German side of the lines; before he could set fire to his machine, the Frenchman, Roland Garros, was captured by German soldiers. The capture of his aircraft with its machine-gun and crude interruptor gear was to alter the course of the war in the air. For this action Udet was awarded the Iron Cross 2nd Class.

On 18 March 1916 Udet was posted to FA68 (which later became *Kek* Habsheim, and in September *Jasta* 15), and on the same day he shot down his first enemy aircraft, a French Farman F40, over Milhausen; it is said that he attacked twenty-two enemy aircraft single-handed. It was a good start but he would only score two more by the end of the year. At the beginning of January 1917 he was awarded the Iron Cross 1st Class and commissioned Leutnant on 22 January. After his sixth victory he requested a transfer to *Jasta* 37 and was posted there on 19 June. On 7 November he was appointed commander of *Jasta* 37 after the death of its commander, his friend Heinrich Gontermann. He was also awarded the Knight's Cross with Swords of the Royal Hohenzollern House Order on 13 November. He continued to score steadily and by the end of 1917 had sixteen confirmed victories.

With his tally at twenty, Udet was made acting commander of *Jasta* 11 on 23 March 1918, a post he held until 8 April. On the 9th he was awarded the *Pour le Mérite* and given command of *Jasta* 4. Most of Udet's aircraft had his fiancée's initials 'LO' painted on the fuselage, and his Fokker DVII had a red fuselage, with the top surfaces of the wings 'candy striped' red and white. Written on the top of his rear tail surface was *Du noch nicht!* ('Not you yet!') On 29 July, with his score standing at forty, he was involved in a dog-fight with a French Breguet two-seater; forced to jump from his aircraft, he landed by parachute in a shell hole. In August 1918 Udet shot down twenty enemy aircraft, including three on the 1st and the 8th, and two on the 9th, 10th, 21st and 22nd. He was awarded the Lubeck Hanseatic Cross in August and the Hamburg Hanseatic Cross in September. Then, on 26 September, after shooting down his sixty-first and sixty-second enemy aircraft, Udet was badly wounded in the thigh, putting an end to his combat days. But he had become the second highest scoring German pilot of the war and the highest surviving ace of the war.

After the war Udet became something of an adventurer, flying all over the world. He was also involved in stunt flying for films and worked as a test pilot. At the start of the Second World War he was persuaded to join the Luftwaffe and attained the rank of Generaloberst. He was awarded the Knight's Cross of the Iron Cross on 4 July 1940. However, he could not deal with the political infighting within the Luftwaffe and on 17 November 1941 he committed suicide. The German propaganda machine announced that he was killed while testing a new aircraft and he was given a state funeral. He is buried in the Berlin Invaliden Friedhof.

Leutnant der Reserve Joseph VELTJENS 'Seppl' (35 victories)

Joseph Veltjens was born on 2 June 1894 in the village of Geldern, west of Duisberg, in Saxony. After leaving school he went to the technical college at Charlottenburg in Berlin to study machine construction. When the war broke out, he enlisted into the Kaiserin-Augusta Guards Regiment Nr 4 on 3 August 1814. He was attached to Lieb Grenadier Regiment Nr 8 three months later and then to 8th Korps Kraftwagen Kolonne. During this time he was promoted to Vizefeldwebel and awarded the Iron Cross 2nd Class.

At the end of October 1915 Veltjens was accepted for the German Army Air Service and was sent to the flying school at Doberitz, graduating at the end of the year. He was then sent to Johannisthal for further training and was posted to FA23 as a reconnaissance pilot on 10 May 1916. He was commissioned Leutnant at the end of 1916 in recognition of his skills as a reconnaissance pilot. In early 1917 he met Rudolf Berthold, who persuaded him to apply for fighter pilot training. He was accepted and on completion of his training was posted to *Jasta* 14 in March. He scored his first victory on 14 April 1917 when he shot down a Spad while on patrol over Craonne. After shooting down three more in May and one in June, he was posted to *Jasta* 18 on 15 August. By the end of 1917 he had raised his tally to nine, including four in September, and had been awarded the Knight's Cross 2nd Class with Swords from Saxony.

On 20 March 1918 Veltjens was posted to *Jasta* 15, and took command there on 18 May. He celebrated this by shooting down a French Breguet XIV over Cauny on the same day, bringing his tally to thirteen, and then came the Iron Cross 1st Class, the Albrecht Order and Knight's Cross with Swords of the Royal Hohenzollern House Order on 20 May 1918. June was good for Veltjens; he shot down another nine enemy aircraft, including two on the 11th, bringing his score to twenty-three. In August he shot down two on the 10th, three on the 11th, two on the 16th (the day he was awarded the *Pour le Mérite*) and one on the 17th. Four more in October would bring his final score to thirty-five.

In 1919 Veltjens joined the Volunteer Corps Lüttwitz and the Gerstenberg Division to fight against the Spartacists in Berlin and Bremen. During the Second World War Veltjens joined the Luftwaffe with the rank of Oberst. He flew Ju52 transport aircraft and was Göring's emissary to Finland.

Veltjens was killed on 6 October 1943 when his Ju52 was shot down by Yugoslav partisans. He is buried in Travemunde.

Leutnant der Reserve Werner VOSS (48 victories)

The son of an industrial dyer, Werner Voss was born in Krefeld on 13 April 1897. He was expected to join the family business but the young Voss had other ideas. He liked nothing more than wearing the uniform of the Krefeld Hussars and when war broke out he was assigned to the Westphalian Hussar Regiment Nr 11 and sent to the French border. On 16 November 1914 his regiment was posted to the Eastern Front and Voss was promoted to Gefreiter on 27 January 1915. This was followed by the Iron Cross 2nd Class and promotion to Unteroffizier on 18 May. Sick of the ground war, he applied for the German Army Air Service in August and was accepted and sent to *Flieger Ersatz Abteilung* Nr 7 at Cologne in September 1915. Then he was sent for pilot training at Krefeld and returned as an instructor to FEA7 in February 1916, a mere five months after his induction to the Air Service.

Promoted again on 2 March, this time to Vizefeldwebel, he was posted to KG4, initially as an observer but soon as a pilot. Voss was commissioned Leutnant on 9 September and posted to *Jasta* 2 on 21 November 1916, where he met Manfred von Richthofen, who, at that time, had ten victories to his credit. Voss opened his score emphatically on 27 November 1916 by shooting down a Nieuport in the morning and a DH2 in the afternoon. On 19 December he was awarded the Iron Cross 1st Class, and two days later he brought down number three, a BE2 from 7 Squadron. Nine more aircraft would fall to him during February 1917, including doubles on the 25th and the 27th. During March he shot down another eleven, including doubles on the 11th, 17th, 18th and 24th; on the 17th he was awarded the Knight's Cross with Swords of the Royal Hohenzollern House Order. Then on 8 April, with his tally at twenty-four, Voss was awarded the *Pour le Mérite*. May saw him bring down another seven enemy aircraft, including three on the 9th. On 20 May, with his tally at twenty-eight, Voss was transferred to *Jasta* 5. By the time his score reached thirty-four Voss was made acting commander of *Jasta* 29, but was posted to *Jasta* 14 on 3 July, also as acting commander.

On 30 July he was given command of *Jasta* 10. He was now flying a Fokker Dr.I, which was factory finished apart from the yellow engine cowling (*Jasta* 10's markings) with a white face painted on it. Voss shot down four enemy aircraft in August, bringing his tally to thirty-eight. In September he shot down ten more, including two on the 5th, three on the 10th and two on the 11th, bringing his total to forty-eight. On the day of his last victory, 23 September, Voss was due to go on leave, and in fact his father and two brothers had already arrived to accompany him home. But he decided on one last patrol before leaving, probably intent on rounding his score up to fifty. What followed became one of the most famous dog-fights of the war. Voss attacked a flight of seven SE5s from 56 Squadron and for ten minutes he almost single-handedly fought them to a stand-still, inflicting damage on all of the enemy aircraft (in fact some were so badly damaged that they were written off). But finally Lieutenant Arthur Rhys-Davids MC got in a fatal burst of fire and Voss went down behind British lines. He was buried nearby but the grave was lost due to heavy shelling. James McCudden (a future VC holder), who was involved in the fight with Voss, said of him: 'His flying was wonderful, his courage magnificent and in my opinion he is the bravest German airman whom it has been my privilege to see fight.'

Voss's remains are buried in a mass grave in Langemark German Military Cemetery, Ypres, Belgium.

Hauptmann Franz WALZ 'The Eagle of Jericho' (7 victories)

Franz Walz was born in Speyer, south of Mannheim, Bavaria, on 4 December 1885. He volunteered for the army at the age of 20 on 15 July 1905, joining Bavarian Infantry Regiment Nr 8 in Metz. It was soon realised that he was a natural leader of men and in 1908 he was promoted to Leutnant. In 1912 Walz applied for a transfer to the newly created German Army Air Service; this was approved some months later and Walz was posted to the German Army's flying school at Munich-Schliessheim, graduating four months later.

On the outbreak of war Walz took command of the Bavarian FFA3, a reconnaissance unit based in the Alsace-Lorraine region, and was promoted Oberleutnant in November 1914. The following year he carried out over 200 reconnaissance missions on the Western Front and in December 1915 was rewarded with command of *Kagohl* I's *Kampfstaffel* 2. Walz opened his score on 9 April 1916 when he shot down a French Caudron while on patrol over Douaumont, and on 21 May he shot down a Nieuport. By the end of June he had flown over 300 reconnaissance missions. He did not score again until July, when he brought down four enemy aircraft, but then on the 30th he was wounded in the foot, being hospitalised for the next few months.

On 5 September he was awarded the Knight's Cross with Swords of the Royal Hohenzollern House Order, and then he left to command *Jasta* 19 on 3 November 1916. On 29 November he was given command of *Jasta* 2 and promoted to Hauptmann on 20 January 1917. Walz's last victory came on 14 May, when he shot down a DH2 from 32 Squadron. On 9 June he was given command of *Jasta* 34, but on 25 August was posted to Palestine to command FA304b, having largely failed as a fighter leader. Here he was awarded the Turkish Silver Liakat-Medaille on 22 July 1918, and on 9 August he was awarded the *Pour le Mérite* for his work in reconnaissance, having flown over 500 missions. On 15 September he was awarded the Osmanie-Orden 4th Class with Swords. This, together with his Iron Cross 1st and 2nd Class, three Bavarian awards and one Austro-Hungarian award, showed the respect felt for him.

On 20 September 1918 Walz's aircraft was forced down and he was captured by the British, being released on 1 December 1919. He returned to Germany and served in the Reichswehr and the State Police. In 1939 he joined the Luftwaffe and reached the rank of Generalleutnant by 1 April 1945. He was captured by the Russians in 1945 and died in December as a POW in Breslau, Silesia.

Leutnant der Reserve Rudolph WINDISCH (22 victories)

The son of a pastry-shop owner, Rudolph Windisch was born in Dresden on 27 January 1897. As a child he built model aircraft. On 14 September 1914 he volunteered for a year's service with Infantry Regiment Nr 177 and after a short period of training was sent off to the Western Front, where on 21 November 1914 he was wounded by shrapnel. While recovering in hospital, he applied for a transfer to the German Army Air Service, being sent to the flying school at Leipzig-Lindenthal on 22 January 1915. Graduating on 10 June, he was promoted to Unteroffizier and posted to FEA6 as an instructor. Soon bored with training, he applied for a combat posting and on 1 May 1916 was sent to FFA62 as a reconnaissance pilot, with Oberleutnant Maximillian von Cossel as his observer. Along with his unit he was sent to the Eastern Front on 15 June.

It was not long before he made his mark with a number of daring reconnaissance missions, for which he was awarded the Iron Cross 2nd Class and gained promotion to Vizefeldwebel. Windisch scored his first victory on 25 August when he shot down an observation balloon, for which he was awarded the Iron Cross 1st Class. Then on the night of 2/3 October 1916 he set out on what was arguably the first air-supported espionage mission, landing behind enemy lines to drop off Cossel near the Rowno–Brody railway line, where he destroyed a vital railway bridge; Windisch then picked Cossel up and flew him back to safety. For this Windisch was awarded the Prussian Crown Order 4th Class with Swords; he was the only pilot to be awarded it, and the Kaiser himself presented it to him on 18 October. He was also awarded the Prussian Cross of Honour with Swords. Cossel was awarded the Knight's Cross with Swords of the Royal Hohenzollern House Order and the Cross of Merit 3rd Class with Swords.

After a short leave Windisch was sent to *Kagohl* 2 on the Western Front on 24 November and on 5 December he was commissioned Leutnant. He continued to fly reconnaissance missions until 20 February 1917, when he was posted to *Jasta* 32 as a fighter pilot. After further training he shot down an AR2 on 18 September while on patrol over Fleury. After his fourth victory, a Spad on 1 November, he was awarded the Knight's Cross 1st Class with Swords of the Albert Order from Saxony on 4 November, and by the end of the month his tally stood at six.

On 3 January 1918 he shot down another balloon and on 4 January another Spad. On 10 January he was posted to *Jasta* 50, but then was given command of *Jasta* 66 on 24 January. During March he shot down five more Spads and a Sopwith, three more Spads following on the 24th. He scored three more times in April and five in May, bringing his total to twenty-two. No fewer than sixteen of his victories were Spad fighters. During this time he was awarded the Knight's Cross with Swords of the Royal Hohenzollern House Order, the Military Order of St Heinrich Medal in Silver from Saxony 2nd Class and the Austrian-Hungarian Bravery Medal in Silver 2nd Class. On the day of his twenty-second victory, 27 May 1918, Windisch was shot down and captured by the French.

On the assumption that he was a POW, his *Pour le Mérite* was awarded on 6 June 1918.

After the war, when the repatriation of prisoners commenced, efforts were made to find Windisch but he was never seen again. His disappearance is shrouded in mystery, the French insisting that there was no record of him ever being in a POW camp. A number of possible explanations have been put forward, including the theory that he was shot while attempting to escape by stealing a French aircraft, but this has never been confirmed. His end remains a mystery.

Leutnant Kurt WINTGENS (19 victories)

The son of an army officer, Kurt Wintgens was born in Neustadt on 1 August 1894. In 1913 he became a cadet with Telegraphen-Battaillon Nr 2 in Frankfurt. He was at the Military Academy at Heersfeld when the war started, whereupon he rejoined his unit and was soon in action, being awarded the Iron Cross 2nd Class. He transferred to aviation in late 1914 or early 1915 as an observer, but due to his experiences in telegraphy he was attached to AOK IX (Army Wireless *Abteilung*) first on the Western Front and then in Poland. In March 1915 he was sent to *Jastaschule* at Schwerin for pilot training. Despite wearing glasses (one of only a few fighter pilots known to have done so), he qualified within four months and was first posted to FFA67 flying Fokker Eindeckers then to FFA6b. He claimed his first enemy aircraft, a Morane Parasol, on 1 July 1915, but it was unconfirmed. Had it been verified it would have been the first German fighter victory in history. Wintgens claimed another Morane Parasol on 4 July, but this too was unconfirmed. The next day he was moved to FFA48 and on 15 July he shot down a Morane Parasol while on patrol over Schlucht; this time it was confirmed. He appears to have had something of a roving commission, as he stated to a friend in a letter that he did not belong to any unit but was independent.

It is not certain if one of his early July victories was later confirmed or if victory number two was scored on an unknown date between 15 July and his third victory on 9 August. Some lists show him with only eighteen victories, so maybe this is the true number. Certainly his eighth victory is noted as 30 June (1916), according to the award of his *Pour le Mérite*. Despite a period of ill-health (a bout of influenza curtailed his flying), he returned in January 1916 and shot down a Caudron G.IV but this too was unconfirmed, and he did not score again for three months. During May and June he brought down another five, bringing his tally to eight and resulting in the award of the *Pour le Mérite* on 1 July 1916. He was only the fourth pilot to be so honoured. In July he shot down another four, including two on the 21st. He was then posted to *Kek* Vaux prior to going to *Jasta* 4 with the rest of *Kek* Vaux's aces on 25 August. Only one victory came in August, on the 2nd. In September he moved again, this time to *Jasta* 1, where he brought down six enemy aircraft, including two on the 14th and 24th, bringing his total to nineteen. He had also been awarded the Iron Cross 1st Class, the Knight's Cross with Swords of the Royal Hohenzollern House Order, the Bavarian Military Merit Order 4th Class with Swords and the Saxon Albrecht Order, Knight's 4th Class with Swords.

On 25 September 1916, while flying escort to a two-seater over Villers-Carbonnel, he fought off an attack by aircraft from *Escadrille* N.3, but in doing so was shot down in flames, probably by the French ace Lieutenant Hurteaux. He is buried in Nord Cemetery, Minden.

Leutnant Kurt WOLFF (33 victories)

Kurt Wolff was born in Greifswald, Pomerania, on 6 February 1895. At the age of 17 he became a cadet in Eisenbahn Railway Regiment Nr 4. He served in the field as an Unteroffizier and was commissioned Leutnant on 17 April 1915. There was an urgent need for pilots so Wolff applied for transfer to the German Army Air Service, although his regiment was reluctant to let him go. In July 1915 he was posted to the *Jastaschule* at Doberitz. He was lucky to survive his first flight when his instructor misjudged the landing and crashed; the pilot was killed outright, but Wolff escaped with only a dislocated shoulder. This did not deter him and he made rapid progress, receiving his pilot's badge in December. Wolff was posted to a *Kampfgeschwader* unit at Verdun, where he was quickly in action. Some time later he and his unit moved to the Somme front, where again he was soon in action against Allied ground troops.

On 5 November 1916 Wolff was posted to *Jasta* 11 and although he carried out a number of sorties against Allied aircraft he failed to shoot any down. Then in January 1917 command of *Jasta* 11 was taken up by Manfred von Richthofen and under his guidance the squadron began to take its toll of Allied aircraft. Wolff shot down his first enemy aircraft on 6 March 1917, a BE2d, over Givenchy, rapidly followed by another four by the end of the month. During April 1917 Wolff shot down twenty-two enemy aircraft, including one each on the 6th, 7th and 8th, four on the 13th, two on the 14th, another two on the 22nd and three on the 29th, beating von Richthofen's own tally of twenty-one for the same month. No wonder the British called it 'Bloody April'. Wolff's tally was now up to twenty-seven. He was awarded the Knight's Cross with Swords of the Royal Hohenzollern House Order on 27 April, and with his score at twenty-nine he was awarded the *Pour le Mérite* on 4 May. Two days later he was given command of *Jasta* 29. On 6 May he shot down a Spad, but only managed one in June, on the 27th, and returned to command *Jasta* 11 on 2 July. Victories on 6 and 7 July brought his total to thirty-three. On 11 July, in a fight with Triplanes of 10

Squadron RNAS, Wolff was wounded in the left hand but managed to fly back to his airfield. This injury prevented him from flying until September, and on 12 September he was promoted to Oberleutnant.

On the afternoon of 15 September 1917 Wolff, who had scored all of his victories in an Albatros, was flying von Richthofen's Fokker Dr.I No. FI 102/17 in combat with fighters from 70 and 10 Squadrons RNAS when he was shot down and killed by Flight Sub-Lieutenant N.M. McGregor. He was just 22 years old. He is buried in the German War Cemetery at Memel, Klaipeda, Lithuania.

Leutnant der Reserve Kurt WÜSTHOFF (27 victories)

The son of a music director, Kurt Wüsthoff was born in Aachen on 27 January 1897. He discovered at an early age an aptitude for all things mechanical, so it was no surprise when he joined the army at 16 and immediately applied for the German Army Air Service. Being accepted, he was posted to the Military Flying School at Leipzig. Wüsthoff took just four months to qualify as a pilot, but was too young for front-line service so he was sent to FEA6 at Grossenheim as an instructor. After much pressure from his superiors, he managed to get a posting to KGI in the Flanders sector in 1915. Later he saw service in Bulgaria, Romania, Macedonia and Greece as a bomber and reconnaissance pilot.

At the beginning of June 1917, after promotion to Vizefeldwebel, he was posted to *Jasta* 4 on the Western Front. He shot down his first enemy aircraft, a Sopwith 1½ Strutter from 45 Squadron, on 15 June. On 23 June he shot down a balloon over Wytschaete, for which he was awarded the Iron Cross 2nd Class. Two more balloons, on 11 and 16 July, and two more fighters would earn him the Iron Cross 1st Class by the end of the month. He also had one unconfirmed kill on 27 July. On 1 August Wüsthoff was commissioned Leutnant, but August must have been a slow month as he only shot down one, on the 5th. But he was awarded the Knight's Cross with Swords of the Royal Hohenzollern House Order. During September he shot down fourteen enemy aircraft, including two each on the 3rd, 4th and 20th, bringing his tally to twenty-one. His *Pour le Mérite* was awarded on 26 November and he was made acting commander of *Jasta* 4 in mid-December, with his score at twenty-six. He was appointed Staffelführer on 22 February 1918 and assigned to the staff of JGI on 16 March, just after shooting down a Sopwith Camel on the 10th.

Wüsthoff was given command of *Jasta* 15 on 16 June, having been with FEA13 for a short time. On 17 June he got into a fight with 23 and 24 Squadron aircraft and was shot down near Cachy. Badly wounded in both legs, he was taken to a French hospital. In 1920 he was released from a prison hospital and returned to Germany on crutches, complaining that the French doctors had deliberately neglected his treatment. He was taken to a hospital in Dresden, and after several operations over two years he was able to walk again. He got a job with an Austrian car manufacturer and was soon able to return to flying.

On 18 July 1926 Wüsthoff took part in an air show at Dresden to raise funds for a memorial to Max Immelmann; during his aerobatic display he crashed and was very badly injured, dying five days later.

The men who missed out on the *Pour le Mérite*

Leutnant Hans Ritter von ADAM (21 victories)

The son of a railway official, Hans Adam was born in Eisenstein, Bavaria, on 24 May 1886. On 1 October 1906 he volunteered for a year's service in Infantry Regiment Nr 4. He then went into business in Munich. By the time the war started he was a married man with two children. He served in the infantry with the rank of Leutnant, being wounded on 2 September 1914. He returned to the front line in 1915 but applied for the German Army Air Service and qualified as an observer on 15 May 1916 and was posted to FF(A)2b, often flying with Eduard Ritter von Schleich, who would go on to shoot down thirty-five enemy aircraft.

Adam was awarded the Iron Cross 1st Class and the Bavarian Military Merit Order 4th Class with Swords, and posted to *Jasta* 34 on 2 March 1917. He scored his first victory on 24 March by shooting down a Caudron G4 over Woevre, followed by one each in April and June. In mid-June he was posted to *Jasta* 6, scoring seven victories in July and three in August, and then he became Staffelführer on 30 August 1917. One of his July victories was over Lieutenant A.W.B. Miller, a six-victory ace. Adam shot down another seven enemy aircraft in September, including two each on the 19th and 20th. His last victory was a Nieuport from 29 Squadron, shot down west of Passchendaele on 6 November 1917.

Adam's luck ran out on 15 November 1917. In combat with 29 and 45 Squadrons, he was shot down and killed by Lieutenant Kenneth B. Montgomery of 45 Squadron. He was also awarded the Iron Cross 1st and 2nd Class and was posthumously awarded the Knight's Cross of the Royal Hohenzollern House Order on 2 February 1918, and on 20 May 1919 the Knight's Cross of the Military Max-Joseph Order, making him a knight. This was backdated to 28 July

1917. Although Adam shot down the required number of enemy aircraft for the *Pour le Mérite*, his death prevented its award.

Offizierstellvertreter Friedrich ALTEMEIER (21 victories)

Friedrich Altemeier was born in Niederbecksen, near Hanover, on 14 June 1886. He went to military school from 1906 to 1908, and worked for Krupps before the war; all of his aircraft would carry their triple ring logo on the fuselage. Altemeier was called up in August 1914 and served in Infantry Regiment Nr 57, as part of a machine-gun company. Wounded on 15 January 1915, he applied for the German Army Air Service, but was not accepted until 11 August. After training he was posted first to FA67 on 21 July 1916, then to *Jasta* 14 in September, and finally to *Jasta* 24 on the Western Front on 1 December, and within days was promoted from Vizefeldwebel to Offizierstellvertreter. His first victory did not come until 3 March 1917 when he shot down a Nieuport 17 while on patrol over Bois Morel. On 30 May he was awarded the Iron Cross 1st Class (the Iron Cross 2nd Class most probably having been awarded during his infantry days), but he did not score again until 7 July, shooting down an RNAS Sopwith Triplane and a Spad VII on 12 July. On 17 August he shot down two enemy aircraft on the same day. He shot down four more enemy aircraft in September, but did not score again for the remainder of 1917.

It was not until 19 February 1918 that he achieved his tenth victory (an SE5a), making him a *Kanone*. He was victorious again on 24 February, and shot down three more in March, one of which was *Jasta* 24's fiftieth victory. He was awarded the Saxon Silver Friedrich August Medal on 4 March, and the Golden Military Merit Cross (the NCO's equivalent of the *Pour le Mérite*) on 11 April 1918. A lean spell followed, but in August he shot down two enemy aircraft. He had two confirmed and one unconfirmed in both September and October, bringing his tally to twenty. Altemeier's twenty-first and last victory came on 10 November 1918, the day before the armistice. He was one of only a few pilots to fly the Fokker DVIII. He was also awarded the Silver Wound Badge, which means he was wounded at least three times.

The rest of his life is a mystery, and even the date of his death is unknown. He just seems to have disappeared. He is included here because he shot down twenty-one aircraft and would have been eligible for the *Pour le Mérite* apart from two things: the war ended the day after he shot down his last enemy aircraft and the *Pour le Mérite* was only awarded to officers.

Oberleutnant Eduard AUFFARTH (sometimes spelt AUFFAHRT) (29 victories)

Eduard Auffarth's date and place of birth are unknown. Based on his service records, he is likely to have been born in or before 1896. Very little is known about his pre-Army Air Service, but he first flew with *Feldflieger Abteilung* 27 and then FA(A)266 as an observer before being transferred to *Jasta* 18 in September 1917 and shooting down his first enemy aircraft on the 16th, becoming an ace by the end of the month. He was then posted to *Jasta* 29 as acting Staffelführer, being confirmed on the 11th with the rank of Oberleutnant, and shooting down his first aircraft with them on 13 November. He would go on to score a quarter of his *Jasta's* victories. He flew a succession of aircraft, including Albatros, Fokker DVIIs and a rare Pfalz DVIII, all of them with his personal colour scheme of yellow nose and green fuselage with a stylised eight-pointed comet on the side.

On 11 April 1918, with his score at ten, he was awarded the Knight's Cross of the Royal Hohenzollern House Order. At the end of May, with his tally at fourteen, he was wounded in the hand and did not return to the front until 21 July. In August he shot down five but two of these were unconfirmed. Auffarth accumulated victories erratically, but with his tally at twenty, on 3 September he was recommended for the *Pour le Mérite*. He was given command of JG3 on 28 September and then in October he had his best month ever, shooting down nine, including two on the 9th and three each on the 14th and 30th, bringing his total to twenty-nine. Auffarth's final score is in dispute as only twenty-six seem to have been confirmed, but the Commander of Army Aviation recorded his twenty-ninth victory over an SE5 at Dottenigs taking place on 30 October (the first of three victories that day), which would make his total thirty-one. It seems to me that they may have counted the two unconfirmed claims in August. Auffarth survived the war, despite being wounded at least three times. His other awards were the Iron Cross 1st and 2nd Class, the Hanseatic Cross from both Bremen and Hamburg, and the Silver Wound Badge.

He established his own flying school in Munster, Fliegerschule Auffarth, in 1924. This was one of ten flying schools that surreptitiously supported covert military training in violation of the Versailles Treaty. Auffarth returned to service in the Second World War, being stationed at Eschenbach in May 1943 with the rank of Oberstleutnant. He died there on 12 October 1946.

Although Auffarth was recommended for the *Pour le Mérite*, the Kaiser abdicated before the award could be confirmed.

Leutnant Hermann BECKER (23 victories)

Hermann Becker was born in Tribus, Upper Silesia, on 10 September 1887. He joined the German Army Air Service in 1916, serving as an observer with FA2, then with FA57 on the Eastern Front. After pilot training Becker was posted to KG5 and then on to *Schutzstaffel* 11, and was involved in operations over the Somme and Verdun. Commissioned Leutnant in November 1916, he was properly awarded the Iron Cross 2nd Class at the same time. He received the Iron Cross 1st Class on 12 January 1917.

Transferred to *Jasta* 12 as a fighter pilot in May 1917, Becker scored his first victory on 6 June. Wounded on 16 June, he was unable to fly for nearly three months. His scoring was very slow, and he had only added two more victories by the end of the year. Two victories in February 1918 started a run, with three more coming in March, one in April and another three in May, but one of these was unconfirmed, brining his tally to eleven. He was made commander of *Jasta* 12 in April 1918 and on 15 May was awarded the Knight's Cross with Swords of the Royal Hohenzollern House Order. He shot down two in August and five in September, including two each on the 18th and 26th. Four Spad fighters fell to his guns during October, bringing his tally to twenty-two. On 2 November he was nominated for the *Pour le Mérite*, and on the 3rd he shot down his twenty-third (and *Jasta* 12's 150th) victory. All but five of his victories were over fighter aircraft. He survived the war, but was never awarded the *Pour le Mérite* due to the Kaiser's abdication on 9 November.

What happened to Becker after the war is not known.

Oberleutnant Hans BETHGE (20 victories)

The son of an officer, Hans Bethge was born in Berlin on 6 December 1890. He tried to enlist in the navy but was turned down due to being near-sighted, so he joined *Eisenbahnregiment* Nr 1 as an ensign. In 1912 he transferred to *Eisenbahnregiment* Nr 4, undergoing more training, and was commissioned Leutnant. When the war started his regiment went into action on the very first day as sappers. Wounded in the ankle and sent back to Germany for recovery, Bethge applied for the Air Service and was accepted, joining *Brieftauben Abteilung Ostende*. On 4 August 1916 he was sent to *Kek* Bertincourt of FA32 with the rank of Oberleutnant. He shot down his first opponent, a BE2c, on 29 August over Auchonvillers, and two days later followed this up with a Martinsyde G100 over Fins. He did not score again until December, with one on the 20th, unconfirmed, and one on the 26th, this time confirmed.

On 14 January 1917 Bethge was sent to command *Jasta* 30. It must have needed some work to get the squadron ready as he did not score again until 28 March. Scoring was slow as he only shot down one each in April and May, two each in June and July, but four in August. He had a lucky double on 17 August: he shot down the British ace Philip A. Johnson (five victories), who then collided with his wingman, giving Bethge two victories. Bethge commented: 'I have my 12th and 13th shot down. The aircraft crashed together and both were gone. I do not

want to hurt anyone, but I fly with an iron will and deepest sense of duty . . .'
Three more in September and one in October brought his tally to sixteen by the
end of the year. Bethge was awarded the Iron Cross 1st and 2nd Class and the
Knight's Cross with Swords of the Royal Hohenzollern House Order.

Early in 1918 Bethge was issued a new Pfalz DIII, painted with tapering longi-
tudinal grey and white stripes along the fuselage and a dark gold diamond by the
cockpit. With this new aircraft he shot down a Sopwith Camel on 19 February
and for his twentieth victory a DH4 on 10 March 1918; this was followed by
nomination for the *Pour le Mérite*. Seven days later he was in combat over
Passchendaele. No one is really sure what happened, but when still 200 metres
from the enemy his Pfalz curved sharply downwards and crashed out of sight. His
body was found and laid out in the church near his *Jasta* before being taken to
Germany for burial. On his death the *Pour le Mérite* nomination was withdrawn.

Hans Bethge is buried in Jerusalem's Church Cemetery near the Halle Gate in
Berlin.

Leutnant Paul BILLIK (31 victories)

The son of a Jewish farmer, Paul Billik was born in Haatsch on 27 March 1891
(some sources say 1881). He left school in 1910 and in 1911 joined Infantry
Regiment Nr 157 based in Brzeg. During the next two years he was promoted to
Unteroffizier and went into action with his regiment at the start of the war. In
November 1915 he was awarded the Iron Cross 2nd Class and given a battlefield
commission to Leutnant for his uncommon courage and ability. He applied and
was accepted for the German Army Air Service and was sent to flying school in
May 1916. On graduation in January 1917 he was sent to FEA4 at Posen, and
then assigned to *Schusta* 4 in January 1917. He trained to fly fighters and on 26
March was posted to *Jasta* 12, being assigned an Albatros DIII which he personalised with a pre-Nazi Swastika.

Billik's first victory came on 30 April 1917, when he shot down an RNAS
Sopwith Pup flown by Flight Sub-Lieutenant John J. Malone DSC, a ten-ace
veteran (and the first of five aces Billik was to shoot down). He shot down three
more enemy aircraft in April and was awarded the Iron Cross 1st Class before
being transferred to *Jasta* 7 on 6 July 1917. His new unit was equipped with the
Fokker Dr.I and with this type Billik scored one victory in August, and two in
September, was wounded in October but scored again on 12 December, bringing
his tally to eight. On 28 December he was given command of *Jasta* 52, a new unit
with new pilots, although he did bring with him four pilots from his old unit.
Jasta 52 was equipped with the Pfalz DIII, a somewhat outdated fighter, but Billik
was able to modify his unit's tactics to minimise the Pfalz's limitations.

On 9 March 1918 Billik began a six-month accumulation of victories by
shooting down his second ace, Major Leonard A. Tilney MC, commander of 40

Squadron, and three more in March. On 19 May, in a dog-fight where the Germans were outnumbered, he brought down his third ace, Major Albert D. Carter DSO from 19 Squadron, who had scored twenty-nine victories; Carter was taken prisoner and Billik was slightly wounded in this action. On 1 June he shot the wing off Captain William J. Cairnes's SE5a, which plummeting earthwards at high speed. Cairnes, a five-ace veteran from 74 Squadron, was killed. On 8 July he brought down his fifth ace, Captain Arthur Claydon DFC from 32 Squadron, who had seven victories to his credit. It was at about this time that *Jasta* 52 was upgraded with the Fokker DVII and Dr.I. On 25 July, with his score at twenty-seven, Billik was awarded the Knight's Cross with Swords of the Royal Hohenzollern House Order.

August 1918 started well for Billik: he shot down an RE8 on the 3rd, a DH9 on the 8th and a DH4 and an SE5a on the 9th, bringing his total to thirty-one. But then, on the 10th, Billik was shot down over Allied lines and taken prisoner. It should be noted that most of his successes came despite the fact that most of his opponents were in superior aircraft. He shot down eight Camels, seven SE5s and two Dolphins; he also shot down six well-armed modern two-seaters.

After the war Billik went into civil aviation, and died in a landing accident at Staaken, Berlin, on 8 March 1926. The location of his grave is now unknown.

Billik had been recommended for the *Pour le Mérite* when he scored his twentieth victory, but when he was shot down it was withdrawn, probably because it was assumed he had been killed. Why it was not awarded when word came through that he was a POW is not known.

Leutnant Gustav DÖRR (35 victories)

The son of a building contractor, Gustav Dörr was born in Blindgallen, East Prussia, on 5 October 1887. When he completed trade school, he began work with Krupp AG at the age of 18. In 1908 he volunteered for military service and enlisted into Infantry Regiment Nr 176, passing out as an Unteroffizier.

On 20 August 1914 Dörr was seriously wounded, taking until November to recover. Upon his return, he fought along the Rawka River near Warsaw. During action on 17 February 1915 he was wounded in the right hip by a bayonet. This wound put him in the hospital at Naumburg, but he returned to duty in May. He was in fact wounded three times while in the infantry. On release from hospital, he was recommended for service with the reserve battalion of his regiment.

When he saw a circular from the War Ministry asking for volunteers for pilot training, he applied and was accepted. He reported for training with FEA2 at Doberitz in July 1915. On 18 March 1916 he was posted to FA68, an artillery observation unit, with the rank of Vizefeldwebel. He was transferred to FA6 on 18 March to help counter heavy Allied air pressure and while with this unit was awarded the Iron Cross 2nd Class on 7 April. He stayed with this unit through its redesignation to FA257 in May 1916, and took part in air operations prior to the battle of the Somme in July.

On 17 April 1917 Dörr, now with the rank of Offizierstellvertreter, was awarded the Iron Cross 1st Class. In June 1917 the elevator on his aircraft failed and he crashed from an altitude of 4,600ft; his observer, Leutnant Bohn, was killed but Dörr survived, albeit with his jaw broken in six places. This injury kept him out of action for three months. He returned to duty as a test pilot at Altenberg in November 1917. Then, in February 1918, he was transferred to *Jasta* 45. His first victory came on 17 March in a dog-fight in which six Germans took on twenty-six French and British aircraft. Dörr shot down a Sopwith 1½ Strutter, a rare victory over a British aircraft for him, as most of his opponents were French. He shot down a Brequet XIV over Vendeuil on 28 May, only to be shot down in flames himself during the same fight, his time from 1,300ft. He landed in no-man's-land, but made it back to the German lines under heavy fire with only minor burns.

Dörr claimed an RE8 on 1 June but this was unconfirmed, although he did shoot down three Spads during the month. July was a very good month: he shot down eleven French aircraft, including two each on the 15th and 18th, bringing his total to seventeen. During August he added six more victories and on 29 August was awarded the Gold Military Merit Cross (the NCO's equivalent of the *Pour le Mérite*). September saw him shoot down seven Spads and he was commissioned Leutnant.

During October he brought down seven more but two of these were unconfirmed, and on 25 October 1918 he was recommended for the *Pour le Mérite*. His tally was now at thirty-five confirmed enemy aircraft. On 4 November he had yet another unconfirmed victory. By the end of the war he was the most successful ace to fly the Fokker DVII: he had shot down thirty enemy aircraft in it. He had been wounded three times in the infantry and twice as a pilot. He had refused an assignment to the rear to stay in the front line. Nevertheless his *Pour le Mérite* was never awarded as the Kaiser abdicated. It was a bitter experience that may have been the root for a false report that he was given the *Pour le Mérite* in January 1919. The fact that all his victories came within the last nine months of the war makes his record one of the best in the German Army Air Service.

After the war Dörr became a pilot for Lufthansa and flew 360,000 miles. On 11 December 1928 he was flying a Junkers G31 on a night flight to Berlin when he attempted an emergency landing, but his plane brushed a tree on his final approach and crashed, killing him and all of the crew.

Leutnant Rudolph von ESCHWEGE 'The Eagle of the Aegean Sea' (20 victories)

Rudolph Eschwege was born in Bad Homburg von der Hohe, near Hamburg, on 25 February 1895. It appears that he was orphaned at a young age. On finishing school he attended the War Academy and was serving with Mounted *Jäger* Regiment Nr 3 as an Ensign when the war broke out. He took part in the Battle of Mulhausen on 9/10 August and in the fighting on the River Yser. Transferred to the German Army Air Service, he had begun pilot training by February 1915, crashing several times before qualifying. Posted to FA36 in August 1915, he saw action on the Western Front as a reconnaissance pilot, and later as escort to the unit's two-seaters. He was then sent to the Macedonian front in the autumn of 1916 with FA66 and promoted to Leutnant.

Eschwege's first claim was for a Nieuport XII shot down over Drama in Greece on 25 October but this was unconfirmed. On 19 November 1916 he shot down his first confirmed enemy aircraft, a Nieuport XII, also over Drama. Eschwege scored only one more in 1916, a Farman on 27 December. Now flying with FA30, he shot down his first enemy aircraft of 1917 on 9 January near Drama. After scoring again on 18 February, and with an unconfirmed one on the 19th, Eschwege was awarded the Bulgarian Bravery Order 4th Class, followed later by the 1st Class. He was wounded in the right arm in May but pressed home his attack regardless, bringing down a British two-seater near Lake Tahino. With his tally at twelve he received the Prussian Knight's Cross of the Military St Henry Order on 8 July. In September, with his score at fifteen, he fell ill with malaria. By the end of October British observation balloons were a target and Eschwege shot down one in late October and another in November. After his nineteenth victory, a Sopwith 1½ Strutter on 19 November, he was recommended for the *Pour le Mérite*. Then on 21 November Eschwege attacked a balloon that was in fact a decoy filled with explosives. This was detonated from the ground, destroying the German aircraft and killing Eschwege. It was assumed by the Germans that Eschwege had shot the balloon down and it was credited to him as his twentieth victory. He was buried by the British with full military honours. The award of the *Pour le Mérite* was cancelled after his death.

The Bulgarians dubbed him 'the Eagle of the Aegean Sea', and later built a monument to him. Among his other awards were the Iron Cross 1st and 2nd Class and the Knight's Cross with Swords of the Royal Hohenzollern House Order. Considering that all of his victories came on the Macedonian front, it should be emphasised that his achievements were of the highest order.

Leutnant Rudolph von FREDEN (20 victories)

Rudolph Freden was born in Berlin on 18 March 1892. Nothing seems to be known about his early life but when war broke out he volunteered and was assigned to Field Artillery Regiment Nr 18. Freden arrived at the front on 19 October 1914 with the rank of Kanonier. He was promoted to Vizefeldwebel in March 1915 and then commissioned Leutnant on 30 July 1915. In January 1916 he was given command of *Flakzug* 64, but later went to *Flakzug* 26. He began training as an observer in 1916, going to FFA48, later designated FA10, on 2 August. He was wounded on 24 August 1916, and then took pilot training in June 1917. On graduating he was posted to *Jasta* 1 in Italy on 27 November.

Freden's first victory came on 29 January 1918 when he shot down a balloon over Spresiano. He shot down two more balloons before being transferred to France to join *Jasta* 72 on 8 March. *Jasta* 1 returned to France on 25 March, and Freden rejoined it the next day. He shot down a Spad on 9 June before being sent to command *Jasta* 50 on 11 June 1918. Freden shot down four during July, including a balloon, and then in September he shot down five balloons and two aircraft, including two doubles on the 15th and 26th, bringing his tally to fourteen. Also on 20 September 1918 he was awarded the Knight's Cross with Swords of the Royal Hohenzollern House Order. He got four more in October, but only one of these was a balloon. In November Freden shot down two fighters, on the 9th and 10th.

Freden had been recommended for the *Pour le Mérite* but due to the Kaiser's abdication it was never approved. He had been awarded the Iron Cross 1st and 2nd Class. Freden died in the great flu epidemic on 30 October 1919, in Stettin, Pomerania, now part of Poland.

Leutnant Friedrich 'Fitz' FRIEDRICHS (21 victories)

The son of a customs official, Friedrich Friedrichs was born in Spark, Westphalia, on 21 February 1895. Fitz, as he was generally known, had ideas about a medical career, but the war put an end to all that. On 14 August 1914 he volunteered for Infantry Regiment Nr 85, going to the Western Front on 9 October. He served with the 85th until he was sent for officer training in Munich, being commissioned Leutnant on 23 September 1915 and posted to Infantry Regiment Nr 32 in the Serbian campaign on 8 October. He was severely wounded in the leg on the 20th and declared unfit for further duty.

Friedrichs then applied for the German Army Air Service, and was sent for observer training from 1 October 1916 to 20 February 1917. On 9 June he was posted to FA(A)264 and while serving with it was awarded the Iron Cross 1st and 2nd Class. At the beginning of January 1918 Friedrichs was sent to *Jastaschule* and then on 11 January was posted to *Jasta* 10. His first combat claim was for a Sopwith Camel on 18 March, but this was unconfirmed. On 21 March, while flying a Pfalz DIII, he shot down an observation balloon over Ruyalcourt for his first confirmed victory; for his second an SE5a followed on the 27th. He did not score in April but shot down four in May, including two balloons each on the 18th and 28th. June was his best month as he shot down thirteen enemy aircraft, with doubles on the 5th, 27th and 30th. Eight of these victories were balloons. Two Nieuports fell to him, one each on 2 and 8 July, bringing his score to twenty-one. Then, on 15 July 1918, one of the more unusual hazards of balloon-busting caught up with him when his incendiary ammunition ignited and set fire to his Fokker DVII's fuel tank. Friedrichs jumped but his parachute got entangled in the tailplane and he fell to his death near Arcq.

His *Pour le Mérite* had just been approved and was announced five days after his death, the staff probably having not realised he had been killed. However, it seems not to have been awarded as his name does not appear on the roll of honour. He was awarded the Knight's Cross of the Royal Hohenzollern House Order. That he shot down twenty-one enemy aircraft in just under four months is an incredible record.

Leutnant Hermann FROMMHERZ (32 victories)

Hermann Frommherz was born in Waldshut, Baden, on 10 August 1891. He studied engineering at Stuttgart, but on 1 October 1911 he joined Mecklenburg *Jäger* Regiment Nr 14. At the outbreak of war he was a Vizefeldwebel. He fought on both the Western and Eastern Fronts, and in February 1915 he was awarded the Iron Cross 2nd Class before being transferred to the German Army Air Service on 1 June 1915.

On graduating, he was sent to *Kasta* 20 of *Kagohl* IV on 1 December as a reconnaissance pilot, with the rank of Offizierstellvertreter, seeing action over Verdun and the Somme. He was then posted to Romania and commissioned Leutnant on 1 August 1916. In December he was sent to Macedonia, where he met Oswald Boelcke.

On 3 March 1917 he was assigned to *Jasta* 2 as a fighter pilot on the Western Front. Flying a light blue Albatros DIII, which he nicknamed 'Blaue Maus', he shot down his first enemy aircraft on 11 April, a Spad VII from 23 Squadron. This was followed by a BE2 on 14 April. On both occasions he forced the aircraft to land and the English crews were taken prisoner.

Frommherz was injured in a crash on 1 May 1917; on his recovery he was reassigned on 29 October as an instructor with FEA3 in Lubeck, being awarded the Hanseatic Cross of Lubeck in December 1917. Returning on 1 March 1918 to *Jasta* 2, and now flying a Fokker Dr.I with the black and white tail of his *Jasta*, a chequerboard pattern around the fuselage just behind the cockpit and black nose, he began a string of victories, with two in June, and six in July. On 29 July 1918 he succeeded Hermann Göring as commander of *Jasta* 27, when Göring moved up to command *Jagdgruppe* 3. He was a caring and popular commander, once bringing a newly awarded Iron Cross to one of his pilots in hospital. Another six enemy craft fell to him in August, including three on the 26th, ten in September, including two each on the 3rd and 27th, four in October and two on 4 November, bringing his tally to thirty-two.

After the war he was active in the German Police Aviation Service. He also flew mail for Deutsche-Luftreederie, the predecessor to Lufthansa. In 1920

Frommherz returned to Baden as a technical chief at the new airfield at Lorach. He spent time in the Soviet Union in 1925 instructing pilots as part of a secret training programme; he also spent time in China instructing pilots in Chiang Kai-shek's new air force during 1931–32.

In 1938 he was commanding officer of I *Gruppe* of *Jagdgeschwader* 134 (reconstituted as JGI42 on I November 1938) with the rank of Oberleutnant, a command he held until I January 1939. From I April until 30 September 1942 he was commander of *Jagdfliegerfuhrer Deutsche Bucht* with the rank of Generalmajor.

He died from a heart attack in his home town of Waldshut on 30 December 1964. Despite his thirty-two victories, he was never awarded the *Pour le Mérite* (although he was seen wearing one after the war) as the Kaiser abdicated before signing the authorisation. However, he was awarded the Iron Cross 1st and 2nd Class, the Knight's Cross of the Karl Friedrich Military Merit Order, the Saxon Knight's Cross of the Military St Henry Order, and the Knight's Cross with Swords of the Royal Hohenzollern House Order.

Leutnant Otto FRUHNER (27 victories)

Otto Fruhner was born in Breig, Schleissen, on 6 September 1893, but sadly very little is known about his life. He started his career as an aviation mechanic on 20 November 1914, but applied for and was accepted for pilot training in 1915. By May 1916 he was flying a two-seater as an enlisted pilot on the Eastern Front, until promoted Unteroffizier in August, before volunteering for fighter training, being sent to *Jasta* 26 on the Western Front on completion of his training in July 1917.

Fruhner's first combat success came when he shot down two Sopwiths in separate actions on 3 September 1917. His next victory came on 3 January 1918 and by the end of March his tally had reached nine. Fruhner was awarded the Iron Cross 1st Class and Golden Military Merit Cross (the NCO's equivalent of the *Pour le Mérite*) and commissioned Leutnant on 3 June 1918. He did not score again until July, when on the 1st he shot down number ten, and became a *Kanone*. In August he added another five, four SE5as and a Sopwith Camel. Then in September he shot down seven, including three Sopwith Camels from 70 Squadron on the 4th.

For his last victory, on 20 September, Fruhner fired into a Camel at close range but then collided with it. Although injured, Fruhner jumped from his damaged aircraft using a parachute and became one of the first flyers to parachute to safety. The Camel crashed and was credited as his twenty-seventh and last victory. Fruhner was recommended for the *Pour le Mérite* but the Kaiser abdicated before the award could be confirmed. He was one of only a handful of enlisted men to become a successful flyer, making his record all the more impressive.

In 1935 Fruhner joined the Luftwaffe with the rank of Major and was given command of a flying school. He remained in training commands throughout the war, ending with the rank of Generalmajor.

He died in Villach, Austria, on 19 June 1965.

Leutnant Walter GOTTSCH (20 victories)

Walter Gottsch was born in Altour, near Hamburg, on 10 June 1896. He volunteered on 1 July 1915 and saw service with FA33 on the Western Front during 1916, with the rank of Vizefeldwebel. After fighter training he was posted to *Jasta* 8 on 10 September 1916. He opened his score on 14 November when he shot down his one and only observation balloon over Oostvlederen. On 17 November he brought down a DH4 from 29 Squadron for his second victory. He did not score again until January 1917, when he shot down a BE2e on the 5th; on the 7th he shot down in flames an FE2d flown by Flight Sergeant Thomas Mottershead DCM and Lieutenant W.E. Gower. Mottershead was awarded a posthumous VC for getting his observer back alive. February started well for Gottsch when he shot down two FE2s from 20 Squadron on the 1st, but he was wounded on the 3rd in combat with an FE2 flown by Second Lieutenant C.G. Davis and Captain R.M. Knowles of 20 Squadron. This wound kept him away from the front for four weeks.

Returning in April with the rank of Leutnant, Gottsch shot down three more enemy aircraft before the end of the month. Three in May and two in July brought his tally to fourteen, and on 23 August he was awarded the Knight's Cross with Swords of the Royal Hohenzollern House Order. He had already been awarded the Iron Cross 1st and 2nd Class. He shot down another three during September but with his tally at seventeen he was wounded again on 25 September. He was back in January 1918 and was given command of *Jasta* 19 on 14 February. By now he was flying a Fokker Dr.I with a yellow '2' on the fuselage. Command must have kept him from flying as his next victory did not come until 31 March 1918. He shot down number nineteen on 1 April and then on 10 April he shot down an RE 8 for his twentieth, flown by Second Lieutenant H.L. Taylor and Lieutenant W.E. Lane. Lane got in a fatal burst and Gottsch went down behind Allied lines near Gontelles. His death while gaining the all-important twentieth victory prevented him being awarded the *Pour le Mérite*.

Leutnant Georg von HANTELMANN (25 victories)

Georg von Hantelmann was born in Rokietnice, Prussia (now part of Poland), on 9 October 1898. He volunteered for the army in October 1916 and was commissioned Leutnant on 15 June 1917 in Hussar Regiment Nr 17 – the Death's Head Hussars. Transferring to the German Army Air Service on 20

September 1917, Hantelmann trained with FEA9 and then went to the *Jastaschule* at Valenciennes. Initially posted to *Jasta* 18 on 6 February 1918, he then went to *Jasta* 15 on 18 March with most of the rest of the *Jasta* 18 pilots. Hantelmann marked his Albatros DV with the 17th Hussars 'Death's Head' insignia.

Hantelmann's first claim was for a Spad fighter on 29 May 1918 but this was unconfirmed. His first confirmed victory was on 6 June when he shot down a DH4 from 27 Squadron. He would shoot down four more in June to bring his tally to five. August was a quiet month as he only shot down one confirmed, a Spad on the 17th. However, September was to be his best month ever. He shot down twelve enemy aircraft, including two on the 12th and three on the 14th, and as if that was not enough there were three aces among them. On the 12th he downed Lieutenant David Putnam, a thirteen-victory ace from the US 93rd Aero Squadron, on the 14th he shot down Sous Lieutenant Maurice Boyau, the fifth most successful French ace with twenty-one balloons and fourteen aircraft to his credit, and on the 16th he shot down six-victory ace Lieutenant Joseph Wehner of the US 27th Aero Squadron, bringing his tally to eighteen by the end of the month.

His good run continued into October 1918 with six more falling to his guns and on 21 October he was awarded the Knight's Cross with Swords of the Royal Hohenzollern House Order. On 3 November he was recommended for the *Pour le Mérite* and he shot down his twenty-fifth and last enemy aircraft the next day. Due to the Kaiser's abdication on 9 November Hantelmann's *Pour le Mérite* was never approved. He was awarded the Iron Cross 1st and 2nd Class.

After the war he took up farming on his family estate in Charcice, Prussia. He was murdered by Polish poachers on 7 September 1924.

Vizefeldwebel Oskar HENNRICH (20 victories)

Nothing is known about Oskar Hennrich's life other than his flying career. He served as an aerial gunner with *Kampfgeschwader* II from 20 April 1916 through to 20 February 1917. He then took pilot training, operating with FA(A)273 from 10 October 1917 and going on to *Jasta* 46 on 6 May 1918; he was soon to be its most successful pilot. Starting on the 14th, he shot down three in May, including two balloons, plus another balloon in July and four balloons and two aircraft in August 1918 to bring his tally to ten. He flew a Fokker DVII with a large 'H' painted on the sides.

September 1918 seems to have been a good month for many German pilots and Hennrich was no exception, with nine enemy aircraft falling to his guns, including six balloons, three of which were on the 24th. Hennrich shot down his last enemy aircraft on 1 October 1918. He was awarded the Golden Military Merit Cross (the NCO's equivalent of the *Pour le Mérite*) on 3 November to add to his Iron Cross 1st and 2nd Class. I have included Hennrich because he shot down twenty aircraft and would have been eligible for the *Pour le Mérite* had he been an officer.

Leutnant Fritz HOHN (21 victories)

Fritz Hohn was born in Wiesbaden on 31 May 1896. Not much is known about his early life. He served in Guards Infantry Regiment Nr 7 prior to joining the German Army Air Service, flying with FA(A)227. Hohn became a fighter pilot in 1917, joining *Jasta* 21. He shot down his first enemy aircraft, a Breguet XIV, near Chattencourt on 1 December 1917. He did not score again until April 1918 when he shot down a Spad and three balloons, two of these on the 20th. That same day he was wounded while attacking a Drachen. This wound kept him away from the front until August 1918, when he returned with the Iron Cross 1st and 2nd Class. Hohn shot down four in August, two of which were balloons. Then, after his tenth victory, he was made acting commander of *Jasta* 81 for the first three days of September, and then posted to *Jasta* 60 as acting commander for the remainder of the month, during which time he shot down another eight enemy aircraft, of which four were balloons.

Hohn was given command of *Jasta* 41 in October, during which month he shot down three more enemy aircraft to bring his total to twenty-one. On 3 October, the same day as his last victory, he was shot down and killed, probably by Adjutant Le Petit of *Escadrille* Spa 67. Had it not been for his death he would have been awarded the *Pour le Mérite*. He was awarded the Knight's Cross with Swords of the Royal Hohenzollern House Order.

Leutnant Joseph MAI (30 victories)

The son of ethnic Germans, Joseph Mai was born in Ottorowo, Galizien (part of the Austro-Hungarian Empire), on 3 March 1887. His military service started in October 1907 with the 10th Lancers, and when war broke out his regiment was part of the offensive aimed at Paris. In 1915 he was transferred to the Eastern Front, taking part in the fighting around Warsaw and the Dniestr river. He did, however, return to the Western Front and fought at Verdun and the Somme. He was promoted to Vizefeldwebel at this time.

Mai joined the German Army Air Service in May 1915 and trained at the Fokker plant at Leipzig. On graduation he was posted to *Jasta* 29 as a reconnaissance pilot on 28 July 1916. Then he underwent training as a fighter pilot and was posted to *Jasta* 5 in March 1917 with the rank of Offizierstellvertreter. It was at *Jasta* 5 that he met two other NCO pilots, Otto Könnecke and Fritz Rumey; later they were known as 'The Golden Triumvirate' and together they shot down a total of 109 enemy aircraft.

Mai scored his first victory on 20 August 1917; flying an Albatros DV, he shot down a Sopwith Camel from 70 Squadron. Another in August and three in November brought his score to five at the year's end, and he would not score again until January 1918. On 25 April he forced down Lieutenant Maurice A. Newnham from 65 Squadron, who survived the encounter and went on to score eighteen victories. This was Mai's tenth victory.

By May *Jasta* 5 was sharing an airfield with *Jagdgeschwader* I, and as the 'Flying Circus' re-equipped with Fokker DVIIs, Mai started flying a cast-off Fokker Dr.I, in which he scored his twelfth victory, shooting down a BF2b from 11 Squadron flown by Lieutenant Herbert Sellars, an eight-victory ace, and his observer Lieutenant Charles Robson. Sellars was killed but Robson survived and was taken prisoner. Mai's Albatros and Fokker DVIIs were painted in a 'zebra stripe' pattern with a star and crescent; he believed the optical illusion would help to throw off his enemy's aim. It is unclear if his Fokker Dr.I had the same pattern. Mai was awarded the Golden Military Merit Cross (the NCO's equivalent of the *Pour le Mérite*) on 24 June to add to his Iron Cross 1st and 2nd Class.

On 19 August 1918 he had his most successful day. He attacked two Bristol BF2b fighters from 48 Squadron, and as he shot up one, the other swerved away from the incoming fire and crashed into the shot-up aircraft. He followed this double victory by shooting down an SE5a from 56 Squadron later the same day. He was commissioned Leutnant on 1 September 1918 but after shooting down a Bristol fighter on 3 September, he was wounded in the left thigh, although it seems not to have been too serious as he shot down another aircraft two days later.

On 27 September he shot down number twenty-nine. Two days later he shot down a Bristol BF2b flown by Lieutenant Nicholson Boulton, an eight-ace veteran, and Second Lieutenant C.H. Chase from 20 Squadron for his thirtieth and last victory. He also had fifteen unconfirmed victories. Although Mai was recommended for the *Pour le Mérite*, the Kaiser abdicated before the award could be confirmed.

Mai is believed to have been a flying instructor for the Luftwaffe during the Second World War. He died on 18 January 1982.

Leutnant Georg MEYER (24 victories)

Georg Meyer was born in Bremen on 11 January 1893. He joined the army in 1911, serving with Infantry Regiment Nr 75, and on the outbreak of war he joined the Guard Ersatz Division. He was transferred to the German Army Air Service on 1 February 1916 flying two-seaters with FFA69 in Macedonia from 18 August, and later with FA(A)253 on the Western Front. He scored his first victory as a two-seater pilot on 7 February 1917 when he shot down a Nieuport over Lemmes. Soon after this he was trained as a fighter pilot and posted to *Jasta* 22 in April. Meyer had one unconfirmed victory in both May and July before moving to *Jasta* 7 on 2 August. Two in August and one in September would bring his tally to four by the end of 1917.

Meyer seems to have had a very dry spell over the winter and did not shoot anything down after 3 September 1917 until June 1918. However, on 25 March 1918 Meyer was posted to *Jasta* 37 and was made its commander on 14 April 1918, which may go some way to explain the absence of victories. In June his unit was re-equipped with Fokker DVIIs and his first victory of the year came on 1 June when he shot down an SE5a over Albert. He only shot down one more in June, a balloon on the 17th, but then things started to get better, and in July he shot down two balloons and two Bristol fighters. The good run continued into August as he shot down three DH9s and an unconfirmed balloon on 8 August and an SE5a on the 11th, bringing his score to fourteen. Another six fell to his guns during September, including two on the 15th. Meyer was lightly wounded on 14 October but managed to stay at the front and shot down three more that month. His last victory came on 4 November 1918 and he was recommended for the *Pour le Mérite* the next day, but the Kaiser's abdication on the 9th meant it was never confirmed. He did, however, receive the Iron Cross 1st and 2nd Class, the Hanseatic Cross of Bremen and the Knight's Cross with Swords of the Royal Hohenzollern House Order.

Georg Meyer was killed in a motor-cycle accident on 15 September 1926.

Leutnant Max NÄTHER (26 victories)

Almost certainly the youngest German ace, Max Näther was born in Tepliwoda, Silesia, on 24 August 1899. He joined the Infantry in 1914, when he was only 15 years old. He was twice promoted, wounded and awarded the Iron Cross 1st and 2nd Class before being commissioned Leutnant on 11 August 1916, just a week before his 16th birthday. He went for basic flight training at Bucharest in the summer of 1917, and was then trained with FEA7 at Brunswick. He went for final training with *Jastaschule* at Valenciennes.

On graduating, Näther was posted to *Jasta* 62 on 31 March 1918 and shot down his first enemy aircraft, a Spad XIII, on 16 May over Trignieres. His Albatros was painted all black with the German flag on a white square on the fuselage. In June he shot down six balloons. Balloons were well defended by anti-aircraft guns and fighter patrols, and attacks on them were often considered suicidal. In July he shot down a Sopwith Dolphin and three Spad XIIIs, bringing his tally to eleven, and on 7 July 1918 he was made commander of *Jasta* 62. He was on leave from 28 July until 21 August. On his return, flying the new Fokker DVII, he shot down two balloons, a Breguet XIV and three Spad XIIIs in September, three of them on the 26th. He was slightly wounded on 27 September but was awarded the Knight's Cross with Swords of the Royal Hohenzollern House Order. October was a good month for Näther, shooting down two each on the 9th and 19th, and one each on the 18th and 23rd, and he ended the month with three more victories on 29 October, bringing his total to twenty-six. He was nominated for the *Pour le Mérite* on 29 October, but it was never approved due to the Kaiser's abdication on 9 November 1918.

Twenty-six victories in just five months (four, if you take away the time he spent on leave) is an impressive record for any pilot, but for some one who was only 18 when the war ended it is incredible. In late 1918 Näther took part in Germany's border war with Poland, being shot down and killed by anti-aircraft fire on 8 January 1919 over Kolmar, Posen, now part of Poland.

Leutnant Friedrich NOLTENIUS (21 victories)

The son of a Professor of Medicine, Friedrich Noltenius was born in Bremen on 8 January 1894. He was studying to become a doctor when the war started but he volunteered for Field Artillery Regiment Nr 13 on 4 August 1914. He served on the Eastern Front from December 1914 until December 1915. During this time he saw action in the assault on Warsaw and in Serbia, and was promoted Gefreiter on 21 June 1915. Then he was transferred to the Western Front, seeing action at Ypres and the Somme, and being awarded the Iron Cross 2nd Class on 17 November 1915. The next day he was promoted to Unteroffizier. Noltenius was awarded the Iron Cross 1st Class on 10 May 1916, followed by the Knight's Cross of the Wurttemburg Military Merit Order on 5 July. Commissioned Leutnant on 5 October 1916, he was wounded on 16 April. On 3 November 1917 he began aviation training with FEA1 at Altenburg, and then went to flying training with FEA10 at Boblingen in February 1918. *Jastaschule* followed in late June and he must have shown some talent as he was posted to *Jasta* 27, one of the better units of the Air Service.

Noltenius's Fokker DVII was painted with red and white stripes around the fuselage and on the middle of the top wing. His first victory came on 10 August 1918 when he shot down a Sopwith Dolphin over Puzeaux. His next victory was a balloon on 20 August, followed by two more fighters by the end of the month. Like so many German pilots he had a very good time in September, shooting down nine enemy aircraft, including two each on the 2nd and 20th. Three of his victories that month were balloons. With his score at thirteen, however, he was moved to *Jasta* 6 on 27 September due to disputes over victories with fellow pilots. A Spad and a balloon on 6 and 10 October brought his tally to fifteen, but a clash with his commanding officer, Leutnant Ulrich Neckel, resulted in him being moved again, this time to *Jasta* 11 on 19 October. On 23 October he shot down two balloons and a Spad, followed by another balloon on 28 October, bringing his score to nineteen. One each on 3 and 4 November brought his final score to twenty-one. On 8 November he was awarded the Knight's Cross with Swords of the Royal Hohenzollern House Order – the last man to receive it. The armistice on the 11th scotched his chances of the *Pour le Mérite*.

After the war he took part in fighting the communists in Germany before becoming a doctor. He went to live in South America with his family in 1923, but returned to Germany in 1933 and began flying again. He died on 12 March 1936 when he crashed on take-off from Johannistal airport in a Bucker Jungmann.

Leutnant Karl ODEBRETT (21 victories)

Karl Odebrett was born in Schneidemuhl, Prussia, on 31 July 1890. A pre-war pilot, he gained his licence on 9 February 1914 and volunteered for the German Army Air Service on 4 August. He went for more training at Posen, and then served with FA47 on the Eastern Front in 1915, shooting down his first opponent on 18 October. Odebrett was wounded on 24 May 1916. He became a fighter pilot on 25 July with FA(A)215 while still on the Eastern Front. On 11 November 1916 he was posted to *Jasta* 16 in France, but it was June 1917 before he shot down a Nieuport over Chattancourt. He shot down another four in August, including three on the 20th. He downed a Caudron G on 4 September but was slightly wounded in the thigh on 7 September by anti-aircraft fire. Upon his return, he was posted to FEA2 and then was given command of *Jasta* 42 on 6 December 1917.

Odebrett did not score again until 18 February 1918, when he shot down a Sopwith 1½ Strutter over Bernecourt, followed by three more successes in March, including a double on the 9th. He was awarded the Knight's Cross with Swords of the Royal Hohenzollern House Order on 28 April 1918, then things seem to have slowed down as he only got one in May and did not score at all in June. Odebrett went on leave in July and this was the only time he did not command *Jasta* 42. His next victory came on 15 August 1918, a Caudron R11 east of Compiegne. This was followed by three more in September. His last five victories appear unconfirmed as the records show no claims by *Jasta* 42 in the last month of the war, which is odd, and suggests some records are missing, as he was recommended for the *Pour le Mérite* in late October, so it must be assumed that the figure of twenty-one victories is correct. Due to the Kaiser's abdication it was never awarded. However, he did receive the Iron Cross 1st and 2nd Class, the Military Merit Order 4th Class with Swords from Bavaria and an Austro-Hungarian Bravery Medal in Bronze.

Odebrett died from kidney failure in Caracas, Venezuela, on 13 February 1930.

Leutnant Hans PIPPART (22 victories)

Hans Pippart was born in Mannheim, Baden, on 14 May 1888. He was one of the few pre-war pilots and had his own aircraft manufacturing company. When the war started he volunteered and was posted to FEA3 as an instructor, but he finally managed to transfer to a front-line unit on 1 February 1916, reporting to FA(A)220 on the Eastern Front. He received the Iron Cross 2nd Class on 11 April and was promoted Vizefeldwebel on 1 July; in November he was awarded the Iron Cross 1st Class and two days later, on 21 November 1916, was commissioned Leutnant.

On 18 April 1917 Pippart was assigned to fly single-seaters with *Kampfstaffel* 1 of FA(A)220 and shot down his first opponent, a Farman, north-west of Silvko on 25 May. His next three victories, two in June and one in August, were all balloons. A Sopwith and a balloon in October brought his tally to six confirmed victories. He was posted to *Jasta* 13 on the Western Front on 4 December 1917. After shooting down a balloon in February, an SE5a in March and another balloon on 1 April, he was given command of *Jasta* 19 on 18 April 1918. He scored once more in April, then brought down four in May and was awarded the Knight's Cross with Swords of the Royal Hohenzollern House Order on 2 May. He also received awards from Austria and his home state of Baden. Pippart only scored once in June but brought down six in July, including a double on the 22nd. On 11 August 1918 he shot down a balloon for his 22nd and last victory. He was then shot down himself; he baled out of his crippled Fokker but his parachute failed to open and he fell to his death near Noyon. He is buried in Mannheim. His death on the same day as his twenty-second victory excluded him from the *Pour le Mérite*.

Leutnant Werner PREUSS (22 victories)

The son of a tax inspector, Werner Preuss was born in Gardelegen on 21 September 1894. After graduating from high school on 6 August 1914, he volunteered for military service on 14 August with Infantry Regiment Nr 85. On 15 May 1915 he attended an officers' training course and returned to the front with the rank of Feldwebel. He was commissioned Leutnant on 16 January 1916, but he was badly wounded on 25 May, and it took him a year to recover from the paralysis caused by the injury. He was most likely to have been awarded his Iron Cross 2nd Class at this time.

Preuss was transferred to the German Army Air Service and began pilot training on 20 September 1917, graduating on 15 October. He was initially assigned to an artillery spotting unit before ending up with *Jasta* 66. He was awarded his pilot's badge on 19 April 1918 and shot down his first opponent on 1 June, earning his *Ehrenbecher*. During July he shot down one each on the 1st, 3rd,

4th, 17th, 18th, 19th and 22nd, bringing his tally to eight. He was also awarded the Iron Cross 1st Class. In August he shot down four Spads, including a double on the 29th. September saw him add another four aircraft to his tally, and he was awarded the Knight's Cross with Swords of the Royal Hohenzollern House Order. By the end of October he had brought his score to twenty-two. In early November he was recommended for the *Pour le Mérite* and at least one photo shows him wearing it, but it was never officially awarded to him due to the Kaiser's abdication on 9 November 1918.

After the war Preuss joined the air component of the Freikorps and on 6 March 1919 was killed in an air crash at Rendsburg.

Hauptmann Wilhelm REINHARD (20 victories)

Wilhelm Reinhard was born in Dusseldorf on 12 March 1891. He entered military service as an officer cadet in 1909 and was assigned to Bavarian Foot Artillery Regiment Nr 14. Reinhard was severely wounded in the leg at Ypres in November, but returned to the front line in June 1915. He was accepted for pilot training, and after completion was sent to a front-line unit, but was wounded in December. He was back at the front in February 1916, now promoted to Oberleutnant and flying with FA(A)205 until he was transferred to the Balkans with FA28. In early 1917 he went to *Jastaschule* and then on 24 June to *Jasta* 11 on the Western Front. His first victory came on 22 July 1917 when he shot down a 45 Squadron Sopwith 1½ Strutter flown by Captain G.H. Cock MC (a fifteen-victory ace) and Lieutenant M. Moore, both of whom became POWs. In August he shot down four more, including a double on the 14th. After shooting down one on 1 September he was wounded, but was back to take command of *Jasta* 6 on 26 November.

The year 1918 started slowly for Reinhard as he only shot down one each in January and February, but he got two each in March, April and May, bringing his tally to fourteen. He was promoted to Hauptmann on 23 March and in April, after the death of von Richthofen, he was appointed commander of JGI, and awarded the Knight's Cross with Swords of the Royal Hohenzollern House Order on the 11th. In June 1918 things started to get better when he shot down six, three of them on the 2nd. This brought his total to twenty and he was nominated for the *Pour le Mérite*.

Reinhard was killed on 3 July 1918 while test-flying a Dornier-designed Zeppelin-Lindau DI. Göring had just flown it, but when Reinhard took it up a strut broke and the top wing collapsed. His death excluded him from the *Pour le Mérite*. However, he was awarded the Iron Cross 1st and 2nd Class, the Bulgarian Bravery Order 4th Class, both 1st and 2nd Class Degrees and the Baden Order of the Zahringer Lion, Knight 2nd Class with Swords. He is buried in Dusseldorf.

Vizefeldwebel Karl SCHLEGEL (24 victories)

Karl Schlegel was born in Wechselburg, Saxony, on 7 May 1893. He attended military school from 1907 to 1912, and on 1 April 1912 he joined Royal Sachsenburg Machine-gun Section Nr 19 with the rank of Gefreiter, later serving with the 8th Section as an Unteroffizier. When the war started he saw action on both the Western and Eastern Fronts. During 1914 he was awarded the Iron Cross 2nd Class and in April 1915 the Silver St Heinrich Medal. During the summer of 1915 he became the first man in his division to be awarded the Iron Cross 1st Class. In the spring of 1917 Schlegel applied and was accepted for flying duties, and was sent to the FEA at Altenberg. After passing his pilot exams he was posted to FEA6 and from there to FA39, flying a two-seater which he crashed, injuring himself. He returned to his unit in January 1918 but at the beginning of May was posted to *Kest* I on the Western Front. He moved again just five days later to *Jasta* 45.

Schlegel's first victory came on 14 June 1918 when he shot down a balloon. After two more balloons in early July, and two Spads on the 15th, he was promoted Vizefeldwebel. His run in June continued with balloons on the 19th and 20th, a Breguet XIV on the 22nd, and another Breguet XIV and a balloon on the 25th, followed by another Breguet XIVs on each of the 29th and 30th, bringing his tally to twelve. Seven more victories were added to his score in August, five of which were balloons, including two doubles on the 12th and 21st. He shot down another three balloons in September to bring his score to twenty-two. He was awarded the Golden Military Merit Cross (the NCO's equivalent of the *Pour le Mérite*) on 15 October. Then on 27 October 1918 he shot down a balloon at 15.40 and a Spad XI at 15.45, before being shot down and killed in the same dog-fight, possibly by Sous Lieutenant Pierre Marinovitch for his nineteenth victory. It is unclear if Schlegel's last two victories were ever confirmed.

His is another fine record of twenty-four victories in just four months. I have included Schlegel because he would have been eligible for the *Pour le Mérite* had it not been for his death and the fact that he was not an officer.

Oberleutnant Otto SCHMIDT (20 victories)

Otto Schmidt was born in Neukirchen-Saar on 23 March 1885. He entered military service before the war with Hussar Regiment Nr 9, being commissioned Leutnant in 1910. Shortly after the war started he was assigned to *Jäger* Regiment zur Pferde Nr 12, but was soon posted to Infantry Regiment Nr 120. Schmidt was wounded in March 1915, after which he was sent to Reserve Regiment Nr 23 and finally to the 33rd Division as Ordnance Officer. He was promoted to Oberleutnant on 9 October 1915. In March 1916 he was transferred to the German Army Air Service and assigned to FA25 on 10 April as an observer. He shot down his first enemy aircraft on 20 June; his only other victory in 1916 was a balloon on 11 July.

On 23 October 1916 Schmidt was sent for pilot training, and on passing out was posted to *Jasta* 7 on 16 March 1917. He shot down two balloons in June, one each on the 25th and 27th, before being given command of Bavarian *Jasta* 32 on 30 June 1917. Schmidt shot down two more with this unit, a Spad on the 6th and another balloon on the 16th, but as he was not Bavarian he was sent to command *Jasta* 29 on 19 August. He was given command of JGII on 24 August and shot down a balloon on the 26th. His eighth victory on 11 September was over Captain L.F. Jenkin MC, a 22-victory ace who was killed; he would shoot down two more, including another balloon, by the end of the month, bringing his tally to ten. Schmidt was also awarded the Knight's Cross with Swords of the Royal Hohenzollern House Order on 19 September 1917. While attacking a balloon on 18 October Schmidt was seriously wounded by anti-aircraft fire, but managed to return to his base. This wound would keep him out of the war until 3 July 1918, when he was put in command of *Jasta* 5. A downed balloon on 26 August was followed by five victories in September, including another balloon on the 7th. He shot down three aircraft in October and was recommended for the *Pour le Mérite* at the end of the month. He also shot down one on 4 November, which may have not been confirmed but is shown as one of his victories. In fact he may have shot down as many as twenty-five, with the last five never being officially confirmed. The Kaiser's abdication on 9 November 1918 stopped any chance of him receiving his *Pour le Mérite*. He did receive the Iron Cross 1st and 2nd Class.

The rest of his life is a mystery.

CHAPTER 7

Pour le Mérite holders listed by victories

This list also includes the men who, although having shot down the required number of enemy aircraft, were not actually awarded the *Pour le Mérite* either because of the Kaiser's abdication, or because they were killed before it could be awarded, or because they were not of officer rank and therefore not entitled to it. They are marked thus *.

Rittmeister **Manfred Freiherr von RICHTHOFEN (80 victories)**

Oberleutnant **Ernst UDET (62 victories)**

Oberleutnant **Erich LÖWENHARDT (54 victories)**

Leutnant **Josef JACOBS (48 victories)**

Leutnant der Reserve **Werner VOSS (48 victories)**

Leutnant der Reserve **Fritz RUMEY (45 victories)**

Oberleutnant **Rudolf BERTHOLD (44 victories)**

Hauptmann **Bruno LOERZER (44 victories)**

Leutnant **Paul BAÜMER (43 victories)**

Hauptmann **Oswald BOELCKE (40 victories)**

Leutnant **Franz BÜCHNER (40 victories)**

Leutnant **Lothar Freiherr von RICHTHOFEN (40 victories)**

Leutnant der Reserve **Heinrich GONTERMANN (39 victories)**

Oberleutnant **Carl MENCKHOFF (39 victories)**

Rittmeister **Karl BOLLE (36 victories)**

Leutnant der Reserve **Julius BUCKLER (36 victories)**

Leutnant **Max Ritter von MÜLLER (36 victories)**

Leutnant **Gustav DÖRR** (35 victories) *

Leutnant **Otto KÖNNECKE** (35 victories)

Oberleutnant **Eduard Ritter von SCHLEICH** (35 victories)

Leutnant **Emil THUY** (35 victories)

Leutnant der Reserve **Joseph VELTJENS** (35 victories)

Leutnant der Reserve **Heinrich BONGARTZ** (33 victories)

Oberleutnant **Heinrich KROLL** (33 victories)

Leutnant **Kurt WOLFF** (33 victories)

Leutnant **Hermann FROMMHERZ** (32 victories) *

Oberleutnant zur See **Theodor OSTERKAMP** (32 victories)

Leutnant **Paul BILLIK** (31 victories) *

Oberleutnant zur See **Gotthard SACHSENBERG** (31 victories)

Leutnant **Karl ALLMENRÖDER** (30 victories)

Leutnant **Carl DEGELOW** (30 victories)

Leutnant **Joseph MAI** (30 victories) *

Leutnant **Ulrich NECKEL** (30 victories)

Leutnant **Karl SCHÄFER** (30 victories)

Oberleutnant **Eduard AUFFARTH** (sometimes spelt **AUFFAHRT**)
    (29 victories) *

Leutnant der Reserve **Walter BLUME** (28 victories)

Leutnant **Walter von BÜLOW-BOTHKAMP** (28 victories)

Oberleutnant **Robert Ritter von GREIM** (28 victories)

Leutnant der Reserve **Arthur LAUMANN** (28 victories)

Oberleutnant **Friedrich Ritter von RÖTH** (28 victories)

Oberleutnant **Fritz BERNERT** (27 victories)

Leutnant **Hans KIRSCHSTEIN** (27 victories)

Leutnant **Karl THOM** (27 victories)

Leutnant **Otto FRUHNER** (27 victories) *

Oberleutnant **Adolf Ritter von TUTSCHEK** (27 victories)

Leutnant der Reserve **Kurt WÜSTHOFF** (27 victories)

Oberleutnant **Oskar Freiherr von BOENIGK** (26 victories)

Oberleutnant **Eduard Ritter von DOSTLER** (26 victories)

Leutnant **Max NÄTHER** (26 victories) *

Leutnant **Oliver Freiherr von BEAULIEU-MARCONNAY** (25 victories)

Leutnant **Georg von HANTELMANN** (25 victories) *

Leutnant **Fritz PÜTTER** (25 victories)

Leutnant der Reserve **Erwin BÖHME** (24 victories)

Leutnant **Georg MEYER** (24 victories) *

Vizefeldwebel **Karl SCHLEGEL** (24 victories) *

Leutnant **Hermann BECKER** (23 victories) *

Oberleutnant **Hermann GÖRING** (22 victories)

Oberleutnant **Hans KLEIN** (22 victories)

Leutnant **Hans PIPPART** (22 victories) *

Leutnant **Werner PREUSS** (22 victories) *

Leutnant der Reserve **Rudolph WINDISCH** (22 victories)

Leutnant **Hans Ritter von ADAM** (21 victories) *

Offizierstellvertreter **Friedrich ALTEMEIER** (21 victories)*

Leutnant **Friedrich FRIEDRICHS** (21 victories) *

Leutnant **Fritz HOHN** (21 victories) *

Leutnant **Friedrich NOLTENIUS** (21 victories) *

Leutnant **Karl ODEBRETT** (21 victories) *

Oberleutnant **Hans BETHGE** (20 victories) *

Leutnant **Rudolph von ESCHWEGE** (20 victories) *

Leutnant der Reserve **Wilhelm FRANKL** (20 victories)

Leutnant **Hans von FREDEN** (20 victories) *

Leutnant **Walter GOTTSCH** (20 victories) *

Vizefeldwebel **Oskar HENNRICH** (20 victories) *

Oberleutnant **Otto KISSENBERTH** (20 victories)

Hauptmann **Wilhelm REINHARD** (20 victories) *

Oberleutnant **Otto SCHMIDT** (20 victories) *

Leutnant **Kurt WINTGENS** (19 victories)

Oberleutnant **Max IMMELMANN** (17 victories)

Leutnant der Reserve Albert DOSSENBACH (15 victories)

Hauptmann Hans-Joachim BUDDECKE (13 victories)

Kapitänleutnant zur See Freidrich CHRISTIANSEN (13 victories)

Leutnant Walter HÖHNDORF (12 victories)

Oberleutnant Hans BERR (10 victories)

Leutnant Max Ritter von MULZER (10 victories)

Oberleutnant Ernst Freiherr von ALTHAUS (9 victories)

Leutnant der Reserve Gustav LEFFERS (9 victories)

Leutnant Otto PARSCHAU (8 victories)

Hauptmann Franz WALZ (7 victories)

Pour le Mérite holders with no combat victories:

Hauptmann Ernst von BRANDENBURG

Kapitänleutnant Horst Freiherr Treusch von BUTTLAR-BRANDENFELS

Oberleutnant Hermann FRICKE

Leutnant der Reserve Wilhelm GRIEBSCH

Hauptmann Jürgen von GRONE

General der Kavallerie Ernst von HOEPPNER

Oberleutnant Erich HOMBURG

Leutnant Hans-Georg HORN

Hauptmann Alfred KELLER

Kapitänleutnant Rudolf KLEINE

Hauptmann Hermann KÖHL

Oberst Hermann von der LEITH-THOMSEN (born Hermann Thomsen)

Hauptmann Leo LEONHARDY

Oberleutnant Albert MÜLLER-KAHLE

Leutnant der Landwehr Friedrich NIELEBOCK

Oberleutnant Paul Freiherr von PECHMANN

Leutnant der Reserve Peter RIEPER

Leutnant Wilhelm Paul SCHREIBER

Fregattenkapitän Peter STRASSER

CHAPTER 8

Alphabetical list of First World War *Pour le Mérite* Holders

The following is a complete alphabetical list of all the First World War 'Air Service' *Pour le Mérite* holders. Each entry starts with the rank, then the name. This is followed by the page number in the main text. Also included in this list are those who shot down the required number of enemy aircraft but were not actually awarded the *Pour le Mérite*. They are marked thus *.

Leutnant Ritter von ADAM * 196

Leutnant Karl ALLMENRÖDER 109

Offizierstellvertreter Friedrich ALTEMEIER * 197

Oberleutnant Ernst Freiherr von ALTHAUS 110

Oberleutnant Eduard Florus Harald AUFFARTH * (sometimes spelt AUFFAHRT) 198

Leutnant Paul BAÜMER 111

Leutnant Oliver Freiherr von BEAULIEU-MARCONNAY 112

Leutnant Hermann BECKER * 198

Oberleutnant Fritz Otto BERNERT 113

Oberleutnant Hans BERR 114

Oberleutnant Rudolf BERTHOLD 115

Oberleutnant Hans BETHGE * 199

Leutnant Paul BILLIK * 200

Leutnant der Reserve Walter BLUME 116

Hauptmann Oswald BOELCKE 118

Oberleutnant Oskar Freiherr von BOENIGK 119

Oberleutnant Fritz HOHN * 209

Leutnant Walter HÖHNDORF 142

Oberleutnant Erich HOMBURG 144

Leutnant Hans-Georg HORN 144

Oberleutnant Max IMMELMANN 145

Leutnant Josef Carl Peter JACOBS 147

Hauptmann Alfred KELLER 148

Leutnant Hans KIRSCHSTEIN 149

Oberleutnant Otto KISSENBERTH 150

Leutnant Hans KLEIN 151

Kapitänleutnant Rudolf KLEINE 152

Hauptmann Hermann KÖHL 153

Leutnant Otto KÖNNECKE 154

Oberleutnant Heinrich Claudius KROLL 155

Leutnant der Reserve Arthur LAUMANN 156

Leutnant der Reserve Gustav LEFFERS 157

Oberst Hermann von der LEITH-THOMSEN (born Hermann
    THOMSEN) 158

Hauptmann Leo LEONHARDY 158

Hauptmann Bruno LOERZER 159

Oberleutnant Erich LÖWENHARDT 160

Leutnant Joseph MAI * 209

Oberleutnant Carl MENCKHOFF 161

Leutnant Georg MEYER * 210

Leutnant Max Ritter von MÜLLER 162

Oberleutnant Albert MÜLLER-KAHLE 163

Leutnant Max Ritter von MULZER 164

Leutnant Max NÄTHER * 211

Leutnant Ulrich NECKEL 165

Leutnant der Landwehr Friedrich NIELEBOCK 166

Leutnant Friedrich Theodor NOLTENIUS * 212

Glossary

Ä Ë Ö Ü	Means the next letter 'E' has been omitted
AFP (*Armee Flugpark*)	Supply Depot
Bogohl (Bombengeschwader)	Bombing Unit
Brieftauben Abteilung Ostende	Carrier Pigeon Unit, Ostend
Eisenbahnregiment	Railway Regiment
Ehrenbecher	Honour Cup, awarded to pilots for their first aerial victory
Escadrille	Squadron (French/Belgian)
Flakzug	Flak Platoon (Anti-Aircraft Battery)
FA (*Flieger Abteilung*)	Flying Section
FA(A) (*Flieger Abteilung Artillerie*)	Flying Section Artillery
FEA (*Flieger Ersatz Abteilung*)	Pilot Training Unit
FFA (*Feldflieger Abteilung*)	Field Aviation Unit
Fliegerschule	Pilot School
Friedhof	Cemetery
Freiherr von	Noble family title of Baron
Jasta (or Jastastaffel)	Squadron
Jastaschule	Fighter Pilot School
JG (*Jagdgeschwader*)	Jasta Wing
Jagdgruppe	Jasta Group
Kanone	'Big gun' – used by the Germans to mean an ace with ten or more victories
Kagohl (Kampfgeschwader der Obersten Heeresleitung)	Combat Squadrons of the Supreme Commander
Kasta (Kampfstaffel)	Fighting Unit or Section
Kek (Kampfeinsatzkommando)	Fighter Group
Kest (Kampfeinsatze Staffeln)	Home Defence Squadron
KG (*Kampfgeschwader*)	Bombing Squadron
MFJ (*Marine FeldJasta*)	Marine Fighting Squadron
Ritter	Knight, title awarded by Royal Decree
Schusta (Schlachtstaffel)	Ground Support Unit

SFA (*Seefrontstaffel*)	Marine Unit
SflS (*Seeflug Station*)	Naval Air base
Sortie	A patrol made by aircraft
Sous	French word meaning 'under', as in 'Sub' Lieutenant
Staffelführer	Flight Leader
Sturmoffizier	Bombing Officer (not actually a rank)

Acronyms and Abbreviations

aka	also known as
CO	Commanding Officer
MID	Mentioned in Dispatches
DSC	Distinguished Service Cross
DSO	Distinguished Service Order
MC	Military Cross
NSFK	National Socialist Flying Korps
POW	Prisoner of War
RNAS	Royal Naval Air Service
OHL	*Oberste Heeresleitung*
USAS	United States Air Service

Comparative Ranks

THE ARMY

German	*British*
Generalfeldmarschall	None
Feldmarschall	Field Marshal
Generaloberst	None
General der Artillerie (of Artillery)	General
General der Infanterie (of Infantry)	General
General der Kavallerie (of Cavalry)	General
Generalleutnant	Lieutenant General
Generalmajor	Major General
Oberst	Colonel
Oberstleutnant	Lieutenant Colonel
Major	Major
Hauptmann/Rittmeister	Captain
Oberleutnant	First Lieutenant
Leutnant	Second Lieutenant
Fähnrich	Officer Cadet

Offiziersstellvertreter	Acting Officer
Vizefeldwebel/Wachtmeister	
Oberfeldwebel	Sergeant Major
Feldwebel	Staff Sergeant
Unterfeldwebel	Sergeant
Unteroffizier	Corporal
Obergefreiter	None
Gefreiter	Lance Corporal
Flieger	Private (in the Air Service)
Jäger	Private (in Alpine unit)
Kanonier	Private (in the Artillery)

THE NAVY

German	*British*
Grossadmiral	Admiral of the Fleet
Vizeadmiral	Rear Admiral
Konteradmiral	Commodore
Generaladmiral	None
Admiral	Vice Admiral
Kapitänleutnant	Lieutenant Commander
Fregattenkapitän (Frigate)	Commander
Korvettenkapitän (Corvette)	Commander
Kapitän zur See	Captain
Oberleutnant zur See	Lieutenant
Leutnant zur See	Sub-Lieutenant
Fähnrich	Officer Cadet
Oberflugmeister	Aviation Senior NCO
Vizefugmeister	Aviation Junior NCO
Flugmeister	Aviation Airman

Bibliography

Baker, David, *Manfred von Richthofen* (Outline Press, 1990)

Edkins, David, *History of the Blue Max* (Ajay Enterprises, 1981)

Franks, Norman, *The Red Baron's Last Flight* (Grub Street, 1997)

Franks, Norman, *Jasta Boelcke* (Grub Street, 2004)

Franks, Norman, Bailey, Frank & Guest, Russell, *Above the Lines* (Grub Street, 1993)

Franks, Norman, & Giblin, Hal, *Under the Guns of the German Aces* (Grub Street, 1997)

Franks, Norman, & Giblin, Hal, *Under the Guns of the Kaiser's Aces* (Grub Street, 2003)

Franks, Norman, & Giblin, Hal, & McCrery, Nigel, *Under the Guns of the Red Baron* (Grub Street, 1995)

Kilduff, Peter, *Germany's First Air Force 1914–1918* (Arms & Armour Press, 1991)

O'Connor, Neal, *Aviation Awards of Imperial Germany in World War I and the Men Who Earned Them*, Vols 1, 2, 3 (Foundation for Aviation, 1988–2003)

Paul, Wolfgang, *Hermann Goring; Hitler Paladin or Puppet?* (Brockhampton Press, 1998)

Richthofen, Manfred von, *The Red Air Fighter* (Greenhill Books, 1990)

Treadwell, Terry, & Wood, Alan, *German Knights of the Air* (Brassey's, 1997)

Wyngarden, Greg van, *Richthofen's Circus* (Osprey Publishing, 2004)